# FIRST
# ENTREPRENEUR

# FIRST ENTREPRENEUR

*How George Washington
Built His—and the Nation's—Prosperity*

## EDWARD G. LENGEL

Da Capo Press
A Member of the Perseus Books Group

Designed by Pauline Brown
Set in 11.5 point Adobe Garamond Pro by The Perseus Books Group

Library of Congress Cataloging-in-Publication Data

Lengel, Edward G., author.
 First entrepreneur : how George Washington built his—and the nation's—
prosperity / Edward G. Lengel.
    pages   cm
Includes bibliographical references and index.
   ISBN 978-0-306-82347-3 (hardcover)—ISBN 978-0-306-82348-0 (e-book)
1. Washington, George, 1732–1799—Career in business. 2. Presidents—United
States—Biography. 3. Mount Vernon (Va. : Estate) I. Title.

   E312.17.L46 2015
   973.4'1092—dc23

                              2015032444

Published by Da Capo Press
A Member of the Perseus Books Group
www.dacapopress.com

Da Capo Press books are available at special discounts for bulk purchases in the US
by corporations, institutions, and other organizations. For more information, please
contact the Special Markets Department at the Perseus Books Group, 2300 Chestnut Street, Suite 200, Philadelphia, PA 19103, or call (800) 810-4145, ext. 5000, or
e-mail special.markets@perseusbooks.com.

10 9 8 7 6 5 4 3 2 1

# CONTENTS

## MAPS

*Illustrations follow page 136*

# A NOTE ON THE TEXT

Modern documentary editors pride themselves, and rightly so, on their scrupulous fidelity to the original source text. At the Washington Papers project at the University of Virginia, where I have worked since 1997, editors prepare transcriptions that faithfully reproduce George Washington's writing with all of its misspellings, abbreviations, contractions, and infelicities of grammar and style. Though he was an intelligent and well-read man, in the liberal arts Washington was largely self-taught rather than formally educated—and this is apparent in his letters (especially those he wrote early in life). His writings also reflected the generally loose and inconsistent nature of eighteenth-century orthography.

Unfortunately, scrupulously literal transcriptions can sometimes appear inscrutable to twenty-first-century eyes and minds. It is enough to interpret eighteenth-century styles of writing and speech without having to wade through inadvertent errors, abbreviations, contractions, and other impediments to understanding. For that reason, in rendering letters to and from Washington I have taken the liberty of silently correcting minor spelling errors and expanding abbreviations and contractions in order to enhance readability.

## CURRENCY

Colonial and early-American currency can be bewildering. Colonial governments sought to and often did issue paper currencies in bids to stabilize commerce, but the British imposition of Currency Acts in 1751 and 1764 undermined their ability to do so. As a result, Americans often had to rely on commodity exchange notes, such as tobacco notes, and hard money minted abroad, such as Spanish silver dollars. For their part, British merchants paid American farmers not in cash but in credit.

Increasing the confusion was the fact that colonial governments typically issued their currencies in British denominations, a practice some states continued during the war and in the Confederation period; consequently, in references to pounds, shillings, and pence the distinction between colonial and state currencies or pounds sterling is often unclear. After the war began and before the adoption of the Constitution, the United States was awash in paper and hard currencies (the latter frequently cut into bills) of all imaginable varieties alongside the new but much-battered dollar. Contemporaries struggled to understand the worth of the different currencies, and so commerce typically degenerated into barter or the exchange of commodities in kind. Even after the Constitution was established with a single national currency, that currency remained unstable for some time and other forms of hard and paper currency did not immediately fall out of circulation.

The confusion is to some degree reflected in this book. Symbols for pounds and dollars appear interchangeably because Washington, like his countrymen, used these and other currencies at different times of his life. In this book, references to pounds almost always refer to Virginia currency rather than to pounds sterling, while dollars are Continental and then (after the Constitution) American dollars. Other currencies, though, sometimes appear as well.

# INTRODUCTION

GEORGE WASHINGTON PROBABLY WROTE THOUSANDS OF safe-passage passes, as was only natural for a man who held so much authority. Most of them were routine: allowing civilians to cross military checkpoints, messengers to enter secured areas, and the like. There were exceptions—like passes for spies. None, though, was more unusual than the one he penned at his presidential desk in Philadelphia on the morning of January 9, 1793. It read:

> The bearer hereof, Mr. Blanchard a citizen of France, proposing to ascend in a balloon from the city of Philadelphia, at 10 o'clock, A.M. this day, to pass in such direction and to descend in such place as circumstances may render most convenient—THESE are therefore to recommend to all citizens of the United States, and others, that in his passage, descent, return or journeying elsewhere, they oppose no hindrance or molestation to the said Mr. Blanchard; And, that on the contrary, they receive and aid him with that humanity and good will, which may render honor to their country, and justice to an individual so distinguished by his efforts to establish and advance an art, in order to make it useful to mankind in general.

Washington would deliver this pass personally.

Cannon fire awoke Philadelphians at dawn that day. The guns—unloaded, thankfully—boomed at regular intervals thereafter, and a growing

1

hubbub embroiled the streets. Curious crowds gravitated toward the prison yard, where people jabbered excitedly about a big event due to begin at nine o'clock. Many probably thought they were about to witness a hanging until they caught glimpses of an immense heap of yellow varnished silk laced with netting lying in the yard's center. A Frenchman gaily dressed in a blue suit and cocked hat bedecked with white feathers strutted around the heap, looking important. Incredibly, the heap began to expand slowly as an orchestra played a slow, solemn accompaniment. Soon an "immense concourse of spectators" had assembled to view the "majestic sight," which they found "truly awful and interesting." Discovering that the heap of cloth was in fact a balloon, and that they were about to witness it in flight, the crowd broke into frenzied applause. Some noticed men hawking tickets—five dollars to enter the prison yard and witness the spectacle up close. This crowd, though, possessed a sort of collective intelligence. Reasoning that once the balloon ascended it would be just as visible from outside the yard as it was inside, spectators spurned the ticket-sellers and scrambled onto window-ledges, shimmied up posts, and stampeded into nearby vacant lots.

At ten o'clock another finely dressed and solemn figure entered the yard—the President of the United States. Washington handed his pass to "the bold ÆRONAUT" and spoke a few words into his ear. After a simple bow, the Frenchman vaulted with amazing agility into his "blue and spangled" boat under the now fully inflated balloon. While the president watched, he dumped some ballast and the craft slowly began to rise. Blanchard furiously waved flags of the United States and France, and then waved his hat to "the thousands of [mostly freeloading] citizens from every part of the country who stood gratified and astonished at his intrepidity." The wind swept up within a few minutes, propelling the balloon off to the southeast. Some local gentlemen whipped their steeds after it but fell quickly behind as it disappeared over the treetops.

Blanchard's intended destination is uncertain, but his balloon landed in a field east of Woodbury, New Jersey. From there he hitched a ride on a passing carriage, arriving back in Philadelphia later that evening. As soon as he entered the city, the Frenchman hurried "to pay his respects to the President of the United States." He told Washington—always a lover of details—that he had spent forty-six minutes aloft and covered fifteen miles. The president congratulated him and turned back to the business of running the country while Blanchard left to square his accounts. What he discovered astonished him. After all the money that he had invested in preparing the balloon and staging a grand spectacle—those artillerymen and musicians all had to be paid—Blanchard's ticket receipts had been miserable. In a single blow he had lost several hundred dollars. He would have to beg for donations just to get back to France.[1]

This amusing but rather sorry event was not Washington's first exposure to lighter-than-air flight. Back in 1784 he had read accounts of balloon flights in Paris, prompting him to joke to the Marquis de Lafayette that he might eventually fly across the Atlantic to "make you a visit in an air Balloon in France." Learning that French adventurers proposed to conduct similar flights in the United States, Washington was curious—but determined that nothing on earth would ever get him up in a balloon. "It may do for young men of science & spirit to explore the upper regions: the observations there made may serve to ascertain the utility of the first discovery, & how far it may be applied to valuable purposes," he wrote on November 25, 1785, to his Irish friend Edward Newenham. "To such *alone* I think these voyages ought at present to be consigned—& to them handsome public encouragements should be offer'd for the risk they run in ascertaining its usefulness, or the inutility of the pursuit." The world needed visionaries—but always with an ample helping of prudence. He might have said the same about the management of his own wealth, and the economy of the United States.[2]

───────────

THIS IS A BOOK ABOUT GEORGE WASHINGTON. It features a diverse and fascinating cast of characters good, bad, and everywhere in between. Some worked in tandem for positive results. Others flew at each other's throats. What they shared in common was humanity, with all its flaws and talents. These talents, applied through steady work, built the foundations of American prosperity. Washington understood and believed in that fundamental truth. As an entrepreneur he was among the pioneers, although many of his contemporaries competed for the distinction. As a national leader, though, he stood first and foremost. He did not have all the ideas, or all of the energy. He did, however, make crucial choices that determined his country's future. Moreover, Washington was not just a national symbol but an outstanding example. Other men built fortunes and made decisions of national importance. No one, however, was more closely watched than Washington—and no one shared his capacity to either discourage or inspire. That is why his picture gazes from the cover of this book.

Washington was a crafty and diligent entrepreneur. He began early, employing principles imbibed from his parents, family, and friends to build his fortune. His first income came from the salary he earned as a surveyor. Saving and investing, he used this to purchase land and grow tobacco. A modest inheritance helped to establish him as a substantial landowner and gifted him with an estate—Mount Vernon—that became his country seat. Marrying Martha Dandridge Custis, a wealthy widow who would become his devoted partner, George acquired the wherewithal to begin operations on an exalted scale.

Today, the word *farmer* has humble connotations. Washington was anything but. Driven by a powerful (but not ruthless or obsessive) ambition, he transformed his estate from a tobacco plantation mired within an oppressive colonial system into a profitable enterprise producing commodities for trade throughout America, the West Indies, and Europe. Hard work—for he viewed industry as both a natural and a moral quality—built his fortune. But so did practices he learned through instruction and experience: prudence, attention to detail, transparency, clear and active communication, honesty, experimentation, and boldness tempered by thrift. Washington's progress toward personal wealth—he left behind a sprawling estate of over 50,000 acres and almost achieved millionaire status at a time when the distinction was rare indeed—makes up part of this story.

Even as he grew personally wealthy, Washington set the course for national prosperity. His personal experiences and abilities as an entrepreneur inspired his policies both as general and as president. Such was the case with his dread of debt. Unfortunately for posterity, Washington never kept a dream journal. In his nightmares, he was probably pursued by hordes of bayonet-wielding redcoats or hounded by Thomas Jefferson and his baying minions of the press. More frequently, Washington must have woken up drenched in sweat after dreaming that he had opened up his account books to discover his estate swamped by unsustainable debt. He spent the balance of his life straining to keep this dreadful experience from becoming reality for either himself or his country. Other principles guiding his economic policies included fiscal stability, national unity, and peace. Never, though, did he aspire to command prosperity. He thought of the economy as a kind of self-sustaining machine. Government's job was to keep it clean, well-oiled, and secure. The people fueled it, set it in motion, and—after a tithe to the government to fund its expenses—reaped the benefits. The operation was both natural and simple. Always, though, he exhorted the people to keep one principle in mind: work together, or perish separately. Washington was the unifier to guide them.

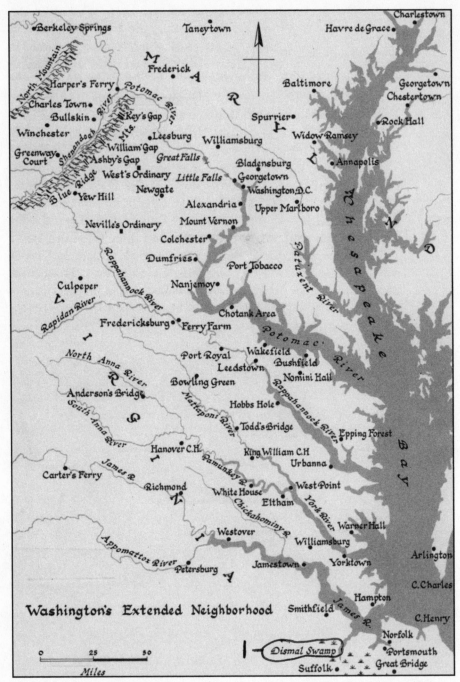

Washington's Extended Neighborhood

0    25    50
Miles

Donald Jackson and Dorothy Twohig, eds., *The Diaries of George Washington* (Charlottesville: University Press of Virginia, 1976–1979), 1:xxi.

CHAPTER ONE

# FAMILY FORTUNES

WASHINGTON FAMILY FORTUNES WERE FOUNDED ON tobacco and land. But ambition was the catalyst for prosperity. George's great-grandfather John Washington, who arrived in Virginia in 1656, was an apparently undistinguished clergyman's son in his mid-twenties who yearned to make his fortune. Rough and ready, he understood instinctively how to roll with fate's punches and make the most of any situation. These were boom years for the Chesapeake region. Tobacco dominated the economy, drawing planters wealthy and poor and laborers free and enslaved, to cultivate the crop and feed Europe's ever-growing demand. The prospects were extensive, but so were the risks. Tobacco prices fell steadily as production increased, but thus far profits had remained solid as efficiencies and technological improvements caused planters' costs to decline. Everyone knew, though, that the boom would not last forever.

Washington must have had this on his mind as his ship, the *Sea Horse of London,* entered the Chesapeake and he caught his first glimpse of America's shores. Prosperity beckoned, and so did ruin. His first experiences were anything but auspicious. Upon arrival in Virginia—the first port of entry remains uncertain—the ship unloaded its cargo of English goods, and the ship's agent debarked to exchange the cargo for good Virginia tobacco. Washington, who as the ship's second master looked to share in the profits, likely watched with interest as hogshead barrels of dried leaf were loaded on board until the holds

7

seemed fit to burst. As the ship readied for its journey home, he could have been excused for mulling over how he would invest his profits. Heading down the Potomac in early 1657, however, the ship ran aground, and before the crew could get it afloat, a howling winter storm lashed the normally placid river into a frenzy. Waves sank the vessel, and its entire cargo was lost.

John was unharmed, but his whole investment had disappeared with the sinking ship, and he had neither the money nor the means of getting back to England. Making matters worse, the castaway soon fell to legal bickering with the ship's master over wages and how to pay for raising the vessel. Such a sudden turn of fortune may have devastated a lesser man. Instead of bemoaning his fate, however, Washington curried supporters among the Virginia gentry and soon befriended a moderately prosperous planter named Nathanial Pope. That worthy not only backed up Washington in his litigation with the ship-master but also approved the young man's union in marriage with his daughter Anne. Along with her hand, John acquired £80 and 700 acres of land—more than enough to make his start. He decided to remain in Virginia.

At the top, seventeenth-century Virginia society resembled the British aristocracy. Power belonged to men with money and political connections. Chief among them were the great Proprietors, who had secured their power from the crown. Over time the wealthy became wealthier as they cornered the best and largest land patents. The rest had to pick up the crumbs as best they could.

John Washington was one of the up-and-comers—a cheeky, ambitious youth who spurned complacency and assembled his fortune piece by piece. Through the headright system—by which a planter received a small land grant for each settler he imported, at his own cost, to the New World—Washington acquired 1,820 acres of potentially arable land. He secured rights to more by barter, simple purchase, or the securing of grants to deserted land and small forest tracts. By 1668, he owned 5,000 acres. In 1675, at one fell swoop, he acquired 5,000 more.

While these land acquisitions were under way, John sought and won a series of lucrative colonial offices, contracts, and appointments—essential for upward mobility in the colonial system. He became a member of Virginia's House of Burgesses, a lieutenant colonel of the militia, and the owner of a mill, a tavern, and a shop. He even collected rent from a courthouse and a prison.

With some of the proceeds from these and other business ventures, John planted and grew tobacco—which served in effect as the colonial currency.

Though he was a success at business, John Washington fell victim to an untimely death—a fate that would also plague his male descendants for many generations. When he passed away in 1677, John was only forty-six. But he left behind a prosperous estate. The bulk of it went to his oldest son, eighteen-year-old Lawrence. A perfectly respectable gentleman, Lawrence nevertheless lacked the family fire for self-improvement. He served as a burgess and in other offices, but in limited business dealings he added only 440 acres to his inheritance. Lawrence married well, however, to Mildred Warner. She came from a prominent Virginia political family. Through her, Lawrence established connections that would serve his family well in the future, even though he died at the early age of thirty-eight in 1698.

Lawrence Washington left behind three children: John, who was seven; Augustine, who was three; and Mildred, who was just a baby. Their mother died a few years later after marrying a second time. Fortunately for the children, a cousin intervened legally to prevent the ill-intentioned stepfather from plundering their estate. Unfortunately for Augustine Washington, as the second son he received only a small portion of his father's legacy—a mere 1,100 acres when he came of age. For his branch of the family, the upward climb would have to start anew from a point much further down the ladder.

Augustine Washington is said to have been tall, strong, blond, and good-natured. Friends called him Gus. In personality, though, he hearkened back to his grandfather John. Astute and ambitious, he refused to rest with his second son's portion of the family estate and set about amassing large holdings of his own. Like his father and grandfather—and like his future sons Lawrence and George—Augustine Washington made a good marriage. Just after turning twenty-one in about 1715, he tied the knot with the teenage Jane Butler. Her marriage portion included over 600 acres. With this and a number of local official appointments to start on, Augustine began trading and purchasing tracts to expand his estate.

At the time, Virginia was in a frenzy of land fever. The Proprietors leveraged their wealth and political connections to secure the largest and richest holdings as the colony expanded westward. Just like his grandfather, though,

Augustine established his personal empire by stages. His new holdings included a tract along Pope's Creek on the south bank of the Potomac River. Here, in 1727, he finished building a house. He kept the structure modest, for it was too early to rest in comfort. Augustine wanted to save his capital for other purposes, such as buying more land, growing tobacco, building a mill, and investing money. As a young entrepreneur who anticipated a long road to fortune, he treated wealth not as an excuse to waste his days in idle luxury but as a means for acquiring more wealth.

In Augustine's day, land was king but iron was trendy. The British government, seeking to end the nation's dependence on Swedish ore, encouraged its New World colonists to build furnaces. Many attempted to do so, but not until the Principio Iron Works were established in Maryland in 1720 did any of these operations earn substantial profits. Spurred by the ministers in London, Principio ironmaster John England began prospecting for more mineral-rich land and soon discovered it along the Accokeek Creek in Virginia—where Augustine Washington owned extensive property. At first, the young planter could hardly believe his good fortune. John England came to Virginia to bargain with him for the use of his land, but Washington hesitated. The ironmaster was an aggressive salesman, and the Virginian may have feared being duped.

Upon discovering Washington's fondness for wine—a proclivity his son George would share—England proffered him "a small present" of it to secure his favor. Gus accepted the gift, but though it may have pleased his palate, it failed to melt his heart. He now believed the venture would be profitable, but was determined to secure a substantial personal share in the ongoing enterprise rather than simply sell out. As he continued negotiating with England, Washington craftily bought up all the iron-rich land along the Accokeek he could find. He also gathered information—perhaps from reading, certainly from interaction with his peers—about the still-infant iron industry. Only after he had a full understanding of its prospects and dangers did he set forth to drive the hardest possible bargain with Principio—one that would maximize his personal profits and minimize his risks.[1]

In essence, Washington sought a partnership that simultaneously placed him at minimum liability for the substantial costs of mining and of constructing and repairing furnaces, secured him one-sixth of the profits for all iron produced, and gave him an opt-out clause to negotiate an even better contract in the future should the venture prove successful. In the winter of 1729–1730, he sailed to England, where he appointed an agent and signed a formal contract with the Principio Company's British owners. The supposedly uncouth colonial had proved a shrewd businessman.

Business success was marred by personal tragedy. On returning to Virginia in the spring of 1730, Augustine discovered that his wife had died the previous November, leaving behind three bereaved children: Lawrence, Augustine, and Jane. Though deeply saddened, he permitted himself little time for grieving. On March 6, 1731, Augustine Sr. married for the second time. His bride was twenty-three-year-old Mary Johnson Ball.

The partnership was beneficial from both points of view. Mary was not rich—she was an orphan of modest means—but her personality fit Augustine's needs perfectly. Posterity, drawing upon her oldest son George's resentment, has given his mother a bad name. In legend—for there are no reliable first-hand depictions of her in youth—she appears as a nettlesome, overanxious, and undereducated woman who ruled her maternal roost with iron discipline and scant indulgence. She would certainly grow hard to handle in her later years. As a young woman, however, Mary complemented Augustine, who was overwhelmed by business concerns and often away from home.

Mary was nothing if not tough. If asked, she probably would have said that she had no time for luxuries like delicacy or sentimentality. As an orphaned youth she had developed a fierce stubbornness and self-reliance that the men of her time must have found intimidating. Not so Augustine. In Mary he sought, and found, a woman who could manage. For her part, she must have been impressed by her husband's shrewd business sense—although he may have invested too near the extent of his means for her comfort. Mary's ruling mantras were thrift and self-discipline. They were qualities that would serve her well, and in which she would steep her children.

Mary's firstborn, George, came into the world on February 22, 1732 (February 11 according to the soon-to-be-outmoded Julian calendar). Five more children would follow and grow to adulthood. Although Augustine's two boys by Jane Butler—his daughter died young—would soon be off to grammar school, Mary still had much to handle, and her husband's ventures didn't make things any easier. In 1735 he moved his family to a larger home on Little Hunting Creek. Three years later, he moved them again to an estate along the Rappahannock opposite Fredericksburg. He had little time to help them settle in.

The Augustine Washington of Parson Weems's fables is a loving father, deeply involved with his children. Loving he may have been—George would remember him fondly—but involved he was not. The prime reason for this was his involvement in the Principio venture, which often lured him away to oversee the furnaces and in 1736 sent him to England to negotiate a better contract. While his business ventures flourished with profits and new land acquisitions, responsibility for managing his home devolved upon Mary.

Contrary to popular imagination, an early-eighteenth-century homemaker of moderately prosperous means spent little time sewing dresses or baking pies. Instead, Mary and other women of her class had to manage day-to-day affairs on the scale of a small business enterprise: overseeing and keeping accounts; directing purchases for everything from food to furniture, clothes, and home improvements and repairs; instructing slaves and workmen; and seeing to the children's needs, discipline, and education. A woman of more delicate sensibilities might have crumbled under the pressure or tried to turn over her responsibilities to someone else, but Mary was unafraid. She ran a tight ship.

George, by all accounts a healthy, vigorous boy, had two primary influences growing up. One was his mother, who irritated him with her strictness even as he absorbed her principles of personal conduct. Another was his older half-brother Lawrence, whom George would come to love despite his fecklessness. Mary and Lawrence presented George with deeply contrasting examples. She probably disapproved of Lawrence and worried about his influence over George. Where she was stern, Lawrence was easygoing; where she was parsimonious, he was extravagant; and where she was prudent, he was careless. Worst of all, she was a realist and he a dreamer. No doubt seeking escape from his mother's hard regimen, George sought refuge in Lawrence's company when he could—although his half-brother was away for long periods, first to be educated in England and then to serve in an American contingent under British command during a military expedition to South America. Upon his return home Lawrence, ever-optimistic, saw opportunity in the hectic rough-

and-tumble business world of eighteenth-century Virginia without sensing the dangers that would eventually blight his fortunes.

Tobacco still dominated production and trade in the Virginia of George Washington's youth. Land was the true foundation of wealth, however, just as it had been in John Washington's day. Proprietors in the Northern Neck and along the James River held hundreds of thousands of fertile acres, and thought nothing of bartering or even gambling away tracts of 5,000 or 10,000 acres at a time. A large social and economic gap separated these proprietors from the upper and middle ranks of the Virginia gentry, who thought themselves fortunate if they could farm 20,000 acres. Below the gentry came smallholders who held a few dozen or a few hundred acres, followed by subsistence farmers and—at the lowest rung of the social ladder—slaves. Between the two poles of proprietors and slaves, however, there was tremendous economic—and, to some degree, social—mobility. Despite more than a century of settlement, land remained abundant—with perhaps as many as 1 million acres remaining unclaimed in Virginia east of the Blue Ridge. Even claimed land east of the mountain barrier remained heavily forested and mostly untilled. The west beckoned with limitless possibility.

By the mid-1740s the costs of tobacco production as well as prices had stabilized at a profitable level for planters, so investment in the colony's main industry remained attractive. Towns sprouted up along waterways to support the tobacco trade—just like steel, oil, or railway towns would do in later centuries—with all their concomitant shops, inns, taverns, and houses of entertainment or ill repute. Young George Washington knew one of these boom towns as a child. Across the Rappahannock he could see and frequently visited Fredericksburg, with its lively shops, bustling quarry, and, above all, its teeming wharf. Hogsheads of tobacco were hauled there from warehouses and loaded onto ships for the first stage of the Atlantic journey. Washington observed another wannabe boom town, Falmouth, rising in direct competition with Fredericksburg just a few miles up the Rappahannock. Though he enjoyed riding, fishing, and games, George had no penchant for wasting his time. There was too much going on around him.

Virginia was awash in entrepreneurs, including indentured servants working out their terms of service before they set off to make their fortunes, small farmers striving to set aside disposable capital, and middling to large planters seeking to amass and cultivate (or mine) land ever more efficiently and profitably. Investment opportunities were plentiful, and speculation rife. Gentry strove to acquire land, increase productivity, corner markets, and beat competitors. They bought, sold, and bartered not only land but also offices, for political patronage was central not only to social standing but also to wealth. In fact, the two were interchangeable. Above a certain level, it was impossible to build wealth without simultaneously buttressing social and political status. Many, unfortunately, fell so deeply into debt in the process of seeking to maintain that status that they collapsed spectacularly, ending up in prison or the eighteenth-century version of Skid Row. But the prospect of ruin dissuaded no one. Some rose, some fell—it was all part of the game. Refusing to play it only invited contempt.

Augustine played the game well but did not live to enjoy his fortune. On April 12, 1743, he died suddenly at age forty-nine, leaving behind a substantial estate to be parceled out among his progeny. As the eldest son, Lawrence received the choicest share, including the land on Little Hunting Creek (the future Mount Vernon) and the iron enterprise along the Accokeek. Augustine Jr.'s share included plenty of good land in Westmoreland County. George was not neglected—he got Ferry Farm and land on Deep Run along with three lots in Fredericksburg—but his three younger brothers also received good portions of their late father's wealth. Besides, by the terms of the will Mary Washington retained control over all her children's property until they reached their majority.

George and his siblings would come to count themselves lucky that their late father's will was as efficient and businesslike as the man himself. The boys would not have to spend years disentangling themselves from legal imbroglios or discharging their father's debts. Just as fortunately for them, their mother was an excellent steward. As a woman she had no power to build the estate, but she could certainly have ruined it by neglect had she so desired. Instead, Mary managed her charge with assiduous care, passing on to each of her children modest but intact fortunes that they could use as foundations for future development.

In the short term, however, Augustine's death was an unmitigated tragedy for George Washington. Nowhere was this truer than in its effect on his education. This, he would have known even at eleven years old, could have established the foundation for his future social standing and prosperity. The best opportunities were abroad. George's half-brothers, Lawrence and Augustine Jr., had both been schooled in England. For George and his younger siblings, though, all such hopes were now dashed. They would have to learn at home, from such tutors and instructors as their mother thought she could afford. There was also no escaping Mary's firm domestic regimen. George became so desperately restless that Lawrence cooked up a scheme in 1746 to sign him up for service on a British seagoing vessel. The boy had his bags packed and ready to go until his mother strictly and sensibly put an end to the nonsense and returned him to his duties.

Though George would bemoan his lack of formal education for the remainder of his life—and work to overcome it—his youthful learning was usefully practical if not comprehensive. He acquired, he later remembered, only the "principles of grammar" and the "rudiments of geography, history, & the studies which are not improperly termed the humanities," but he also received instruction in "the highest branches of mathematics." This doubtless reflected both his mother's sense of priorities and his own inclinations. She was concerned that he should learn the practical principles of estate management—for which an ability to work with numbers was vital—alongside the virtues of diligence and hard work. But he also enjoyed it. The overall effect of this upbringing was to produce a man who was somewhat awkward and uncouth, but with a can-do readiness to make his way in the world.[2]

George's surviving school exercise books reveal his growing young mind and its many outstanding qualities. At math, he was studious and efficient. He competently learned the basic principles of economics, management, and geometry. And he was a diligent copyist. The much-ballyhooed "Rules of Civility" that he penned as a child were likely a copybook exercise—perhaps dictated by his mother—from an old sixteenth-century French Catholic handbook. But he also copied complex legal documents. His mother insisted on attention to detail, and George discovered that he had a talent for it. With little leisure to read for pleasure, he learned to study books for practical knowledge—a habit that would remain with him for the rest of his life.

Native self-awareness, carefully cultivated, allowed him to visualize both his strengths—such as his tremendous memory and capacity for hard work—and his deficiencies—such as his irritable temper. Such habits constituted a recipe for self-improvement that would reach perfection in the oven of ambition. From his mother and the entrepreneurial society of his day, George acquired an abiding ambition to improve himself. But he also developed—perhaps from Lawrence—a dreamer's sense of the possible. A recently discovered picture that he may have drawn as a teenager depicts a sailing ship of the type that plied the tobacco trade—a symbol of American commerce and hopes of prosperity. Washington spent his youth training to become a self-made man.

To the teenage Washington, fame and fortune seemed within easy reach. This was no mere adolescent fantasy. In July 1743, just a few months after his father's death, George's gadabout half-brother Lawrence scored a coup by marrying into the most powerful family in Virginia. Lord Thomas Fairfax—sixth Baron Fairfax—was sole Proprietor of Virginia's vast Northern Neck of some 5 million acres. Few men outside Europe's royal dynasties combined greater wealth, political power, and social influence. His cousin Colonel William Fairfax, who served as Lord Thomas's land agent and administrator for the Northern Neck, was the direct instrument of that power in Virginia. With the wealth and prestige emanating from his post and family prestige, Colonel Fairfax built the magnificent Belvoir plantation in 1741 along the banks of the Potomac River. Fortuitously, Belvoir was just a short four-mile ride from Lawrence's property on Little Hunting Creek. In the spring and summer of 1743, Lawrence galloped that path eagerly and often until the object of his attentions became apparent: Colonel Fairfax's eligible young daughter Ann.

The two were married in a sumptuous ceremony that must have bedazzled eleven-year-old George. After it was over, far from brushing the boy away, the easygoing young couple welcomed him to the estate they now called Mount Vernon, and let him tag along on their frequent visits to Belvoir. No one admonished George to stand aside and keep away from the furniture. Instead, good-natured Colonel Fairfax encouraged the boy to saunter with him among the magnificent gardens; ride to inspect farms, mills, and other operations;

and marvel at the mansion house's grandiloquent furnishings. The colonel even read with George, regaling him with the dramas of antiquity. In time, the boy also became fast friends with the colonel's son George William Fairfax—eight years his senior—and later with George William's lovely wife Sally Cary Fairfax. The Fairfaxes must have found George Washington well-behaved, or at least easy to correct. By instruction and example they trained him in the mores of genteel deportment.

There were practical lessons, too. At Belvoir, Washington learned how to build wealth through the selling and purchase of land. Though land in Virginia sometimes changed hands by fairly casual means, in the Northern Neck it was a precise business. Lord Fairfax and Colonel Fairfax both demanded precise knowledge of the dimensions, topography, and resource potential of the land under their control. It was probably on his rides with the colonel that George developed a "nose" for good land, including knowledge of how the best tracts were situated with respect to soil quality, vegetation, and the proximity of navigable waterways.

Young George also learned the challenges of cultivation, management, and, above all, improvement—not just how to acquire land but how to make it more profitable. It all started with the basics. Surveying was among the most vital trades in colonial Virginia. Accurate surveying could make the difference not only between good and bad land but also between a clear title of ownership and legal disputes that could bankrupt farmers and encumber tenants for generations. Colonial Virginia was a litigious society, as George would learn to his sorrow in the future when he consented against his better judgment to serve as executor for the disposal of ill-defined estates.

Surveyors were in high demand as expert technicians, and well if not handsomely paid. Educated young men on their way up in the world often took to surveying as an entry-level profession. They started as apprentices before moving on to freelance work or salaried appointments—preferably, of course, with one of the great Proprietors. Surveying was interesting work for a healthy youngster who enjoyed the outdoors and had a talent for mathematics, geometry, maps, and other detail-oriented tasks. When he was about fourteen, perhaps after observing a surveying operation while accompanying the colonel and his son, George dusted off some old surveying instruments left behind by his father and tinkered with them, learning by experiment. Fredericksburg abounded with local surveyors, and perhaps after talking with them he set out to practice on and around Ferry Farm.

Padding about fields and woods, setting up equipment and drawing measurements, George discovered that he had a talent for the craft. For the first time, and to his great relief, he could put to use his talent for exactitude and efficiency outside school exercises and copy books. After several months of tests, he completed his earliest known formal survey on August 18, 1747. He was still too inexperienced to survey professionally in his own right, but he took the first step by signing on as an assistant to a local surveyor. His first teenage job—in contrast with the employment experiences of most of humanity—was a huge hit.

Each survey earned George small handfuls of cash or tobacco notes, and the feel of money in his pocket whetted his appetite for more. He kept careful records of every penny he earned or spent. With obvious pride he began lending small sums to relatives—afterward noting each transaction and the date of repayment in his accounts. But he soon learned to appreciate the dangers of unrestrained munificence. As his savings grew, close and distant relatives and friends plied him with hard-luck stories or investment schemes, seeking small loans. Some were genuinely needy, but of course many just wanted to take advantage of a successful young man who might be developing a case of swollen head. As would happen later in life—in fact, to his very last days—Washington fell victim to shysters. With experience, though, he became increasingly adept at distinguishing between trustworthy prospects and cheats. He developed a sense of his resources—and their limits.

In 1748 Lord Fairfax, concerned about enforcing his claims to land in a poorly surveyed portion of the Northern Neck, directed Washington's friend George William Fairfax to lead a surveying party that would delineate his properties along the Potomac River's South Branch in the upper Shenandoah Valley. The party set out on March 11, under the direction of an experienced surveyor named James Genn, with Fairfax acting as the Proprietor's representative. Sixteen-year-old Washington joined them, both for his pleasure and because the expedition gave him an opportunity to serve as a junior apprentice under experienced professional surveyors.

With Virginia's forests and fields on the cusp of spring, life bloomed around the little party as they rambled over the mountains and into the fertile but partially uncultivated valley. As he smelled the rain-freshened earth and pulled up handfuls of turf and soil, Washington prospected the land's beauty and potential. Writing in his diary on March 13 after an excursion south of what would become the town of Winchester, the boy rhapsodized about how he "went through most beautiful Groves of Sugar Trees & spent the best part of the Day in admiring the Trees & richness of the Land." The next day's journey was similar, as "the Land exceeding Rich & Fertile all the way produces abundance of Grain Hemp Tobacco &c."[3]

As the party passed along the magnificent northern Shenandoah amid intermittent downpours, Washington learned how to camp in the open and gaped in astonishment at a group of Native Americans who obligingly performed a war dance. But he worked hard alongside the other men, assiduously laying out lots as their mission demanded. By the time the expedition ended in April, he had proven himself a hard worker. He also learned how to look beyond his immediate surroundings toward future development and profit. Opportunities to perfect these developing skills would follow in short order.

After returning home from this expedition, George hung about with Lawrence, whose easygoing nature diluted Mary Ball Washington's souring influence on the boy's personality. Lawrence's lack of thrift and diligence hindered him in business, but he was an amiable companion. Riding alongside his half-brother on fox hunts and countryside jaunts, George laughed and told stories, and sought out the liveliest parties. Away from Lawrence, he prowled towns and villages with male and female friends, checking out who had the finest or speediest horse and gambling at billiards, whist, and loo. Inevitably, he wasted money; but these were mere diversions. George continued to perform surveys when he could—in July 1749 assisting a survey of much of the newly established town of Alexandria—and his purse got fatter. He was still too unsure of himself, though, to invest it in any quantity. Lawrence and other young men snapped up lots in Alexandria with dreams of developing them for a profit, but George chose to save the bulk of his money.

George had just finished assisting the survey of Alexandria when news arrived that his application for the post of surveyor for newly formed Culpeper

County had been approved. It was an unusual stroke of fortune for a teenager who was cheeky even to apply for the post, given his lack of experience. The Fairfax family's support of his application trumped George's inexperience, however, and he was formally commissioned on July 20. He applied himself to the work with gusto, and the quality of his performance justified the trust that his mentors had placed in him. Although his wages varied depending on weather and the number of hours he worked per day, his earnings easily approached £100 or more per annum—more than the income of many small merchants or planters. And while the job allowed him to perfect his trade, it did not consume him. Between surveys George had time left over to manage his business affairs and pursue political connections throughout the colony.

One thing led to another and in November 1749 the Proprietor himself commissioned Washington to lead a survey near Frederick in the Shenandoah Valley. Memories of the magical trip that he had taken to the region as an assistant to George William Fairfax just a year and a half earlier must have danced through his mind as he departed. This time, however, Washington could not bask in the Shenandoah spring—it was winter, the best time for surveying. Also, this time he was in charge. There was no time to admire the landscape; instead, he had to tend to all of the needs, large and small, of himself and the team under his care.

Griping was inevitable as the young man—still only seventeen—sorted out the basic equation of work and reward. He wrote to a friend known to posterity only as "Richard":

> I seem to be in a Place where no real satis[faction can] be had. . . . I have not sleep'd above three Nights or four in a bed but after Walking a good deal all the Day lay down before the fire upon a Little Hay Straw Fodder or bairskin which ever is to be had with Man Wife and Children like a Parcel of Dogs or Catts & happy's he that gets the Birth nearest the fire there's nothing would make it pass off tolerably but a good Reward and Dubbleloon is my constant gain every Day that the Weather will permit my going out and sometime Six Pistoles [a form of hard currency]. the coldness of the Weather will not allow my making a long stay as the Lodging is rather too

cold for the time of Year I have never had my Cloths off but lay and sleep in them like a Negro except the few Nights I have lay'n in Frederick Town.[4]

Despite his complaints—and poor spelling and rambling grammar—the expedition was a success, and he received a "good Reward" of doubloons and pistoles sufficient to make his work "pass off tolerably."

Rewards grew over the next three years as Washington conducted over 190 surveys, mostly outside Culpeper County. Since he had the authority to survey wherever opportunity offered, and since his host county was largely well-settled and already surveyed, he spent much of his time in the Shenandoah Valley. By the time his commission expired in 1750, he had all the skills he needed to freelance successfully. His solid work practically guaranteed a litigation-free landowning experience for his many customers, and word got around. Washington successfully demanded high fees even when they exceeded terms set by Virginia's colonial government, which mandated that surveyors could charge up to £1 11s 3d (one pound eleven shillings and three pence) for surveys of less than 1,000 acres in frontier counties like Frederick. Washington, however, let the open market set his terms of employment. He demanded £2 3s, and his clients paid without demur.

Surveying served Washington well. From 1749 to 1752, he probably earned at least £400 from the trade alone. Liberated as he was now from his mother's penny-pinching supervision, he must have delighted in beginning to spend some of his money for pleasure. After all, purchasing finer clothes and accoutrements, along with surveying equipment and handsome tack and saddlery, not only satisfied in the short term but also provided incentive for earning more. It also gave him a sense of the increased social status that he could look to enjoy as he cut a finer figure among his friends.

Above and beyond tending to his daily comforts, Washington relished the experience of investing his newfound wealth in land. He dreamed of becoming a large landholder rather than a tradesman. Fortunately he both had a knack for and enjoyed assessing, bartering, and developing land. Like his father and grandfather, he went about the process one step at a time. For his first purchases in the fall of 1750, he bought tracts of 93 and 456 acres on Bullskin Run in what is now West Virginia for £122. In March 1752 he acquired another 1,312 acres along Bullskin Run, followed a year later by 240 acres along the Potomac in Frederick County. Continuing this pattern of investment in the fertile Shenandoah Valley, in the spring of 1753 he bought two lots for development in the town of Winchester. Overall during this period George acquired a total of 2,315 acres by purchase and grant in the valley and other parts of Virginia—about equal to what Lawrence held at Mount Vernon. Some of it George leased out to tenant farmers, but he planned to develop most of it for his own use.

Lawrence optimistically pointed toward even grander possibilities. Disdaining to build his fortune incrementally—possibly because of his obviously declining health—he invested in a venture called the Ohio Company. Launched in 1745 with a grant from the Virginia House of Burgesses of 200,000 acres in the Ohio River valley, the company aspired to foster trade, commerce, and eventual settlement throughout the region. It also sought to keep meddlesome entrepreneurs from Pennsylvania out of the valley. Prospects were uncertain despite support from the colonial government. The Ohio Company took little account of French and Native American claims to the land it hoped to develop. Worse, investment costs grew exponentially as the company expanded its claims to half a million acres within five years. There was no guarantee that settlers could be found to develop the land, that they would do so effectively, or that they would be able to develop and sustain ready markets for their produce. The investors nevertheless forged ahead. Lawrence became president of the company in 1751, by which time it had established trading posts and forts meant to pave the way toward permanent settlement. George—restrained by Lawrence or possibly his mother—did not invest in the company but served it as a clerk and followed developments closely.

George and Lawrence's hopes faltered during the difficult year of 1751, when misfortunes small and large threatened to derail their fortunes. That summer George went to Fredericksburg to sell the lots that he had received through his father's will. It was a sweltering day, and on the way home he went swimming in the Rappahannock, trustingly leaving his clothes—and his purse—on the riverbank. While he splashed about, two serving girls rifled his possessions and made off with his valuables—possibly including his clothes. The girls were caught and punished, but George soon had much bigger problems to worry about. Lawrence—his half-brother, friend, and mentor—was dying.

The disease was probably tuberculosis. It had been worsening for some time, with its tell-tale hacking cough. Lawrence had sought medical treatment in England and taken the waters in the warm springs of western Virginia, but nothing helped. In desperation, fearing that another winter would kill him, Lawrence decided to seek a cure in the warmer climate of the West Indies— specifically, the island of Barbados. George, now nineteen, would accompany him. On September 28, 1751, the half-brothers departed the Potomac on the hopefully named 40-ton sloop *Success*, with an 8-man crew and a cargo that included 4,480 barrel staves, 7,627 feet of planking, 984 bushels of corn, and 31 barrels of herring, destined for sale in Barbados.

The mixture of emotions probably gripped George as the *Success* plied the Caribbean. Though his beloved half-brother's health weighed heavily on his mind, his nerves must have tingled with excitement at the journey (it took place in the midst of hurricane season) and the exotic destination. In his baggage he carried a blank memorandum book for use as a diary, but not for recording tourist attractions and idle conversation. Instead, George intended to keep an exact account, based on close observation, of seafaring, trade, economics, and the political and social life of the West Indies. Barbados was at this time not primarily a vacation paradise but a major trading partner with Virginia, importing goods essential to its plantation economy and exporting fruits and sugar. George likely wanted to perfect his knowledge of this system so that he could apply what he learned for his own advancement in the future.

The *Success* made way while George stalked the deck, observing sailors at work in the rigging and shielding his eyes to gaze at passing merchant vessels. He recorded his observations on knots, course, and wind direction and velocity. Sailors caught dolphins and a shark complete with pilot fish, which George sampled during dinner at the captain's table. More often than not, the weather was miserable—which must have been torture for Lawrence—and the ship took thirty-seven days to make port in Barbados. Inevitably George must have experienced seasickness for the first time, though he said nothing of it in his journal.

Finally, at 4 A.M. on November 3, George tumbled out of bed to "the cry of Land." Clambering on deck, he discovered Barbados looming before him. After the brutal journey, he and Lawrence must have been eager to get ashore. The hospitable British commandant invited the half-brothers for breakfast, but George attended warily for "the smallpox was in his family." Afterward, a cool evening ride with a local merchant left him "perfectly enraptured with the beautiful prospects, which every side presented to our view,—the fields of cane, corn, fruit trees, &c. in a delightful green." After a brief search the half-brothers took handsome and expensive lodgings, for with Lawrence's low health this was no time for frugality. Once his brother was safely at rest, George set out to explore.[5]

Entertainment beckoned at every quarter. George attended plays and dances, explored the country and shore, and sampled local delicacies such as pineapple. He inspected the British fortifications and watched the garrison drill. The island's economic potential fascinated him. George waxed poetic on the soil, which "in most parts is extremely rich & as black as our richest." Sugarcane production fascinated him—not just the process, which he observed closely, but its profitability as well. Long conversations with planters familiarized him with labor, production, and transportation costs; the fluctuating prices that sugar could command on the market; and its relation to the price of rum. Planters amazed Washington by telling him that in a good year, a single acre of sugarcane could return as much as £170 in profits.[6]

Good estate management, though, meant not just earning profits but reinvesting them. Above all, it meant avoiding debt. George was moved by the "Hospitality" and "Genteel" manners of the planters and their families. He was less impressed by their habits. Instead of working to plow profits back into the land and improve their estates, they luxuriated in high living at expenses that vastly outstripped their earnings. For many of them the results were disastrous. "How wonderful such people shou'd be in debt! & not be able to indulge themselves in all the Luxurys as well as necessarys of Life," he scribbled in his diary; "yet so it happens Estates are often alienated for debts." Though disgusted by their lack of thrift, George nonetheless thought he might persuade the planters to purchase more goods from Virginia.[7]

George's top-to-bottom assessment of the Barbados economy and West Indies trade briefly distracted him from grim personal realities. As he had

feared, he fell sick with smallpox. He survived thanks to his robust constitution, but Lawrence showed no signs of improvement. With nothing left to
do but watch helplessly as his brother faded away—and probably hoping that
he could still squeeze in a few surveys before the season ended—George left
Lawrence behind and sailed for Virginia in December. On the way he finished
his notes on Barbados. The surveys he conducted after returning home would
be his last. Virginia governor Robert Dinwiddie had informed Lord Fairfax in
the spring of 1752 that an old regulation requiring all surveyors to pay a sixth
of their income to support the College of William and Mary would now be
strictly enforced. Washington reacted to the news by quitting a profession that
had served its purpose but could bring him only limited social and political
prestige.

Lawrence returned home just as George was packing away his surveying
tools. The family helped the dying man to prepare a clear and comprehensive
will, but time was not on their side. He died on July 26, 1752, after complet-
ing a serviceable will, allowing the family to sort out the complexities of his
estate. George and three other assistants to the primary executor, John Carlyle,
discovered that Lawrence had no gift for record-keeping. He had not squandered his fortune, but his tangled investments left the family encumbered
with nettlesome debts and legal imbroglios. George would grapple with them
for years to come. In the short term, though, Lawrence's bequests provided
significant benefits. George received lots in Fredericksburg and temporary
control of both the Principio enterprises on the Accokeek and Lawrence's
stake in the Ohio Company. Tantalizingly, he also would receive the estate at
Mount Vernon if Lawrence's widow and infant daughter Sarah died without
heirs. Even with Mount Vernon's ultimate disposition yet to be determined,
George, still only twenty years old, now held possession of some 4,291 acres.
This brought him firmly within the ranks of the upper Virginia gentry.

Membership in the gentry bestowed both privileges and responsibilities.
By holding public office, a gentleman like Washington could influence policy;
establish political, business, and social connections; and bestow and receive
patronage. The more prestigious offices he held, the more likely he was to
boost his personal fortunes. But public service also entailed moral obligations.
No man of ability could shirk it without losing face among his peers and even
his social inferiors. George knew all of this very well. He had no choice but

to seek public office. The way he went about it, however, signified his surging ambition. George had only just laid down his surveyor's tools, and now had to toil over Lawrence's legal affairs while managing his own landholdings. As soon as he learned that Governor Dinwiddie intended to replace Lawrence's former adjutant general post with four new offices, however, George immediately applied for one of them. He was successful, becoming adjutant for the Southern District in February 1753 at an annual salary of £100.

The decent salary and prospects of military adventure only partially inspired this practical career move. Washington could not have predicted, after all, the two major wars looming on the horizon. Instead, he likely saw the adjutancy primarily as an entrée into public service, with all the benefits that this offered. Promising to "render myself worthy of the trust reposed in Me . . . by a constant application to fit myself for the Office," he hoped to get the attention of the governor and others in positions of power. When the far more prestigious adjutancy of the Northern Neck opened up a few months later, Washington successfully lobbied for a transfer to that office. He had hardly time to get a grasp of his new responsibilities before even more exciting prospects appeared.[8]

By 1753, the Ohio Company had become a venture of public concern. The previous year Governor Dinwiddie had assumed personal control of it, setting a new course that focused not on expanding its land claims but on tightening its grip on the land already theoretically under company control. This looked to be problematic, because the French and their Native American allies did not recognize Ohio Company claims. In 1752, the French razed a company trading post and commenced building their own chain of forts in the Ohio Valley. Dinwiddie resolved to send an expedition to the region with a message formally declaring Virginia's claim—and hence Great Britain's—to the valley and shooing away interlopers. Washington, whose efficient performance as adjutant had impressed the governor, requested to lead the expedition and was quickly accepted.

The journey west offered Washington adventure and a chance to prove his worth to the colonial authorities while cutting a public figure. His family's involvement in the Ohio Company also gave him a personal stake in rousting the French. Just as he had on his trip to Barbados, Washington would keep a personal diary. This time, he intended to publish it—provided, of course, that the expedition succeeded—in order to cement his prestige in Virginia. His goal was to present himself as a man of vision and energy who could be trusted with public office and—crucially—as an advocate for Virginia's economic interests. Though still awkwardly self-conscious, he was learning the qualities of leadership.

The expedition lasted from October 1753 to January 1754 and proved a formative experience. Washington managed a sometimes unruly band of seasoned trader-frontiersmen who balked at serving under a greenhorn. He oversaw wilderness travel and supply, negotiated with wily French officers and Native Americans, delivered Dinwiddie's message to the regional French commandant, and survived a harrowing return that included a dunking in the icy Allegheny River. The leadership and management lessons were many, and sometimes he learned them the hard way. But all of them were necessary.

During his journey to Barbados, Washington had endured the vagaries of oceangoing commerce in the Atlantic trade. In his expedition to the Ohio Valley, he encountered the West's promise and dangers. His diary expounded on the region's wealth and suggested how Virginia might exploit it commercially. Published in the newspapers, Washington's testimony enhanced his reputation and induced Virginians to identify their interests with western expansion and development. A grateful House of Burgesses knew that his public relations efforts advanced its agenda as well as his own and voted Washington a £50 reward.

Dinwiddie hardly expected the French to run away. He ordered his adjutants to raise militia to protect the frontier, but they offered recruits little monetary incentive and no one enlisted. Dinwiddie then raised £10,000 from the House of Burgesses to form a regiment of well-paid volunteers. Washington applied for and was given the post of lieutenant colonel and second in command of the regiment. In practical terms, he would be responsible for raising, equipping, and training it. All went easily enough—at first. A healthy number of volunteers enlisted on the colony's promise that they would receive daily pay equivalent to fifteen pounds of tobacco, plus land for settlement in the Ohio Valley. Unfortunately, the government knew little about military administration and was dilatory in issuing payroll funds. This neglect left Washington to face the protests of his "selfwill'd" and "ungovernable" men. Their discontent, he wrote to the governor on March 9, 1754, "is now grown to a pretty general Clamour, and some of those who were amongst the first Enlister's; being Needy, and knowing it to be usual for His Majesty's Soldiers to be paid once a Week, or at most every Fortnight, are very importunate to receive their Due."[9]

Military service is a social equalizer. In civilian life, Washington would have had nothing to do with the plebes—farm laborers, dockworkers, drifters, and immigrants fresh off the boat—who enlisted in his regiment. But circumstances now forced him to confront the basic realities that encompassed their daily lives. He learned about the hardships that a day's lost pay or going without a meal—hardly gentlemen's concerns—could impose on common folk. He was not without empathy, and became their advocate. To a degree, he shared their hardships.

An officer's expenses were significant. In addition to absenting himself from his personal business affairs, he had to pay many of his own expenses for equipment, clothing, horses, food, and other needs. Without an adequate salary, officers faced potentially ruinous consequences. The colony paid its officers only slightly more efficiently than it paid enlisted men. As Washington's purse shrank and his officers grumbled, he confronted the colonial authorities. Writing to the governor, he threatened resignation:

> Let me serve voluntarily; then I will, with the greatest pleasure in life, devote my services to the expedition without any other reward, than the satisfaction of serving my country; but to be slaving dangerously for the shadow of pay, through woods, rocks, mountains,—I would rather prefer the great toil of a daily laborer, and dig for a maintenance, provided I were reduced to the necessity, than serve upon such ignoble terms.

Washington's impudence irritated Dinwiddie, but he agreed to compensate some of the Virginians' daily expenses. Pay also flowed in a little more regularly, ensuring that the regiment remained intact.[10]

By the spring of 1754, Washington had endured loss and hardship but not personal failure. Physical challenges, minor military adventures, investments, and financial ventures had all ended well. As he climbed life's ladder, his imagination conjured destinies gilded with fortune and fame. Now, however, his overconfidence fueled a series of ego-scorching reverses. With his colonel absent, Washington marched the regiment toward the frontier, and at Jumonville's Glen in western Pennsylvania on May 28, he launched a successful and bloody attack on what turned out to be a French negotiating party. Annoyed, the French military authorities dispatched a punitive expedition that deftly routed Washington's tiny unit and forced it to capitulate at Fort Necessity on July 4. In the course of these events it became glaringly apparent that Washington understood little about sound management. The force he commanded was poorly supplied, unruly, and inefficient, and he had not done much to improve it. When Fort Necessity surrendered, the Virginians degenerated into a mob, breaking into the fort's liquor supply and ignoring the imprecations of their shame-faced young commander.

Washington admitted no wrongdoing but nevertheless resigned his military commission after returning to Williamsburg. Afterward, he looked over his military accounts and discovered to his horror that he had either overspent on entertainment or lost some of his money to theft, for his purse was short a pound and six shillings. It was another minor embarrassment for an unhappy year. Forced—maybe for the first time in his life—to beg a friend for some petty cash to pay off his account, Washington returned to northern Virginia. Legal negotiations over the disposition of Lawrence's remaining slaves and the status of Mount Vernon eclipsed past reverses for a time. A shipment of fripperies from London provided further distraction. These included military and civilian dress items befitting a man of quality, such as gold shoulder knots, gold regimental lace, gold embroidered loops, plated gold vellum, gold wire, four large chamois skins, fine glazed Irish linen, a crimson silk sash, crimson velvet, gilt coat buttons, and a gold-laced hat—altogether costing £28 10s 3d.

Washington's "inclinations," he wrote, were still "strongly bent to arms." But he had much to prove—in particular, whether he could learn from adversity. Establishing himself as a successful estate manager was a prerequisite to any future accomplishments, civil or military. After prolonged haggling involving Lawrence's widow, Ann, and her new husband, George Lee, as well as other members of the Washington and Fairfax families, Lawrence's estate was finally settled. First, his slaves were separated among their claimants. George

Washington then agreed to lease Mount Vernon at the rate of 15,000 pounds of tobacco per year or its equivalent in Virginia currency—in effect, £98.10 per annum. The price was not cheap, but he could pay off the first year from his salary as adjutant while continuing to earn money from his other land and investments. Meanwhile, whatever he earned from the 2,500-acre Mount Vernon estate would accrue to his own profit. The essential thing, though, was the status that came with having not just land but an established and substantial country seat under his personal control.[11]

Prudence would have suggested that Washington concentrate on improving his new domain. But aside from purchasing some necessary furniture and animal fodder—and slaves—he focused on retrieving his reputation from the embarrassments of the previous spring. On February 20, 1755, British general Edward Braddock arrived in Virginia and set about organizing a fresh expedition to confront the French on the frontier. The British invited Washington to accompany them, partly as a scout but in the formal role of Braddock's aide-de-camp. The new master of Mount Vernon accepted their offer—partly, as he told his younger brother John Augustine, because the role offered "a good oppertunity . . . of forming an acquaintance which may be serviceable hereafter, if I can find it worth while pushing my Fortune in the Military way." He might thus not only repair his military image but also achieve further success if the opportunity seemed "worth" his "while."[12]

———————

MARY WASHINGTON RARELY SAW EYE TO EYE with her eldest son. To her, military service was mere adventurism, a waste of time and money that generated neglectful business habits. Much "alarmed" at his impending departure for the frontier, she hurried to Mount Vernon in hopes of convincing him to stay home and work the estate. She failed. George, too old to heed her scolding, ventured off. Privately, he must have known she was right—he *had* left Mount Vernon a mess, being "much embarrassed with my Affairs; having no person in whom I can confide, to entrust the management of them with." He certainly wasn't going to let his mother take over, however, and asked his brother John Augustine to steward the estate.[13]

George's concern at "how unprepared I am at present to quit a Family, & an Estate I was just about to settle which was in the utmost confusion" barely veiled his real worry: money. Writing to his influential friend (and noted wastrel) William Byrd, Washington expressed relief that his role as aide-de-camp would "ease me of expences that otherwise must have accrued," leaving him responsible only for his personal gear; but he fretted that abandoning Mount Vernon would "be the means of my using my private Fortune very greatly." Even as he departed, Washington petitioned the government in Williamsburg to compensate him for various items, including a valuable surveying instrument called a theodolite, that he had lost during the disastrous campaign of 1754—amounting to "50 odd pounds."[14]

Setting out, Washington took "real delight" in corresponding with Sally Fairfax, "to whom I stand indebted for so many Obligations." He sent his mother terser communiqués to keep her up to date. Money and expenses continued to worry him. Having lost three horses to illness or accident early in the campaign and finding himself short of money adequate to answer "all contingent expenses that may arise," he begged Lord Fairfax for "About 40 or 50£ [which] will supply my wants, and for which I should gladly pay your Lordship Interest." His Lordship promptly sent Washington £40, which he would repay—without interest—two years later. Meanwhile, even as he adjusted to life in the saddle as Braddock's aide, Washington's enthusiasm for military affairs waned. Pestering John Augustine for frequent updates on the "State of my Affairs" at Mount Vernon, George admitted that the perusal of business matters offered "no small degree of satisfaction to a Person in my situation." The campaign, he feared, would proceed "not advantageously; as I conceive a little experience will be my chief reward."[15]

"A little experience," much of it negative, nevertheless sufficed to hone Washington's management skills. Braddock was an irritable man, and his gruff style with civilian suppliers hurt his army. British military administration was well-tried if not always true, however, and as aide-de-camp Washington handled correspondence and accounts for the entire expedition. This gave him practice in handling sums of money—up to several thousand pounds at a time, more than he had encountered in one place before—and trained him how to deal with the complex business of procurement and supply. Personal expenses and financial affairs troubled him throughout the campaign, dovetailing with his concerns for the finance and supply of a military enterprise that impacted the livelihoods of thousands of men. Hardly a letter crossed Washington's camp table in the spring and summer of 1755 that did not address money problems in some form.

Braddock's catastrophic defeat along the Monongahela River on July 9, 1755, and Washington's heroic conduct in rallying the remaining troops and leading them off the field after the general's mortal injury are the stuff of legend. The experience was both educational and traumatic. Washington would remember for many years his "gloom & horror" at the "dead—the dying—the groans—lamentations—and crys along the Road of the wounded for help." In the battle's aftermath, though, he had little time to rest or to reflect. As the only unwounded member of Braddock's staff, he bore responsibility for the continued supply of the broken army. One thing was certain, though: Washington no longer pondered the military life with any sense of joy. He returned home at the end of July exhausted and nursing bitter reflections. Chief among his regrets was the personal cost he had endured, "having suffered much in my private fortune beside impairing one of the best of Constitution's [his health]." George even went so far as to assure his mother, who probably muttered a few "I told you so" remarks, that "if it is in my power to avoid going to the Ohio again, I shall," unless "the general voice of the Country" insisted upon his return.[16]

It did insist, and with an offer that Washington found difficult to refuse. Toward the end of August, Dinwiddie proposed to appoint him colonel of 1,200 soldiers organized into a new Virginia Regiment. The terms included an aide and a secretary along with a "small Military Chest" that Washington could use as he wished and—crucially—reimbursement of £300 for his past expenses.[17]

Over the following three years in command of the regiment, he honed his skills as a military administrator and money manager. Running the unit efficiently entailed things like command, discipline, drill, weaponry uniforms, and tactics. Washington also understood—thanks to his previous experiences with Braddock and his own instinctive prudence—that success ultimately depended on money. Even the littlest tasks reinforced this basic fact. On days when his troops prowled the dense frontier woods in search of Native Americans, Washington often had to sit moping at his headquarters desk, counting stacked sheets of paper money and cutting them into bills. Working with civilian politicians, government officials, commissaries, and contractors took up his time, as did negotiating with the colonial government to maintain the flow of funds. Washington succeeded at these tasks and improved his managerial maturity and fortitude.

British general John Forbes arrived in America in early 1758, tasked to command a new expedition to eject the French from the Ohio Valley. Washington looked forward eagerly to the expedition's success. The prospect of westward development had interested him for many years. His half-brother Lawrence's early investment in the Ohio Company, moreover, had enticed entrepreneurial Virginians into developing western pathways destined to serve as trading routes. Dinwiddie had ordered the French to get out of the way back in 1753–1754 at the behest of Ohio Company interests. Braddock's subsequent construction of a route to the Forks of the Ohio River, which Washington recognized as a potential commercial and navigational hub, suited the Virginians nicely. Appealing visions of wagon trains trundling along that road, laden to bursting with goods bound from Virginia to the frontier and back again, tempted Washington's ambition. His complacent assumption that Forbes would use the same route in order to save his army expense and time, though, would be disappointed. Advised by his officers and probably also by northern politicians and entrepreneurs, Forbes decided to hack a new, more direct route to the Forks through the wilderness of southwestern Pennsylvania.

Washington was incensed. The new route, he complained, "seemed to forebode our manifest Ruin." For him and other Virginians, a campaign fought for purely military reasons—or, worse, to benefit rival entrepreneurs—was hardly worth supporting. Forbes brusquely dismissed his complaints, but Washington refused to back down. Soon the two entered the written equivalent of a shouting match as military matters took second place to the commercial rivalry between Virginia and Pennsylvania. Washington pushed his luck to the point of going behind the general's back to American and British politicians and even seeking an audience in London with the king. Forbes finally savagely rebuked his upstart deputy in person, declaring that he did not value "provincial interest, jealousys, or suspicions, one single twopence." The general chose the Pennsylvania road, and though his route to the frontier was slow, it ultimately succeeded in forcing the French to burn Fort Duquesne and abandon the Forks of the Ohio. Washington refused to celebrate. For the first time, he had come to look on British colonial authority as indifferent to if not actually opposing Virginia's and his own financial prosperity.[18]

Washington buried his resentment over the abandoned Braddock route and served efficiently as a good military man. Both he and his Virginia Regiment served creditably on the road to Fort Duquesne. But he was done with the military life. When the campaign ended he abruptly resigned his commission and, glowing with the hearty praise offered by his officers and men, returned to Mount Vernon. He was a mature man of twenty-six, a combat veteran and seasoned administrator who knew how to handle, among other things, large sums of money. He understood the fundamentals of procurement, purchase, and efficient allocation to maximize efficiency. And he was a leader. Though still concerned with his personal and financial well-being, Washington had grown adept at negotiating with powerful men and organizations in the interests of those who depended on him.

Early in 1756, he took a journey to Boston to petition the royal governor there (unsuccessfully) for British army commissions for himself and his fellow officers. The request was not only personal but also a symbolic assertion of the colonials' right for equality with the mother country. His procession to Boston was proud if not ostentatious, with gaily equipped carriages and resplendently attired servants. Washington spent large sums of money on items of personal display. He even gambled conspicuously. Such displays served both to feed Washington's youthful vanity and to cement his status as a leader. To lead well—especially in the world of the eighteenth century as the Virginia gentry understood it—one had to appear well.

Nattily dressed, wealthy, and basking in the praise of his subordinates, Washington glowed with confidence. Fort Necessity seemed ages away. Complacency, though, never tainted his character. No one was more aware than Washington of his many imperfections. Everywhere he looked he saw rough edges. At times of stress, he tended to gripe or lose his temper. Thanks to his practically useful but still limited education, his handwriting, grammar, and spelling were mediocre at best. His discomfort with subjects like languages and the classics made it problematic for him to maintain erudite conversation in educated society. The demands of business and politics, where the uncouth were pushed to the sidelines, made it imperative that he rectify these deficiencies. At Mount Vernon, meanwhile, Washington possessed a potentially profitable estate that had yet to be developed. Working toward the dual targets of refining his personality and enhancing his prosperity would force him to broaden his horizons and encompass the affairs of Virginia and—eventually—a new nation.

All of these concerns paled into insignificance, however, next to the glaring reality that Washington remained a bachelor. Finding amiable women willing to share his company had never been a problem. His teenage years had probably seen their share of affairs, and the personal fame that came with military service enhanced Washington's magnetism in feminine society. For a brief period he carried on some sort of liaison—how intimate will probably never be known—with Sally Fairfax, the wife of his good friend George William Fairfax. A gentleman, though, could not behave like this for long. Washington not only wanted but needed a wife—to share his life with, and to provide him with a family that would further motivate him to succeed. For three generations, George's forefathers had married well. Lawrence had married *very* well. George, though, would marry the best of all, partnering with a woman who would become the love of his life—and help establish his fortune.

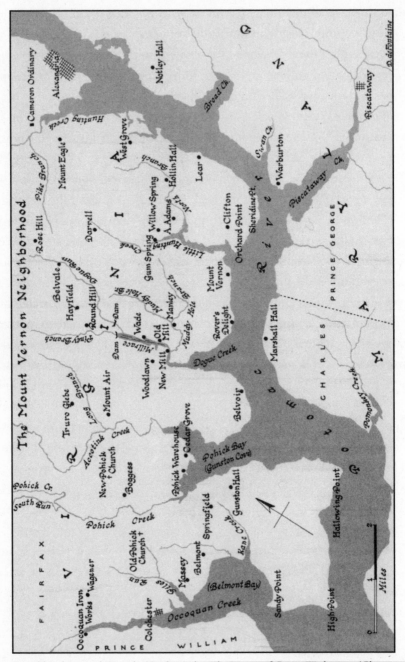

Donald Jackson and Dorothy Twohig, eds., *The Diaries of George Washington* (Charlottesville: University Press of Virginia, 1976–1979), 1:213.

CHAPTER TWO

# LOVE AND INVESTMENT

THOUGHTS OF HOME TEMPTED WASHINGTON LONG BEFORE he left the frontier. Warfare, he knew, threatened rather than promoted his fortune. In April 1757, while still serving on the frontier at Fort Loudon following a brief visit to Alexandria, Washington had griped to his distant cousin Richard Washington, a London merchant: "I have been posted then for twenty Months past upon our cold and Barren Frontiers, to perform I think I must say impossibilitys. . . . [B]y this means I am become in a manner an exile." Hopefully anticipating his return, George asked his cousin to order on his behalf an extensive shipment of items for the renovation of Mount Vernon, such as a chimney piece, 250 window panes, wallpaper, tables, chairs, and door locks. No doubt with a grunt of irritation, he then rode off to confront the French and Native Americans with all their "hellish Arts." George's ill-tempered bickering with Forbes over the wilderness road partly reflected his frustration with military affairs and his yearning to settle down to domestic business.[1]

Washington took another leave of absence from the frontier in March 1758 and rode, sick and grumpy, to Williamsburg to consult with a physician about his lingering dysentery. The doctor found nothing seriously amiss, and it was a more hopeful Washington who attended dinner that evening and heard that the colony's wealthiest widow resided nearby. Her name was Martha Dandridge Custis, and her husband, Daniel, had died the previous July. She was exceptionally rich and had already attracted other potential suitors.

Charles Carter, more than twenty years older than Washington but unlike him a planter of the first rank and a prominent politician, called her "the object of my wish." Perhaps concerned that he had no time to lose before the prospect vanished, Washington resolved to visit her immediately. On March 16, the morning after his visit to the doctor, he hopped into the saddle and rode straight for the widow Custis's plantation at White House on the Pamunkey River in New Kent County.[2]

The first meeting was a great success from both points of view. Washington, well-dressed and amply tipping the servants, cut a good figure. For this he could thank Sally Fairfax—with whom he was still infatuated—and the society at Belvoir, where he had learned gracious manners. Martha and George spent the afternoon and evening together—probably in the company of others—and he may have spent the night. The next day Washington returned to Williamsburg, where he ordered elegant new tack for his horse, including a "Sumpture Saddle" and silver-embroidered holster caps.[3]

On March 25, encouraged by Martha, he reappeared at White House for a brief layover before galloping off to the frontier. Some time that day or perhaps during a return visit in early June they probably exchanged promises, for not long afterward Washington initiated plans to expand Mount Vernon's mansion house—an unlikely investment unless he both had extensive financial prospects and intended to settle down in the near future. He and Martha separately and simultaneously ordered fine new sets of clothing.

Marriage with Martha offered George a shortcut to fortune. Her wealth had primarily originated with her late husband. The story of the Custis estate was well known in Virginia, and must have inspired Washington. Martha's father-in-law John Custis began with an inheritance of 5,000 acres on the Eastern Shore. He doubled that when he married the equally well-endowed Frances Parke, acquiring land along the York River. Though an ill-tempered and sometimes brutal man, John Custis was a talented entrepreneur and a believer in scientific agriculture. He ran his estates efficiently, earning ample profits on their produce. He also scrupulously avoided borrowing, leaving his son Daniel Parke Custis an extensive string of plantations along with ready, liquid assets.

Daniel, who married Martha in 1749, emulated his father in managing his wealth. He died suddenly and intestate in 1757 but left a massive inheritance to his wife and two children, Jacky and Patsy. Together they could claim title to almost 18,000 acres, including newly acquired land in King William County. This acreage, along with slaves, improvements, and personal property, was valued at £30,000. But that was not all. Additional assets that he had squirreled away in the colonies and England amounted to another £10,000. Since Daniel's death Martha had been managing this vast estate on her own—efficiently on the whole, but with a weakness for lending money to friends and relatives.

Some said that Martha and George married for love; others, that he just desired her money. For Martha, who turned down the financially more eligible (and obviously besmitten) Charles Carter in favor of George Washington, personal preference, even love, must have held some sway. George may not have known his own feelings. Martha was certainly a worthy match. Though not well-educated, she was intelligent, personally amiable, young, and physically attractive. But she was also very wealthy. And while most of her estate would go to her children if they survived—although it would take years to settle Daniel Custis's complex legacy—George would be responsible for managing the entire estate. Merged with his considerable holdings, it would become quite a substantial enterprise. In an instant he would become one of the most financially powerful men in Virginia. If he had children, they could expect to follow in his stead.

George was in a frivolous mood the night before his wedding, relaxing with friends at a tavern and losing magnificently at cards. He could afford the hit to his pocketbook. On January 6, he and Martha exchanged vows at the White House plantation. They spent the next few weeks there, enjoying a bitterly cold but gloriously snow-draped Virginia landscape. The couple then moved to Williamsburg, where George took his seat in the House of Burgesses on his twenty-seventh birthday. Martha meanwhile pondered what she should bring to Mount Vernon.

George, not yet having made the full conversion from bachelordom, still absconded occasionally to local taverns to drink and play cards. But he also took Martha to balls, bought and sold horses, began drawing cash from the Custis estate, and crafted ambitious plans for expansion. George and Martha intended to arrive at Mount Vernon in early April, and he wrote ahead to his overseer to have the mansion house "very well cleaned" and aired.[4]

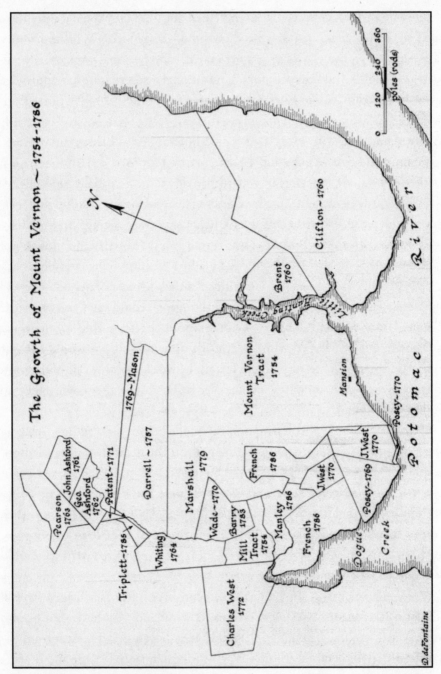

The Growth of Mount Vernon ~ 1754-1786

N

0    120    240    360
poles (rods)

Potomac River

Little Hunting Creek

Clifton ~ 1760

Brent 1760

Mount Vernon Tract 1754

Mansion

Posey ~1770

1769 ~ Mason

Patent ~ 1771

Darrell ~ 1757

Marshall 1779

French 1786

J. West 1770

Posey ~1769

J. West 1770

Triplett ~1785

Pearson 1763

John Ashford 1761

Geo. Ashford 1762

Whiting 1764

Wade ~1770

Barry 1763

Mill Tract 1754

Manley 1786

French 1786

Dogue Creek

Charles West 1772

D. daFontaine

Donald Jackson and Dorothy Twohig, eds., *The Diaries of George Washington* (Charlottesville: University Press of Virginia, 1976–1979), 1:240.

On their journey the young couple may have toured some of the Custis lands and taken in the old neighborhood at Fredericksburg and Ferry Farm. Then, pushing northeast, they crossed the Occoquan to enter a region defined by three great estates—Gunston Hall, Belvoir, and Mount Vernon—and one town, Alexandria. Almost twenty miles separated the first from the last, encompassing an interdependent community of towns, villages, and estates.

Leaving Belvoir, the Washingtons crossed Dogue Run to enter their home neighborhood. After passing through the isolated, 172-acre Mill Tract, they traversed a number of privately owned smallholdings—on which George may have cast a covetous eye—before entering the central estate. Approaching it amidst the splendor of springtime as they did in 1759, George and Martha could gaze with the satisfied benevolence of proprietors over the center and foundation of their new domestic empire.

Vertically rectangular, bounded by the Potomac on the south and Little Hunting Creek on the east, the original Mount Vernon estate had comprised some 2,126 acres. To this George added a 500-acre tract at its northern tip in 1757. Much of the land was still forested, but the fields seemed good and fertile, and the ground was level and just fifty to a hundred feet above sea level. Only later did Washington understand the limitations that the red clay beneath the topsoil placed on the estate's fertility.

Nothing otherwise distinguished the place except the site of its mansion. Riding toward it past fields in which slaves, white workers, and their overseers were busy with spring planting—mostly tobacco—he must have marveled again at its magnificent situation on a bluff overlooking the Potomac. From there, whether in his study or on the piazza he eventually built, his mind could encompass the interconnectedness of the surrounding large and small estates on both sides of the river.

The mansion house was impressive by the standards of the time. Lawrence had substantially expanded the original humble structure, so that by 1759 it stood one and a half stories tall with four ground-floor rooms and four smaller chambers above them. George intended to embellish the mansion further, and it needed extensive repairs. First, though, there was the land to tend to.

Washington's first months at Mount Vernon with Martha established habits that would last a lifetime. Just after rising, and before breakfast, he would dress himself and dispatch servants to prepare his gear (including, if necessary, surveying equipment) and saddle his horse. Then he would ride out to get a feel for his estate. Those first rides must have been exhilarating. Warmed by spring sunshine or soaked by rain—for he was not the type to shelter from inclement weather—he took the circuit of his estate, examining boundaries; inspecting timber and soil quality; praising or reproving slaves, workers, and overseers; and looking over the existing crops. From the mansion house, a typical day's circuit could have taken him ten miles. Only after it was done would he return home to eat.

These journeys certainly included the exploration and careful delineation of the local waterways. Several years earlier, he had stood at the falls of the Ohio and marveled at not just their beauty but their commercial potential. Now he traced the Potomac and its numerous tributaries, conscious that they formed the arteries and veins carrying his estate's lifeblood. All he had to do was step out onto his piazza to enjoy a view—perhaps the grandest anywhere—of the Potomac.

Or he could simply ride along the shore. The portion he initially owned was small, but in 1760 he would purchase 2,000 acres of good river land on the other side of Little Hunting Creek, and in subsequent years his acquisitions would expand his estate west along the shoreline to Dogue Run. On any given day the riverbank would have been dotted with slaves and servants fishing for the master's table. Washington also frequently availed himself of the numerous river ferries to visit friends and business associates in Maryland.

The Mount Vernon estate was much more than a mansion house surrounded by land. It lived and breathed as an active community. At its center stood Washington and his family, who both directed and depended upon the people around them. These included temporary workers of all sorts hired on contract, overseers, and visitors such as couriers and deliverymen. But the largest single group of people inhabiting his estate consisted of enslaved African Americans. From a few dozen whom Washington owned at Mount Vernon in 1759—in addition to Martha's dower slaves, who mostly worked the Custis estates—this population eventually grew by purchase and procreation into the hundreds.

Like his peers, Washington primarily viewed slaves as commodities. At the same time, however, he regarded them as personnel to be managed. Though slaves, they were still people, and so needed motivation to be productive. As a slaveholder Washington tried to be reasonable but firm, demanding hard work and obedience but without the excesses of cruelty that characterized many other estates. Moderation was for him at this time less a moral than a business principle. Put simply, he thought the slaves would work harder if he treated them well—such as providing decent food, shelter, and medical care—than they would if he managed them cruelly. Savage discipline was from his perspective both wrong and counterproductive. Recognition of the moral injustice of slavery, and of the perverse logic of attempting to motivate people who were denied their freedom, would come to Washington only slowly.

Mount Vernon's population, free and enslaved, formed part of an extended social and political network of multiple estates, smallholdings, farms, and towns. Washington often rode southwest from his estate to sumptuous Belvoir, filled with friends and youthful associations. Continuing south along the Potomac, a short ride took him to Gunston Hall, George Mason's newly built Georgian masterpiece that was beautifully situated overlooking a bay formed by the mouths of the Pohick and Accotink Creeks. Social and business associations with the Fairfax and Mason families meant short day trips or, more often, the dispatch of a messenger with a brief letter, receipt, or account. On any given day the roads between these estates would have bustled with horses, carts, and people carrying all manner of mutually enriching goods and communications.

While exploring this network's potential, George wrestled with the Custis estate's legal settlement. He was determined that not one shilling of it would escape him or his family. He peppered Stafford County lawyer John Mercer with incisive questions on his and Martha's legal rights respecting the estate. Taking thorough inventories of the Custis property, Washington noted slaves (with names, locations, relationships, and valuations), livestock, tools, furniture, clothing, and china—even pots of raisins. With all the meticulous care with which he had composed surveys in his youth, he detailed, classified, and valued every item. In a separate account, he listed the goods that Martha had taken from the Custis estate for her own use, including even "a little Brandy

& some old Cyder" that he valued at £1. He also prepared a full catalog of Daniel Parke Custis's extensive library. There were good legal reasons for copying or composing these inventories—George was no miser counting his pennies—but the work must have taken many days and nights in which he came late to bed or not at all.[5]

For the first few months after his marriage, Washington still gambled (and lost up to £5 at a time) at horse racing, billiards, and cards, and the inevitable first postmatrimonial quarrel may have occurred at about this time. His accounts reveal that shortly afterward his expenditures on cards ceased entirely, and that he played at billiards only occasionally (and perhaps surreptitiously). Martha might well have peremptorily ordered him to stop gambling, only to relent a few years later when George's expenditures on cards resumed at a low level while billiards ceased—perhaps as a quid pro quo.

George was no gambling addict, however, and his idle pursuits never diverted him from business. In his household economy he emulated the woman he affected to resent—his mother. Like her, he emphasized practical efficiency and thrift. Mount Vernon was a gentleman's seat, not a miser's abode, and so there were frequent visitors and parties. But there also were standards to maintain. Washington adhered to these more strictly than anyone else in his family. The gentry had its share of dissolute scoundrels who shamed their families and ruined their estates. He was determined not to be one of them. Mount Vernon had to be a beacon of prosperity, not a bitter example of neglect. Martha felt the same, and proved an energetic and effective household manager.

Leaving Mount Vernon's domestic machine humming smoothly under his wife's oversight, George often took the easy eight-mile ride to Alexandria. In 1759 the town was hardly a metropolis, but it was young and had a bright future. The town's political importance had been established just five years earlier with the opening of the Fairfax County Courthouse. Now it was becoming not just an administrative but a commercial center. Alexandria was perfectly situated for navigation, as described by a gentleman who visited it shortly after George and Martha married. "The Potomac above and below the town is not more than a mile broad," he wrote, "but it here opens into a large circular bay of at least twice that diameter. The town is built upon an arc of this bay, at one extremity of which is a wharf; at the other a dock for building ships; with water sufficient to launch a vessel of any rate or magnitude." Trustees oversaw Alexandria's development with a view toward making it a major commercial center for the enrichment of all the communities, including Mount Vernon, along the Potomac.[6]

Ships docked at the Alexandria wharf and unloaded boxes addressed to "Mount Vernon Potomack River Virginia"—the former being, as Washington explained to a merchant, "the name of my Seat the other the River on which 'tis Situated." Goods-laden wagons escorted by servants and slaves trundled from Alexandria to Mount Vernon and returned with hogsheads of tobacco from the Custis and Washington estates. At Alexandria, workers unloaded the tobacco and stacked it in warehouses, where it awaited inspectors bearing stamps of rejection or approval. Heaved on board transatlantic vessels, this tobacco was destined for London, where it was transformed into cigars and snuff for the enjoyment of British lords and ladies—maybe even the king himself. Much of it eventually was sold in the markets of continental Europe.[7]

Washington visited Alexandria to oversee the exchange of goods in both directions, and stood at the wharf to watch the work under way and worry about the handling of his tobacco. Mostly, however, he managed this ongoing business from his desk at Mount Vernon. He had been corresponding with British merchants since his earliest days as an estate proprietor. After his marriage, Washington entered into a relationship with the prominent firm of Robert Cary & Company, which had worked with the Custis family for many years. This relationship merged his own inheritance—enhanced by personal acquisitions, the fruit of his labor as a teenage surveyor, thrifty money management, and investment—with the Custis estate that had fallen to his stewardship by marriage. Quite apart from his love for Martha, as a conscientiously responsible man George felt compelled to properly manage and enhance his wife's and stepchildren's inheritance even as he leveraged it to build his own fortune.

On May 1, 1759, George addressed Cary & Company—enclosing a certified copy of his marriage certificate—as the new manager of all commercial affairs relating to the Custis and Washington estates. In transactions that both sides carefully documented, Washington shipped tobacco to the care of Cary & Company, which sold it on consignment in Europe and credited

the proceeds to his account. Meanwhile, he ordered from the firm all of
the European manufactured goods that he needed for the improvement of
his estate and his own enjoyment. George developed ongoing relationships
with other English merchants as well, such as John Hanbury & Company
of London and James Gildart of Liverpool.

Imported British goods were vital to the improvement and expansion
of the Mount Vernon mansion house, a project dear to Washington's heart.
His younger brother Jack, who had managed it in George's absence, was well
meaning but not up to the job. After returning from the war, George was
shocked at the "rundown" appearance of the place. Outbuildings were crum-
bling, the lawn sprouted patchy and rank with crabgrass, and the main mansion looked barely habitable.

George and Martha prioritized redesigning the bedchamber according to
her wishes, with blue and white themes for the new tester bed with canopy and
curtains, chairs, draperies, and other furnishings. The young couple ordered
a "Fashionable Sett of Desert Glasses, and Stands for Sweet Meats Jellys &ca
together with Wash Glasses and a proper stand for these," along with cutlery,
carpets, fire screens, and other items—enough to put on a decent show of
gentility until the house could be expanded.[8]

In the same letter to Cary in which he requested new furnishings for the
mansion house, George asked for "the newest, and most approved Treatise of
Agriculture . . . called a new System of Agriculture, or a Speedy way to grow
Rich." The title was revealing. For Washington and his fellow planters engaged
in the competitive world of Virginia farming, it was no prosaic rural pastime.
Farming was a business, a venue for entrepreneurs to show their worth and talent
for innovation. Acquiring wealth was the goal, and the devil took the hindmost.[9]

Just as Washington loved being fashionable and up to date in all his oc-
cupations, including his dress, he knew that falling even a little bit behind
in business could pave the way to ruin. Throughout his life, he sought the
latest books on agriculture and husbandry, and corresponded with the leading
agriculturalists of his day. It was in this spirit that Washington ordered "the
latest Edition" of William Gibson's manual on the treatment of horses; Batty
Langley's *New Principles of Gardening;* and "One neat Pocket Book, capable
of receiving Memorandoms & small Cash Accounts."[10]

Washington still had much to learn about entrepreneurship. Among other things, he had yet to diversify his investments. Visitors to his estate would have been immediately impressed by the green fields of tobacco and the barns in which cut leaves were hung to dry. This crop had been the staple source of profit for Washington and other planters for many generations. Growing and preparing the finest possible tobacco was a source not just of potential profit but of social standing in colonial Virginia. He did not initially consider chancing a switch to some other crop.

Many farmers preferred to play it safe with tobacco, selling it to Virginia merchants for a modest but steady return. But Washington was eager to extend his profits, and so gambled on the riskier but potentially much more lucrative trans-Atlantic trade. The danger of lost cargo was real, thanks to French naval activity—the war did not end until 1763—and the frequent storms during the fall and spring shipping seasons. Costs for insurance and freight were likewise high, and British import duties were even more onerous. Then there were handling duties, and the cuts taken by the merchants managing the business. Still, the earnings could be good if market prices held, although British regulations prevented planters from selling to non-British buyers.

There was another temptation to sticking with tobacco: easy credit. Currency of any sort, but especially hard currency, was exceptionally difficult to find in colonial Virginia. Credit, however, was plentiful for interested planters thanks to British tobacco merchants. The credit they offered provided the needed capital for the purchase of land, slaves, and the British manufactured goods necessary for production and maintaining the Virginia gentry's opulent lifestyle. Credit was financed with tobacco. In the short run, easy credit seemed to offer the means for enrichment via the ever-expanding production of tobacco. But it reinforced colonial dependency on the mother country, and it depended in turn on the continuing profitability of tobacco in British and European markets. If tobacco prices plummeted or even fluctuated, planters faced ruinous debt and bankruptcy. The risk was theirs alone.

Washington stuck with tobacco despite some troubling signs in the air. The Virginia tobacco crop's yield for 1758 was low, but scarcity gave no substantial boost to prices in London markets. Despite this stagnancy, he remained cautiously optimistic that tobacco would soon return to profitability.

The crop of 1759 promised a "favourable aspect at present," Washington told the London merchant John Hanbury, and "self Interest" would predispose him in favor of whatever merchant demonstrated the "greatest Exertion in the Sales" of his tobacco.

Not all tobacco was created equal, of course. Leaf grown on the Custis estates along the York River, Washington learned, was particularly sweet smelling and sold more rapidly and for higher prices than other tobacco. He therefore considered planting York River tobacco seed at Mount Vernon and on his "fine Lands" in the Shenandoah, provided that the crops would be "managed in every respect in the same manner."[11]

The system seemed simple—for a time. Washington could maintain the tried-and-true tobacco system—being sure to keep up with the latest practices—and reinvest a portion of his profits in more land, better equipment, more paying tenant farmers, more livestock, and ultimately more tobacco. At the same time he could purchase shiploads of fine cloth, elegant saddlery, expensive home furnishings, and dainties such as mangos, "best Porter," "perfumed Powder," and packs of playing cards.[12]

Washington's taste for such items reflected a growing American fascination with consumer goods. His interests were both personal and symbolic. He ordered a collection of busts of military heroes as well as statues of two "Furious Wild Beasts" (though because the military busts were unavailable he had to settle for busts of more peaceable luminaries alongside "Two Lyons after the antique Lyon's in Italy"). As the busts emphasized, Washington was a retired military hero, a lion of the battlefield now taking his place as a civil leader. He even spoke of sating his "longing desire" to visit the "great Matrapolis" of London.[13]

Such complacency would not endure for long. Over the following months and years, Washington's English agents tested his patience with apologies that the "Crop of Tobacco in General was but ordinary," that sales were "too light," and that "it gave us a good deal of trouble to get the price it sold for." By the early 1760s, tobacco was unmistakably failing as a trade commodity. The primitive farming practices of the day played a role in the decline. Tobacco rapidly drains soil fertility, and although Washington directed regular crop rotations the nutrient-poor and clayey Mount Vernon land soon lost its potency.

All he could do was let old fields lie fallow—for up to twenty years—and clear new land for planting. That practice could not continue indefinitely.[14]

Nor could he rely on the sweet-smelling tobacco from the Custis plantations to take up the slack. Plantation manager Joseph Valentine wrote Washington on August 9, 1760, that the tobacco there had been "drownded" by heavy rains. Drought followed in 1762, forcing Washington to write to Cary on June 20: "We have had one of the most severe Droughts in these parts that was ever known & without a speedy Interposition of Providence (in sending us moderate & refreshing Rains to molifie & soften the Earth) we shall not make one Oz. of Tobacco this Year." Or, as he wrote with bitter sarcasm to his friend and relation Burwell Bassett on August 28: "Our growing Property— meaning the Tobacco—is assailed by every villainous worm that has had an existence since the days of Noah (how unkind it was of Noah now that I have mentioned his name to suffer such a brood of Vermin to get a birth in the Ark)." Plenty of other tobacco was damaged in transit or lost to French predators or bad weather, and insurance was expensive—another knock against an international trade that had at first seemed so lucrative.[15]

Washington also began to suspect that British tradesmen were hoodwinking him, for price tags on imports rose even as tobacco prices wilted. "I cannot forbear ushering in a Complaint of the exorbitant prices of my Goods," he complained to Robert Cary. It was shoddy merchandise too, and sometimes even—horrors—out of date. "You may believe me when I tell you," Washington griped, "that instead of getting things good and fashionable in their several kind we often have Articles sent Us that could only have been used by our Forefathers in the days of yore." It appeared that British merchants were palming off their refuse for the export trade while deliberately jacking up prices as much as 20 percent.[16]

Washington hated the thought of being cheated. In desperation, he told his agents to order goods from tradesmen without revealing that they were for export. The ineffectiveness of this prescription solidified his suspicion that agents and tradesmen were working in tandem. A creeping resentment against the mother country stole into his mind.

Peace seemed to promise a better future. At the end of the French and Indian War, Washington looked forward to the prospect of free and uninterrupted commerce. "We are much rejoiced at the prospect of Peace," he told Cary, "which 'tis hoped will be of long continuance, & introductory of mutual advantages to the Merchant & Planter, as the Trade to this Colony will flow in a more easy and regular Channel than it has done for a considerable time past." Experience quickly showed, however, that in the colonial system trade was not free. America served as a source of raw materials for Great Britain, and as a market for British manufactured goods. Imperial regulations dictated that this should remain so in perpetuity.[17]

American entrepreneurs like Washington did not enjoy unfettered access to the world market and could not react freely to the laws of supply and demand. American exporters had to ship goods demanded by Continental European markets to Great Britain, where they were subject to heavy duties and tolls before being transmitted through middlemen—of course at higher prices—to the Continent. Likewise, European exports to America had to go through Great Britain, again incurring duties and tolls, before traveling on British ships to America. British merchants were subject to no such liabilities. The system was designed to protect and enrich them, not their American suppliers.

The colonial system humiliated Americans and stifled their natural yearning toward prosperity. Some began to face not just stasis but poverty. By the mid-1760s, Washington's accounts were falling out of balance. Low tobacco profits were only part of the problem. Upkeep and repairs to Mount Vernon led to a steady flow of heavy expenses. So did his proclivity for purchasing land, which brought his total holdings to 9,381 acres by the summer of 1763. Washington's excessive lending to family and friends—a habit he never entirely cured—also came back to bite him, as debtors kept finding excuses to delay repayment. And as the prices of imports continued to rise, so did his debts. These became worse every year until 1764, when he discovered to his alarm that he owed £1,800 to Cary & Company alone. With perhaps the greatest sense of shame he had felt since the surrender at Fort Necessity a decade earlier, Washington penned an abject letter of apology to Cary, confessing that it is "an irksome thing to a free mind to be any ways hampered in Debt."[18]

The situation was especially galling because in 1762 Washington had finally come into his own as the master of Mount Vernon with the death of

Lawrence's widow. In most respects it was a dream fulfilled. There now rose before him, however, the prospect of becoming what he had long despised—a profligate, debt-ridden planter. Washington often bought lottery tickets for "prizes" from the property of heavily indebted fellow planters and merchants seeking to liquidate their estates, and might well have wondered whether he would soon be selling tickets instead of buying them. Never, though, did he blame his predicament on his own management or open-handed spending. Instead, he grew convinced that the unequal colonial relationship with Great Britain placed an unfair economic burden on American planters.

Washington was slow to change his personal habits. His heavy spending on luxury goods, including large quantities of wine and other alcoholic beverages, reflected not just his and Martha's personal tastes but his belief in and enjoyment of entertaining. Until his later years, when the cares of public life had worn him down, Washington was known as a genial and gracious host who danced well, conversed freely—especially with the ladies—and spent lavishly to ensure that his guests enjoyed themselves. Foxhunting, which Washington enjoyed, was another social function that made up part of the display. Always, though, his parties and other events served a purpose.

In his early days visiting Belvoir, Washington learned how balls and other less formal gatherings—including even cockfights and card games—served to maintain the social and business relationships so vital to the gentry. Such events took on added importance during the political campaigning season, when candidates were expected to treat voters to a good time in the form of music, games, food, and, above all, rivers of alcohol. In the days-long festival preceding his first election to the House of Burgesses in June 1758, Washington paid £39 out of his own pocket for 160 gallons of booze. During the polling for his reelection in May 1761, he navigated the surging crowd at a cockfight to press hands, show his affinity for the common people, and get out the vote.

Writing in his diary on April 9, 1760, Washington recorded the arrival of one Doctor Laurie, "I may add Drunk." In an age of prodigious alcohol consumption and widespread alcoholism, such encounters were all too common. Though no alcoholic, Washington drank freely if not prodigiously. Later in life he would develop a fondness for wine, particularly the fortified Madeira variety.[19]

Domestic production intrigued him as well. Just before the onset of the Revolutionary War, he invested £50 in Italian wine merchant Philip Mazzei's project to establish an experimental agricultural venture near Monticello "for the Purpose of raising and making Wine, Oil, agruminous Plants and Silk." Mazzei's venture failed, but Washington proved prescient in his prediction that "from the spontaneous growth of the vine, that the climate and soil in many parts of Virginia were well fitted for Vineyards & that Wine, sooner or later would become a valuable article of produce."[20]

As a young man, Washington's alcoholic beverage of choice was beer. For a time he even experimented with brewing it. A recipe for "Small Beer" appears in his memorandum book of 1757:

Take a large Siffer full of Bran Hops to your Taste. Boil these 3 hours. then strain out 30 Gallns into a Cooler put in 3 Gallns Molasses while the Beer is Scalding hot or rather draw the Molasses into the Cooler & Strain the Beer on it while boiling Hot. let this stand till it is little more than Blood warm then put in a quart of Yest if the weather is very Cold cover it over with a Blanket & let it work in the Cooler 24 hours then put it into the Cask—leave the Bung open till it is almost done woring—Bottle it that day week it was Brewed.

Nothing came of these experiments—possibly, as modern duplications of his recipe indicate, because George Washington brand beer was awful stuff—and he ultimately relied on others to cater to his needs. He preferred his beer good and strong—preferably porter—but sampled a good number of varieties.[21]

Domestic brews were available in places. The brewer John Mercer of Frederick County supplied Washington with a cask of beer for almost £4 in April 1768. Imports, however, were usually of higher quality. London brewer Benjamin Kenton sent him a hogshead of "fine old Porter" for £2 5s in March 1760, and Londoner Thomas Dale shipped four casks of "Dorsett Beer" (a staggering 492 bottles) to Mount Vernon in April 1762. Here too, however, Washington discovered that British merchants were not always honest, and that the long route for goods from London to Alexandria presented ample opportunities for accident and thievery. On July 26, 1762, he eagerly opened a cask of porter and three casks of Dorsetshire beer only to discover that they contained dozens of broken, partially full, or empty bottles.[22]

In the House of Burgesses, delegates generally behaved with decorum, although when deliberations ended they adjourned to local taverns for long nights of gossip, gambling, and drinking. Washington reveled in these affairs but diligently carried out his legislative duties, which included frequent attention to matters concerning the domestic and international dimensions of commerce, finance, and trade. His habits of prudence and moderation impressed the burgesses as they carried out their deliberations. Even as tensions with the mother country heated up, radical firebrands were frowned upon. Washington was attentive and deliberate without being dispassionate or detached.

As a burgess he increasingly identified his personal and economic interests with Virginia and, more broadly, America. He did not expect his country to remain in tobacco, or even primarily in agriculture, forever. In the burgesses he advocated schemes to boost domestic manufacture, and he invested small sums of his own money (for he was too prudent not to be cautious) in ventures for the establishment of wine and silk production in Virginia. These were the first hesitant steps toward what would eventually become a public, and for Washington a personal, crusade.

In the House of Burgesses there is no record of Washington getting bent out of shape over political, legal, religious, or military issues. Economic disputes, however, could get him thoroughly riled. This was especially so when the disputes involved British merchants. Washington continued to rely on their services for his own needs, but he had come to distrust them as a body.

In May 1763, British merchants who were creditors to Virginia for French and Indian War debts petitioned the Board of Trade about the Virginians' irksome habit of paying them in suspect paper treasury notes. Virginia had no choice: because hard currency was so rare and planters lived mostly on credit, there was no way for the colony to pay debts except by issuing increasingly large quantities of paper currency, which the burgesses declared legal tender. The merchants' demand that debts be paid in sterling was nonsensical since none was available. Eventually, Washington (himself in growing debt to British merchants) warned, such behavior would "set the whole Country in Flames. . . . [T]his stir of the Merchants seems to be ill timed and cannot be attended with any good effects—bad I fear it will." He stood with the burgesses in resisting any change. Two years later the Stamp Act, coinciding with deepening financial woes that Washington blamed on unfair trade practices, would bring his feelings of resentment against the merchants to a near-fever pitch.[23]

Washington had to cope directly with the consequences of this controversy. The stubbornness of the burgesses about paper currency annoyed both the royal governor and the British Board of Trade. As a tit-for-tat, when Native Americans began large-scale attacks on Virginia's frontier shortly afterward, the British government withheld military assistance. Virginia had to raise its own militia to fight the natives, even though the British told the burgesses they could not print paper money to pay the militiamen.

In 1764, Washington was placed directly in charge of the House of Burgesses commission tasked with wrangling a way to pay the soldiers. He had to do so even as Parliament passed, in April, the Currency Act that expressly prohibited the colonies from printing paper currency. To raise funds, the colonials would just have to find hard currency somehow—practically impossible in the prevailing system—or accept further credit and fall even more deeply in debt to the British. The currency crisis profoundly impacted Washington's thinking, and threatened his fortune. Another year would pass, though, before the Stamp Act set in motion events that would lead to a final break.

———————

AS THE 1760S PROGRESSED, Washington's mind matured. His education, as we have seen, was practical. No amount of catching up would ever make him an intellectual. Nevertheless, as an adult Washington attained a genius ideally suited to his own and his nation's future prosperity. Grand ideas counted for little, he understood, without a good deal of plain common sense. He believed in more than a few high-flown principles, such as liberty, justice, and freedom. The difference with Washington was that he realized ideas meant and could achieve nothing without close attention to the minute realities of day-to-day life. If the devil dwelt in the details, so did hope.

As a surveyor, Washington had perfected his knowledge of tools and techniques, becoming a brilliant draughtsman. As a military leader during the war, he had learned to devote close attention to fundamentals, a skill that would become a foundation of future greatness. And as a planter-businessman, he carefully tabulated his profits, investments, and expenses down to the last penny. Like his father in dealing with the Principio Iron Works, George Washington made certain to evaluate a proposition from all the angles before deciding to invest (or sometimes to cut his losses), but once his mind was made up he was methodical and remorseless. Let others deride his attention to detail as mental slowness if they so desired—hasty decisions, he had learned the hard way at places like Jumonville's Glen, could lead to disaster.

The same practical mindset had helped Washington to understand both that his education was lacking and that he would have to improve it substantially if he was to achieve success in any realm of endeavor. His shallow training in the liberal arts had caused his letters to betray uncouthness that probably led some to dismiss him as a country bumpkin. Now, as an adult in the 1760s, he applied himself to polishing his written and oral communication skills. The results were tangible. His writing ability, including handwriting, grammar, and organization, improved profoundly from 1759 to 1775.

Washington also spent many a quiet hour in his study at Mount Vernon, simply reading. A lifelong news junkie, he perused weekly papers, especially the *Virginia Gazette* for up-to-date information on business and politics. The *Gazette* was not just any newspaper—it was *the* source of information on market prices, currency values, investment opportunities, mercantile activities, ship departures and arrivals, conditions for trade, estate sales, lotteries, and so on. Washington advertised in it regularly.

Books were a growing but not yet primary interest at this stage in his life. He would later write, "I conceive a knowledge of books is the basis upon which other knowledge is to be built," but a list of the books in his library that he painstakingly compiled in 1764 reveals a collection that was something of a jumble. Most of the volumes had been inherited from the Custis estate and included a good number of classic works of literature and history, as well as many on theology and medicine. To this Washington added a modest collection of bound periodicals and books on agriculture, husbandry, law, geography, travel, and arithmetic as well as a copy of *Mr. Hoyle's Games,* no doubt to inform his card-playing. More usefully, he had purchased Henry Crouch's *A Complete View of the British Customs* (1731, though he probably possessed a newer edition), containing everything an exporter needed to know about trade with Great Britain.[24]

This purposefully directed, bricks-and-mortar reading style reflected Washington's growing conviction that economics was the fundamental reality that underpinned everything else, including politics and war. He had learned this as a soldier, as a burgess, and as a planter. In the political crises that were to wrack the late 1760s and 1770s, Washington would regard his, Virginia's, and America's economic and political interests as one and the same. His actions and words demonstrated his belief that political prosperity depended on economic prosperity, and that political freedom depended on economic freedom. Soon enough, he would have to decide whether they were worth fighting for.

———

BY 1765, WASHINGTON WAS FAR MORE POLISHED and politically astute than he had been when he married Martha. He was also a savvier planter and businessman. Tobacco planting was second nature, and if trade with Great Britain was not equally so, he at least understood how it worked. But change was in the air. Washington's expensive tastes in consumer goods and land were beginning to haunt him. Expenses rose faster than profits. Merchants charged higher prices for the manufactured goods that George, Martha, and the children desired. Meanwhile, income fell as prices continued to fall even as tobacco harvests repeatedly failed, reducing supply.

A naturally creative man, Washington understood that innovation was a key to getting back on track. But although his available capital for new investments remained adequate, it was steadily shrinking due to his increasing debts. If this continued for much longer, he realized, he would no longer have sufficient capital to diversify away from tobacco even if he wanted to. Wrapped in the leaf's deadly embrace, his estate would strangle. Financial disaster would be slow but inevitable.

Washington's mounting worries provoked him to increased frustration with British merchants. He blamed them for his troubles more than he did his own spendthrift ways. Financial uncertainties also coincided with a growing political crisis with the mother country driven largely by questions of debt and trade. By the mid-1760s Great Britain's national debt approached £130,000,000, and the country owed £4,500,000 worth of annual dues in interest on those debts alone. Much of this debt derived from expenses incurred by the British while conducting far-flung campaigns in North America during the French and Indian War. And even though peace had been concluded in 1763, expenses would remain heavy so that the colonial governments could continue to defend the frontier against Native Americans. Washington and many others had resented the royal proclamation of that year prohibiting settlement beyond the Appalachians, but projects such as the Mississippi Company that assumed massive British military protection for western settlers were shockingly naïve.

What would become known as Pontiac's War erupted in the Northwest Territories in May 1763 and would last for three years, sucking in thousands more British troops for frontier defense. It was in this context that the British chancellor of the exchequer, George Grenville, rose in Parliament in the spring of 1764 to propose the imposition of a stamp act on the colonies. By its terms, Americans would be forced to use paper—imported from Great Britain, of course—bearing a special revenue stamp for official documents as well as pamphlets, newspapers, and even playing cards. From the British perspective the proposal seemed reasonable. The colonies demanded much, and they should therefore bear part of the burden themselves.

What seemed reasonable or even benevolent from the British point of view looked punitive to the Americans. The new taxes directly reinforced America's subservient colonial relationship. American assemblies such as the House of Burgesses had been used to thinking of themselves as smaller versions of Parliament with jurisdiction over their own territories. The Stamp Act, ratified in March 1765 and scheduled to enter operation in November of that year, overrode colonial legislative autonomy on taxation even as the Currency Act of the previous year had removed Americans' ability to control their own currency.

For the burgesses as a body, and Washington as an individual, the time had come to take a stand. In the House of Burgesses, Patrick Henry introduced his Stamp Act resolutions that in effect asserted the colonists' equality to residents of the British Isles, and thus their right to tax themselves through their own assemblies. In response, the governor dissolved the legislature and called new elections for the summer, providing Washington with an opportunity to move himself closer to the political center of resistance in Virginia. He left his Frederick constituency and campaigned successfully for election in Fairfax. Political opposition to the Stamp Act was not going away.

Even as the burgesses sought to achieve political autonomy over economic issues, Washington issued his own declaration of financial autonomy. In fact, the two processes dovetailed. On September 20, 1765, as he began developing plans to diversify away from tobacco, Washington wrote to Cary complaining about the "pitifully low" sales of his sweet-smelling tobacco in England. His Virginia neighbors, working through other London agents, seemed to be earning more than him even though their tobacco was of worse quality. In addition, English tradesmen still charged Washington ridiculous prices. From where he sat, it looked like Cary was doing nothing to counteract this outrageous behavior. Instead, the agent simply suggested that Washington return overpriced items to London—a process both expensive and ridiculously inconvenient.[25]

Not just individuals, it seemed, but the British in general were cheating Americans on "matters of the utmost consequence to our well doing." Consciously or otherwise, Washington increasingly adopted the voice of an aggrieved people as he commenced a strident denunciation of not only the "ill Judged" Stamp Act but all of the recent legislation "and other Acts to Burthen us" that had tightened the squeeze on colonial commerce. Moreover, the measures seemed self-defeating. So far, he pointed out, "the whole produce of our labour . . . has centred in Great Britain." New taxes would reduce imports and hurt British manufacturers to the detriment of the "Common Weal." And he hinted at a boycott:

> The Eyes of our People (already beginning to open) will perceive, that many of the Luxuries which we have heretofore lavished our Substance to Great Britain for can well be dispensed with whilst the Necessaries of Life are to be procured (for the most part) within

ourselves—This consequently will introduce frugality; and be a necessary stimulation to Industry—Great Britain may then load her Exports with as Heavy Taxes as She pleases but where will the consumption be? I am apt to think no Law or usage can compel us to barter our money or Staple Commodities for their Manufactures, if we can be supplied within ourselves upon the better Terms.[26]

What else had Washington done over the past five years but expend his "Substance"—the produce of his lands—to Great Britain in return for overpriced "Luxuries" that he was well aware he could do without?

Resistance to these policies did not just represent a protest of the aggrieved. On the whole, it resulted from people thinking not negatively but optimistically. Americans sensed instinctively that they were on the verge of great things—in modern parlance, that their economy was approaching takeoff. The mother country itself provided the inspiration. Under the right conditions, the opportunity was there for America to enter into a whole new phase even as Great Britain had reached the height of an Agricultural Revolution and was in the first throes of the Industrial Revolution. It was no secret that the boom in British agricultural prosperity with the adoption of better farming methods and new technologies had enriched a whole generation of entrepreneurs with ample capital to invest. As investment led innovation and further promoted prosperity, a chain reaction seemed under way. The growing sense of excitement transmitted itself across the Atlantic. American entrepreneurs wanted to join in and share the prosperity. Instead, even as they saw the first glimpses of daylight, they were manacled with onerous restrictions that would force them at best to endure decades of incarceration in an agricultural backwater, and at worst to enter a whirlpool of debt slavery.

Public self-criticism was not in Washington's line. Privately, however, he recognized that his own spending habits had helped to reinforce the problem. He was not the only one to feel this way. In the aftermath of the Stamp Act, which Parliament grudgingly repealed in March 1766, Americans everywhere were looking at how their addiction to imported British goods made them slaves of the colonial system. Just as later generations were transfixed by the catchphrase "Buy American," so were the colonials of the 1760s and 1770s.

Wearing homespun rather than imported fineries became a matter of pride. At Princeton University (then the College of New Jersey), undergraduates such as James Madison and Henry (later "Light Horse" Harry) Lee pledged their honor to don only American-made clothing.

Old habits die hard, however, and domestic manufacture, neglected for so long, could not be conjured into existence overnight. For many years Washington had spent a good deal of his income on baubles and fripperies. In the morally simplistic thinking of his youth, this had been both a just reward for hard work and prosperity and a necessity to maintain his social standing. But his growing debt made him aware that he was projecting a prosperity he did not in fact enjoy, and the specter of crushing debt and possible bankruptcy, bitterness against British agents and tradesmen, and his growing political awareness convinced him it was time for a change. Henceforward the goal would be self-sufficiency.

The first order of business was to decide how to replace tobacco. Parliament had issued a bounty for American production of hemp and flax. As with other American-produced raw materials, these were to be destined primarily for British markets and the manufacture of rope and cloth. Washington was briefly intrigued with the idea, and asked his agents to tell him what prices he could expect to fetch "as they are Articles altogether new to us & I believe not much of our Lands well adapted for them, and as the proper kind of Packages, Freight, & accustomed charges are little known here." The prospect of engaging once again in a relationship of dependency with untrustworthy British agents, merchants, and tradesmen cannot have appealed to him. Nevertheless, he experimented with both crops for a time after 1765.[27]

After careful consideration and extensive research, however, Washington decided to turn his estate over to wheat. There were many considerations behind the decision, not least among them being that although some of his wheat and flour would be destined for overseas markets, he did not have to deal with British merchants directly. Instead he contracted, beginning in 1764, to sell his wheat to American merchants in Alexandria. In following years he simply dealt with merchants in any location who could offer him the best prices.

The changeover involved some expense—fields and farms, buildings and equipment, would have to be reconfigured. But the benefits multiplied in ways that he could not have foreseen immediately, especially with respect to labor. Tobacco had been very labor-intensive, absorbing much of the time and energy of his slaves and white workmen. Wheat, relying more heavily on animal power, did require the devotion of more resources to livestock (and especially the growth of corn and other plants for fodder), but it freed his workers to do other things. This in turn furthered Washington's dual goals of reducing expenditures and increasing his economic self-sufficiency.

The changeover was extremely rapid. In 1764, his estate produced 257 bushels of wheat; in 1766, 2,331 bushels; and in 1769, 6,241 bushels. By 1774, he could truly say that "the whole of my force is in a manner confined to the growth of Wheat, & Manufacturing of it into Flour." By 1766, he had eliminated tobacco from his Mount Vernon farms, although he would continue to raise a small crop from rents and his Custis lands until the 1770s. Even so, tobacco production on the Custis estate fell from 133 hogsheads in 1763 to 51 hogsheads in 1767.[28]

Once he committed to wheat, there would be no turning back. Improvement was rapid but the statistics did not suffice to satisfy Washington's ambitions. He wanted to maximize production. For this, experimentation and investment were essential. Experimentation particularly tantalized Washington, who possessed a scientific bent of mind.

Back in 1760, he had laboriously constructed a large wooden box divided into ten compartments. Into each of these he shoveled soil, being certain to take all of the soil from the same field "without any mixture." One box he left unenhanced. Into each of the others he added a different kind of fertilizer, including horse, cow, and sheep dung; "Mud taken out of the Creek"; "Riverside Sand"; clay; "Black Mould"; and marl (clay with silt of fossil shell or lime). To ensure regularity, Washington mixed the fertilizers and soil "in the most effectual manner by reducing the whole to a tolerable degree of fineness & jumbling them well together in a Cloth." Into each compartment he planted three seeds each of wheat, oats, and barley, using "a Machine made for the purpose," to ensure that they were "all at equal distances in Rows & of equal depth." Then he sat back to wait, watering each of the compartments equally for two weeks. On May 1, he evaluated the experiment and concluded that sheep dung and "Black Mould" were the most productive; but the experiments would continue.[29]

Machinery fascinated Washington. He was aware of innovations developed overseas from reading the newspapers. Though he also read plenty of books on the subject, he always preferred using his hands. On any given day in the 1760s he could be found puttering about the workshop, often side by side with a slave, trying out some new contraption aimed at improving production.

He began with the most fundamental of all agricultural implements: the plow. Shortly after moving to Mount Vernon, he worked on designing a new model plow partly of his own design. The gadget didn't work at first, but after more tinkering he proudly went out to draw it behind his large bay mare. Over the following years he built more plows and had them used across all of his fields while still seeking to improve them. Experiments also continued on a new harrow for his grain.

Larger labor-saving devices intrigued Washington, complex though they were by the standards of the time. In 1764 he investigated reports of an "engine" that had been developed for tearing up trees by the roots, allowing for more rapid clearing of land. He also looked into developing a forge and ironworking industry on his estate, although nothing would come of this until after the Revolution.[30]

The most important and complex machinery at Mount Vernon was in the gristmill. The building was originally located on the Mill Tract east of Dogue Run about two miles northwest of the mansion. It was an elderly construction, having been acquired by Lawrence in 1738 when he bought the surrounding property. He then transferred it to his father. When Augustine died in 1743, it reverted to Lawrence and he made some improvements to it, expanding the property for the growing millpond. By the time George moved to Mount Vernon with Martha in 1759, though, the mill was little more than a junk pile. Watching its operation closely, Washington was shocked to discover that it took the old machinery almost an hour to grind a single bushel of grain.

At first all he could afford were stopgap repairs. Characteristically, he brought in expert help but participated personally in every undertaking, whether digging a new mill dam alongside his slaves and hired labor or working alongside his carpenters to replace decayed machinery or make delicate adjustments to the mill operations. In so doing, he acquired a minute understanding of how everything worked.

With the changeover from tobacco to wheat, updating the gristmill became imperative. After a thorough inspection of the old building, Washington concluded it was hopeless. Instead, in 1769 he decided to construct a new mill half a mile downstream and on the other side of Dogue Run. He chose the site with the expert advice of John Ballendine, a successful local mill owner, and then devised a plan for constructing the building. Traveling to the falls of the Potomac, Washington selected large river rocks, and had workers excavate and float them down to Mount Vernon. These would serve as the building's foundation. He directed others to quarry stone for the walls, and cut timber from his estate for the roof and interior. Another team, also under the master's close supervision, dug the millrace.

The equipment was expensive, but Washington did not scrimp. His goals were loftier than just grinding his own grain; he also intended to earn profit from his neighbors by constructing a modern mill that could grind theirs as well, producing varying grades of meal for added profit. To that end, instead of purchasing the substantially cheaper but inferior-quality local millstones, he had two stones imported from France. These were not only superior but the best to be found anywhere, since they were exceptionally hard and held a good sharp edge for many years. The flour they produced would be the best in northern Virginia, and would command commensurate prices. It was worth the investment of £38, almost twice what he would have paid for local stones. By the time the stones were in place and the new mill was fully operational in 1771, Washington's own wheat production was at its peak and he had a highly profitable and growing concern of domestic manufacture. Here too, though, experiments would continue, both with different kinds of wheat and other grains and with different means of harvesting and grinding it.

Wheat and flour could be sold domestically far more easily than tobacco, so that he could operate outside the colonial system. But American merchants were not necessarily easier to deal with than British ones. As he moved over to wheat, the first major firm Washington contracted with for sale was Carlyle & Adam of Alexandria. The relationship quickly went sour, however, and on February 15, 1767, Washington sent the unlucky partners one of the angriest and longest letters he ever wrote, lashing them savagely for their inability to procure a fair price for his wheat. At its end, he promised never to write them again. Ironically, though, Washington and the partners soon settled their differences. Carlyle & Adam would serve for many more years as his primary contractor for wheat and flour. A primary difference between the Alexandria merchants and the British, of course, was that the former were available for personal interaction while the latter were not. Also, with less money on account with the likes of Cary thanks to the decline of tobacco, Washington could concentrate his British purchases on necessities rather than luxuries.

As his productivity multiplied—some twenty-five times by the end of the 1760s—Washington's flour production became a going concern. His finely equipped mill ground grain for other farmers at a fee, and plans were under way to construct similar operations in other parts of Virginia. Quantity, however, could not be allowed to impinge on quality. Washington's insistence on high production standards paid off as his "G. Washington" brand of flour became known for its reliable superiority. A Norfolk merchant reflected the views of his peers in gratefully telling Washington that his brand had "the preference of any at this market."[31]

By the 1770s, Washington was selling corn and meal for slaves in the West Indies. Even sailors gnawed Washington-brand biscuits as they plied the Atlantic trade. Here too, not all his experiences were positive. In 1772, Washington formed a partnership to sell flour refined at his and others' mills in the West Indies via a Jamaican merchant. Unfortunately, the incompetence of his supercargo Daniel Jenifer Adams—whom Washington called a "worthless young Fellow"—doomed the venture. Expecting Adams's ship to sink, he abandoned it quickly in an eighteenth-century harbinger of the modern "fail-fast" technique—but not before losing money that he recovered partly by seizing 500 acres of Adams's land.[32]

Missteps of this sort were inevitable companions of bold entrepreneurship. But though the risks were substantial, the opportunities were too good to ignore. Increasingly large numbers of Washington's countrymen followed his example or, more often, set examples of their own. Those willing to forego tobacco found that their profits went to their own pockets instead of to the British. As more planters moved to wheat and other profitable crops, America experienced an economic explosion. Productivity of staple goods boomed while enterprises for preparing, marketing, and transporting them via land or sea appeared in towns like Alexandria. As the American economy grew in size, however, the colonial shackles restraining it squeezed all the more tightly.

———————

The move to wheat spurred Mount Vernon's transformation. Riding around the estate in 1759, Washington had scanned a vista awash in green, and would not have heard much more than birdsong, the clop of his horse's hooves, and the calls of men in the fields. The same scene a decade later presented him with a bedazzling variety of sights and sounds. Production was everywhere. In the past, Washington's slaves had depended almost entirely on others to supply their basic necessities, such as food and clothing. Now that they were free of tending tobacco, he expected them to provide for themselves. Fields echoed to hammers and saws as they built and maintained their housing, becoming skilled carpenters and masons. They constructed pens to raise hogs and chickens; tanned hides; cobbled shoes; constructed carts and wagons; cut stones; and made and laid bricks. The blacksmith shop, where a hammer or two had been wont to ring from time to time, now expanded into a hive of activity where skilled men not only shoed horses but also manufactured and repaired tools and household implements of all varieties. Before long, the smithy became a profitable enterprise. All of these crafts took training, but because Washington moved quickly over to wheat once he had made the decision to do so, he trained his labor more quickly than many of his neighbors, who now trekked to the Mount Vernon smithy with cash in hand to purchase manufactured goods and services.

As Mount Vernon's slave population grew, so did the need for clothing. Demand was in fact increasing throughout the region as rising numbers of free and enslaved laborers worked to expand estates. Washington, keenly aware of the growing tide of European immigration, anticipated that the increased demand for standard consumer items like clothing offered him another venue for profit. To that end he hired a supervisor named Thomas Davis to train and oversee a team of women—slaves and indentured servants—to labor in a specially constructed spinning house. Soon Mount Vernon's spinning wheels and looms were adding their voices to the chorus of industry at the estate.

The scribble of Washington's pen joined in as he took careful records of costs, production, and profit. In his spinning and weaving account for 1768, he noted that his laborers had churned out 1,365 yards of flax linens, woolens, linsey (wool cloth), and cotton fabric during the year. Beneath the account he tabulated what it would have cost him to import and prepare the same amount of material during the same period, and concluded that by manufacturing at home he was saving more than £50 per annum over and above what he earned by selling his excess production to neighbors for cash and barter goods.

The Mount Vernon community now could also take advantage of a rich natural resource close at hand—the Potomac River, abounding with fish. Washington had been sensitive since childhood to the importance of waterways not just as highways of commerce and trade but as resources in their own right. Water had been close at hand where he lived at his birthplace and on Ferry Farm, and fishing was one of his favorite pastimes. The same applied at Mount Vernon, which Lawrence had named after an admiral.

Given his druthers, George would have been a devoted fisherman. Throughout his life he had a particular fondness for fish on the table. In January 1760, he braved bitter weather to trek down to the river landing, where he "Hauled the Sein and got some fish." Unfortunately, on his return to the landing a thuggish "Oyster Man" ambushed Washington and "plagud me a good deal by his disorderly behavior." Inwardly seething—his spirits worsened by the fact that Martha and much of the family were sick with measles—George carried his fish home; but when he returned to the landing a few days later, the surly oysterman popped up again, this time accompanied by friends. Washington—whose temper befitted his imposing physique, but who usually refrained from initiating physical combat (especially when outnumbered)—"was obliged in the most preemptory manner to order him and his Company away which he did not incline to obey till next morning."[33]

With the oysterman out of the way, Washington marveled at the river's bounty. His diaries and letters abound with references to teeming fish. "The Sturgeon are now jumping," he told Charles Washington on August 15, 1764; and on May 16, 1768, he spent the day "Fishing for Sturgeon from Breakfast to Dinner" although alas he "catched none." On April 22, 1769, his sole diary entry expostulated on how "The Herrings run in great abundance."[34]

Exploiting this resource was initially a simple matter. He would watch attentively as two men rowed out into the channel, drawing out behind them a seine up to 450 feet long, weighted with lead on one side and floated by corks on the other, and tied on each end with hauling ropes. Once the seine was fully deployed, men on shore would pull in the hauling ropes. Thousands of fish trapped in the net would then be pulled ashore, where slaves would wade in with bushel baskets to harvest the catch. Some fish ended up on the evening's table in the mansion house and in slave quarters, but slaves would preserve the majority of the catch by cleaning and gutting the fish, salting them, and packing them in barrels either for future use at Mount Vernon or for sale in Alexandria.

With increasing labor and financial resources available to him after the switch away from tobacco, Washington expanded the fishery. His slaves added shipbuilding to their other skills as they constructed boats and even a fine schooner under the master's supervision. Slaves and hired boatmen manned this small fleet (and eventually operated a river ferry), exponentially increasing production. By the 1770s, he was not only selling fish to neighbors but also shipping barrels of salted fish to the West Indies via Alexandria merchants.

Although restrictive British policies continued to create annoyances—forcing him, for example, to bypass fine Portuguese salt for fish-curing in favor of lower-quality Liverpool salt—the fisheries soon became one of his most valuable enterprises. In 1772 alone, his men caught a million herring along with ten thousand shad and other fish; and after meeting the needs of his own community at Mount Vernon, he sold the rest to merchants, clearing a profit of £184. The profits, and fortunately the fish, would remain ample throughout his lifetime. On December 12, 1793, he wrote to the Englishman Arthur Young: "This River, which encompasses the land the distance abovementioned, is well supplied with various kinds of fish at all seasons of the year; and in the Spring with the greatest profusion of Shad, Herring, Bass, Carp, Perch, Sturgeon &ca. Several valuable fisheries appertain to the estate; the whole shore in short is one entire fishery."[35]

As for tobacco, it had become a sidelight. British merchants still tried to entice him back into the old system, but he informed one of them on May 5, 1768, that "Having discontinued the growth of Tobacco myself, except at a Plantation or two upon York River, I make no more of that Article than barely

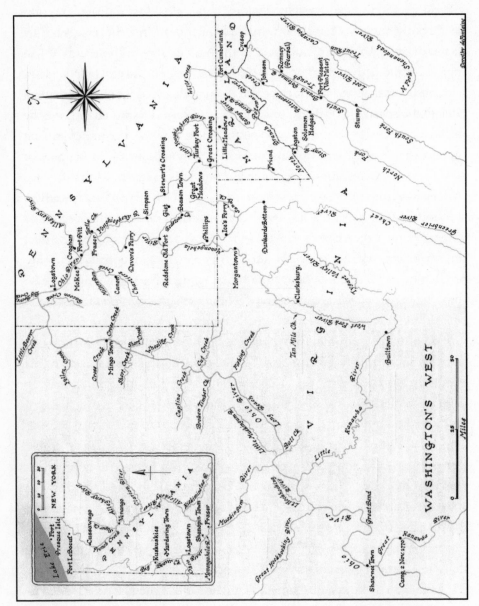

Donald Jackson and Dorothy Twohig, eds., *The Diaries of George Washington* (Charlottesville: University Press of Virginia, 1976–1979), 1:124–125.

serves to furnish me with Goods [and] necessaries wanted for my Family's use." In effect, he regarded it as disposable income.[36]

That spring and summer, tobacco enjoyed a brief spike in prices, and Washington wrote to Cary of his belief that "Tobacco would rise & sell almost as high as it ever had done, was as clear to me as the Sun in its meridian height." Instead of rushing to plant more leaf, however, he just exploited the temporary windfall as an opportunity to purchase extravagances that he would not otherwise have considered, such as a secondhand English chariot that he ordered through Cary. His correspondence with British merchants from then on concerned only his shrinking tobacco crop and the small quantities of hemp and wheat that he also produced for export to England.[37]

Washington had never been busier—or happier. Though not exactly a workaholic, he was industrious and the sensation of expansion and profit gave him deep satisfaction. Instead of joining in the public craze for consumer goods, he profited from it. His success in this arena helped to compensate for his disappointment at Martha's not bearing him any children. Another cause for satisfaction was the revelation that by the early 1770s he was free of debt. The income from Mount Vernon's many industries provided Washington with a modest but growing source of capital that allowed him not only to throw off the British credit system but also to look to other investment opportunities. Almost instinctively, he looked to the west.

———

WASHINGTON'S FINANCIAL INTERESTS transcended the boundaries of his far-flung and growing estate. Even as he attempted to make his farming and trading interests more profitable, he sought to buy, sell, and invest wherever the winds of commerce and his inclinations took him. His goal remained simple: to get rich as quickly as possible. He was not the only one to think that way, and in late colonial America there were more investment schemes available than a planter could shake his cane at. But when it came to large sums of money, Washington was an educated investor rather than a gambler. When opportunities arose, he would take their measure firsthand rather than relying on biased third-party information.

Extended interests also converged with Washington's vision of the physical expansion and financial future of America as a whole. Above all, land was still a primary commodity of economic growth. It could be bartered, rented, settled, and developed in a variety of ways. Commercial towns could be founded and profits controlled. Opportunities for expansion abounded—at least insofar as the British government permitted their exploitation.

In May 1763, at the height of spring and before the flies and mosquitoes began to frolic, Washington and a small band of "adventurers" visited the Great Dismal Swamp. This aptly named quagmire was an odd feature on the landscape. It was higher than the surrounding land, so water drained out of it rather than into it. Other than that it was like a typical swamp, only a hundred times worse. Straddling the Virginia–North Carolina border along a twenty-mile stretch from south of Chesapeake to near present-day Elizabeth City, North Carolina, it was choked with standing cypress and white cedar trees surrounded by thousands of rotten trunks and branches clogging the muck amid clumps of reeds. But it had potential for those with eyes to see.

Taking a break from the General Assembly then meeting in Williamsburg, Washington and his friends Fielding Lewis, Burwell Bassett, and Thomas Walker—all young and equally bent on profit—rode south from Suffolk along the western edge of the swamp. At one point they dared to venture half a mile into the stinky expanse as their horses sank up to their fetlocks in the muck. They withdrew with some difficulty and continued their circuit east, crossing a small bridge across the Perquimans River and turning north up the great swamp's eastern edge. Along the way there would have been plenty of young men's banter, but they also took careful notes on water drainage and soil quality.

Far from being repelled by his little adventure through the wastes, Washington was refreshed and intrigued. Some corners of the swamp had already been drained, cleared, and settled on what he observed to be "prodigious fine land." Given patents to the wasteland and the right of passage across already-settled territory, Washington and his friends were convinced they could make a profit from it. The soil seemed "excessive rich," and the thousands of trees and logs were as good as money in the bank. While the land was being drained, they could harvest and sell the lumber, and once the draining was done, they could farm the rest to their mutual profit. Washington imagined the construction of a canal from the swamp to Norfolk that could both drain the morass and serve for commerce.[38]

The explorers joined with outside partners in forming a company optimistically dubbed "Adventurers for Draining the Dismal Swamp" and successfully petitioned the Assembly for the right to construct canals and causeways across private land to facilitate their work. Legal and practical difficulties would eventually sink the venture in a morass as intractable as the swamp itself. Washington nevertheless invested enough money into it to secure the rights to 4,000 acres of swampland. He would hold on to these until 1795, when he sold them to "Light Horse" Harry Lee.[39]

Just a few weeks after returning from this trip, on June 3, 1763, Washington joined another hardy band of "adventurers" in an organizational meeting of the Mississippi Land Company. The objectives of this company were considerably more grandiose than those of the Dismal Swamp Company. With the disappearance of the French from the Mississippi territory at the end of the war, land there seemed ripe for the taking. Property along the Mississippi looked especially attractive because of the advantages the river offered for interior and exterior trade and commerce. The adventurers invested funds to appoint an agent who would travel to England and secure rights to enough territory along the river to provide 50,000 acres per man. The king, it was assumed, would graciously provide military protection against the Native Americans, whom the settlers would brush aside before clearing and developing their land.

To Washington, still saddled at the time with tobacco-related debt, the gamble must have seemed small and the potential profits enormous. Unfortunately for the speculators, the crown didn't see eye to eye with their schemes. On October 7, 1763, a royal proclamation restricted settlement to east of Appalachia. This wrecked the Mississippi Company's aims, at least for a time. But Washington, like the many settlers who swarmed west across the mountains despite the royal prohibition, saw the measure as doomed to fail by default. "I can never look upon that Proclamation in any other light . . . than as a temporary expedient to quiet the Minds of the Indians," he informed his western land agent William Crawford on September 17, 1767. It "must," he was convinced, "fall of course in a few years especially when those Indians are consenting to our Occupying the Lands. any Person therefore who neglects the present oppertunity of hunting out good Lands & in some measure Marking & distinguishing them for their own (in order to keep others from settling them) will never regain it." In some respects this was the logic of an opportunist. But Washington knew he would never attain or hold a fortune by following all the rules.[40]

However enticing these schemes, the Potomac held the key to Washington's aspirations. The river brought life to his estate. Its fish fed master and slave alike, and generated additional profits. Its waters carried his trade. But Washington had long been intrigued by its potential for inland commerce. The end of the French and Indian War generated hopes not just along the Mississippi but in the Midwest as well. Made fully navigable, the river could be made to link up with the Ohio, creating boundless opportunities for venturesome entrepreneurs.

The potential for Washington was even greater because of his extensive western landholdings. Nothing had come of the Ohio Company scheme that had so interested his family before and during the French and Indian War. However, a royal proclamation of 1754 had set aside 200,000 acres along the Ohio River for those who served in that year's western expedition—as, of course, Washington did. The Proclamation of 1763 further mandated the award of western lands to veterans depending on rank, but simultaneously shut settlers out of the trans-Appalachia region. In so doing it killed a project that an investment group, eagerly supported by Washington, had founded a year earlier for developing western navigation via the Potomac. He and other Virginians could neither claim their western lands nor pursue schemes to improve them.

Frustration at royal restrictions on western expansion threatened to boil over until 1769, when the British government declared, after successful Native American treaty negotiations, that it might after all fulfill the promises of 1754. Washington quickly petitioned royal governor Lord Botetourt and his council to honor the land claims of Virginia Regiment veterans. The petition was granted, with the 200,000-acre territory being delineated in territory that Washington had earlier explored at the confluence of the Great Kanawha and Ohio Rivers.

The race to stake claims was on, and Washington pursued it with gusto. Working on his behalf, Crawford hurried to the frontier to identify and survey the best tracts. Washington followed him in October 1770 and kept a detailed journal of the nine-week journey that expressed his mounting excitement over the region's potential. With a fine appreciation for land resources and soil quality that he had honed as a surveyor, he appraised tracts for both potential productivity and the beauty of their situation. He liked hilly tracts best, not just for their "charming" aspect and "beautiful white Oaks," but for the earth he found there "as black as a Coal."[41]

Rich earth was not the only consideration. Others included the quality of timber, mineral resources (he visited a mine that produced coal "of the very best kind, burning freely"), and proximity to waterways. Navigability was especially important, for it determined whether the lands could be linked to eastern markets. With the growing productivity of Mount Vernon's fishery in mind, he also cast lines to see what he could bring up from western waterways. At one spot Washington was amazed to find the "River cats" so huge that their fry could have gobbled up the largest adults in the river back home. He even scoped out the best areas to find game, including buffalo and wild fowl.[42]

Returning to Mount Vernon at the beginning of December, Washington tabulated his travel expenses, and then set to work laying claim to a western empire. Crawford had made a start, but it was only that. In addition to grants under the terms of his own military service, Washington bought up the grants of several fellow veterans who were in financial distress. He also asked his brother Charles and his cousin Lund to acquire more land surreptitiously on his behalf. Nothing he did was illegal—many others were doing the same—but of all the western land investors, Washington was among the most successful. Between 1772 and 1774 he amassed holdings of over 20,000 acres along the Great Kanawha, and subsequent acquisitions in the region as late as 1790 would net him over 10,000 more.

Still, however, Washington was dissatisfied—not least because of apparent British machinations to outflank American investors and deny them their rights. Revelations of an English investment scheme to build a new western colony, Vandalia, that would interpose itself between American Ohio lands and further western expansion—as well as attempts to restrict grants under the 1763 Proclamation only to British royal army veterans—led Washington to expostulate against the colonial overlords' "malignant disposition towards us poor Americans; founded equally in Malice, absurdity, & error." Such frustration could not, however, curtail Washington's far-reaching hopes for western expansion. With the purchase of his gigantic western tracts, he had irrevocably committed himself to developing inland navigation to link up the Ohio region with the east. The Potomac River, he firmly believed, held the key.[43]

---

THE MID-1760S FORMED THE HIGH-WATER MARK of Washington's ambition and productivity. By this time it was apparent that Martha probably would never bear him any children. Other men in his place might have sought solace in affairs, travel, or dissipation. George, however, was not only a faithful husband and responsible stepfather but also a level-headed man who knew how to channel his energy productively. It is safe to guess that business created a positive outlet for some of his frustration at being unable to generate a line of progeny. He also certainly enjoyed entrepreneurship, and believed that industry was the natural expression of a man of character.

X The passions that fueled Washington's business endeavors help to explain the anger with which he reacted when his efforts were frustrated. He had little sympathy or patience for incompetent employees or business partners. In the decade from 1765 to 1775, though, Washington increasingly directed his ire against the colonial rulers in Great Britain. At every turn, it seemed, they conspired to restrain Washington's industry. As he looked around him, moreover, he saw that he was not alone. Everywhere Americans seemed to be straining through the bars of their colonial prison, grasping at a prosperity that seemed always tantalizingly close but just out of reach. No wonder that he soon joined with them in not just dreaming of freedom but working to make it real.

# CHAPTER THREE

# THE ROAD TO
# ECONOMIC FREEDOM

ON JULY 21, 1766, WASHINGTON PENNED ANOTHER OF HIS long series of letters to British merchant Robert Cary. He was in a conciliatory mood. British authorities had recently decided to repeal the Stamp Act, and Washington may have felt obliged to temper his earlier angry denunciations of colonial policy. "The Repeal of the Stamp Act, to whatsoever causes owing, ought much to be rejoiced at," he wrote. "Had the Parliament of Great Britain resolved upon enforcing it the consequences I conceive would have been more direful than is generally apprehended both to the Mother Country & her Colonies—All therefore who were Instrumental in procuring the Repeal are entitled to the Thanks of every British Subject & have mine cordially."[1]

A return to business as usual was nevertheless out of the question. The Stamp Act had been withdrawn in part, Washington rightly suspected, because colonial resistance had hurt British merchants and forced the royal government's hand. Feeling their strength, Americans determined to achieve economic equality, commercial freedom, and the opportunity to promote domestic manufactures. Writing to Capel & Osgood Hanbury on July 25, 1767, Washington celebrated the British ministry's apparent "opposition to any Act of Oppression" and elaborated on his unwillingness to accept the status quo. Putting "the Commercial System of these Colonies . . . upon a more enlarged and extensive footing than it is," he argued, "would, ultimately, redound to the advantages of the Mother Country so long as the Colonies pursue trade and Agriculture, and would be an effectual Let to Manufacturing among themselves—The Money therefore which they raise would centre in Great Britain, as certain as the Needle will settle to the Poles."[2]

British debt remained heavy, however, and although the Stamp Act had been canceled, the Declaratory Act of 1766 had reasserted Parliament's right to tax the colonies at will. The next year, it did. Seeking to force the Americans to pay their share of the financial burden of colonial administration, Parliament approved Chancellor of the Exchequer Charles Townshend's recommendation to impose duties on tea, paper, glass, lead, and paint. Part of the revenue from the new taxes would pay for the establishment of a Board of Customs Commissioners for North America. It would also pay for the salaries of royal governors and other officials from customs duties, making them fully independent of colonial assemblies.

The legislation, which would go into effect on November 20, 1767, included a provocative authorization for colonial courts to enforce the duties through the use of general search warrants. Although the Virginia courts declined to use these powers—for now—the threat dangled over the heads of colonial businessmen. The duties worried not just Americans but also the British merchants who handled their needs and knew how strongly they would react. Capel & Osgood Hanbury, replying to Washington from London on October 20, lamented that the Townshend Acts were "inconsistent therewith & contrary to our sentiments as well as that of many others."[3]

Ironically, given the stakes, Washington's initial public reaction to the Townshend Acts was muted. He did not attend the House of Burgesses meeting of April 1768 at which the burgesses strongly but courteously asked the king and Parliament to repeal the acts, and he kept no record of his position in his existing correspondence. Why he chose to fade into the shadows at this sensitive time is uncertain. He may have done so because he had no direct commercial interest in the items being taxed, and because his intercourse with British merchants was declining as he shifted away from tobacco. Preoccupied with his own thriving commercial activities and the prospect of western expansion, he may not at first have understood the wider implications that the acts would have for colonial government and commerce. More likely,

Washington may have deliberately shied from controversy. Still reliant on the royal government to grant his petitions for western land—cherishing hopes for the Mississippi Company about which he petitioned the king in December 1768—and hoping to expand the sales of his estate's produce in the West Indies and potentially in Europe, he may have felt it disadvantageous to take an active role in the opposition.

Inside, however, he was seething. A decade later Washington's friend Arthur Lee wrote to him reminiscing about a visit to Mount Vernon in July 1768, when the furor over the Townshend Acts was at its height. "I never forgot," Lee recalled, "your declaration when I had the pleasure of being at your House in 1768 that you was ready to take your Musket upon your Shoulder, whenever your Country call'd upon you." Reelected to the House of Burgesses in December 1768, Washington remained restrained in his correspondence and public remarks; but the break was not long in coming. Ultimately it would not be the passage of the Townshend duties but the revelation of widespread colonial opposition to them—through both protests and the formation of nonimportation associations—that set Washington in motion.[4]

In February 1769, the British government upped the ante in the colonial dispute by reviving a sixteenth-century statute providing for the transportation of accused criminals to England for trial and punishment. This meant that recalcitrant colonials could expect not to be judged by their peers but, rather, to be shipped off to Europe where they would receive neither sympathy nor mercy. Two months later, one of Washington's friends from Bladensburg, on the Maryland side of the Potomac, sent him some papers detailing how Pennsylvania and Maryland merchants and planters proposed to form a nonimportation association that would effectively boycott British goods from American markets. After reading the papers, Washington passed them on to his friend George Mason at Gunston Hall. His accompanying comments showed how far his thinking had advanced:

At a time when our lordly Masters in Great Britain will be satisfied with nothing less than the deprivation of American freedom, it seems highly necessary that something should be done to avert the stroke and maintain the liberty which we have derived from our

Ancestors; but the manner of doing it to answer the purpose effectually is the point in question. That no man should scruple, or hesitate
a moment to use ＿＿ in defence of so valuable a blessing, on which
all the good and evil of life depends; is clearly my opinion; Yet ＿＿
I wou'd beg leave to add, should be the last resource; the dernier
resort. Addresses to the Throne, and remonstrances to parliament,
we have already, it is said, proved the inefficacy of; how far then their
attention to our rights & priviledges is to be awakened or alarmed by
starving their Trade & manufactures, remains to be tryed. The northern Colonies, it appears, are endeavouring to adopt this scheme—In
my opinion it is a good one; & must be attended with salutary effects,
provided it can be carried pretty generally into execution.[5]

Washington's politely veiled reference to the possibility of ＿＿ in defense of
American liberties detracted from his real point: that economic liberties were
at stake, and that a commercial war was the best means of securing them.
There were, he thought, "private, as well as public advantages to result from"
nonimportation. The primary public advantage was the reduction of debt.
"That the Colonies are considerably indebted to Great Britain," he wrote, "is
a truth universally acknowledged. That many families are reduced, almost, if
not quite, to penury & want, from the low ebb of their fortunes, and Estates
daily selling for the discharge of Debts, the public papers furnish but too many
melancholy proofs of." Nonimportation would force planters to live within
their means. "The extravagant & expensive man"—or an earlier version of
himself, he might have admitted—"has the same good plea to retrench his
Expenses." The private advantage was the growth of manufacture. The British,
he thought, would probably crack down on colonial manufacturing anyway,
"it being no greater hardship to forbid my manufacturing, than it is to order
me to buy Goods of them loaded with Duties, for the express purpose of
raising a revenue." Unity, he concluded, was essential. Those who refused to
participate in nonimportation "ought to be stigmatized, and made the objects
of publick reproach."[6]

With his declaration of support for the nonimportation agreements,
Washington became more politically prominent than he ever had been before. The burgesses convened in Williamsburg in May 1769, and he joined

his colleagues in formally resolving that the colonies alone had the right to tax themselves, and that they would petition the king on the subject. On May 17, however, Washington and the burgesses strode into the Council Chamber in response to a blunt summons from the royal governor, Lord Botetourt. "Mr. Speaker, and Gentlemen of the House of Burgesses," the governor lectured them, "I have heard of your Resolves, and augur ill of their Effect. You have made it my Duty to dissolve you; and you are dissolved accordingly."[7]

Dissolved they may have been, but they would not disband. From the Council Chamber, the burgesses—with Washington towering over the rest—marched down Duke of Gloucester Street to Raleigh Tavern, where they convened in the Apollo Room. There they debated all the elements of the crisis. Washington must have spoken most vociferously on the issue of nonimportation, for the speaker Peyton Randolph appointed him to a committee to consider that problem.

Appropriately, Washington dined that evening with Virginia's treasurer, Robert Carter Nicholas, and then spent hours working out the details of the Virginia Association. Back, bleary-eyed, in the Apollo Room the next morning, he and the other committee members declared their agreement that Virginians would boycott a broad range of British goods until Parliament lifted the noxious duties. A boycott was now in effect. Toasts were drunk dutifully to the king, queen, and royal family, and to union, but also pointedly to "the constitutional British Liberty in America, and all true Patriots, the Supporters thereof." There they adjourned.[8]

Washington determined to adhere to the nonimportation association "religiously," even if it was "ten times as strict." But he was no fanatic. When the new prime minister Lord North engineered the repeal of the Townshend duties except for those on tea in 1770, Washington was among those who worked out a compromise new Virginia Association in June 1770 that somewhat reduced the scope of the boycott. In his view, he was not appeasing the British, but simply recognizing that a long and excessively rigid application of the boycott might lead American planters to abandon it altogether. The compromise was an act of sympathy to Americans, not to the British.[9]

Washington and Mason worked vociferously over the next several months to keep their fellow Virginia planters united, even as nonimportation associations collapsed in the north and many southern planters began ignoring them.

Only in July 1771, after the Assembly recognized the obvious by dissolving the Virginia Association (while maintaining the boycott on a few symbolic items), did Washington again import British goods to his own estate and household, including a range of long-deferred luxury items.

Life went on. Washington continued to develop his western land schemes, and to expand his own estate's production. He even continued to sell small amounts of tobacco overseas from the Custis plantations, despite his strident complaints about British merchants. As a man who loved stability, he may briefly have imagined that he would be allowed to trade in peace. With his western schemes largely dependent on imperial favor, it was best not to rock the boat unnecessarily.

Again, though, the peaceful interlude would not last. The spur to renewed protest was once more economic. In 1773, Parliament aimed to help the East India Company out of a massive tea surplus, gain new revenue, and incidentally reassert its "right" to tax the colonies, by arranging to ship large quantities of tea to America. In the process the British would bypass American middlemen, crush competition from alternative sources of tea—and also impose a new tax. Tea would be cheaper for Americans, but in purchasing it under such terms they would implicitly abandon their right to tax themselves.

Washington, who preferred beer to tea, stood by while riots broke out in New England culminating in the notorious tea party of December 16, 1773. It was what followed that bothered him. Enraged by the destruction of property (which Washington also decried) and the precedent it set, Parliament voted in March 1774 to close the port of Boston on June 1. Preoccupied with his western lands—including a scheme to import thousands of Palatine Germans to settle his Ohio estates, which he was toiling industriously to develop and rent—and still currying royal favor for more grants, Washington at first took little public notice of these portentous events. After arriving in Williamsburg on May 16 for the meeting of the burgesses already in session, however, he tumbled into the center of a spreading firestorm as Americans everywhere—driven by their shared interests as producers and consumers in the Continental economy—stood in solidarity with the Bostonians. At first he attempted to play the role of moderator, socializing equally with radicals and conservatives, and with the new royal governor Lord Dunmore. But on the afternoon of May

26, after Washington had dined politely with the governor, Dunmore shocked him and the other burgesses by abruptly dissolving the Assembly.

For some time afterward, Washington behaved like a man in a daze. Meeting outside the chambers during the last two weeks of May, the burgesses considered demanding an outright embargo on all trade with Great Britain until Boston Port was reopened. Even so, Washington mulled expanding his trade with Great Britain, hedging his bets in case of reconciliation. On June 1, he wrote to Cary asking whether, since "the whole of my force is, in a manner confined to the growth of Wheat, & Manufacturing of it into Flour," wheat would fetch good prices in London, providing "our Commerce with Great Britain is kept open (which seems to be a matter of very great doubt at present)."[10]

Washington's fury swelled, however, as he pondered the arrogance of Parliament and its royal appointees in America over the following days. "The Ministry may rely on it that Americans will never be tax'd without their own consent," he wrote George William Fairfax (now living in England) on June 10, adding that "the cause of Boston . . . is and ever will be considered as the cause of America." In a savage temper, he continued: "those from whom we have a right to Seek protection are endeavouring by every piece of Art & despotism to fix the Shackles of Slavery upon us."[11]

Whatever his feelings, by late June nothing remained for Washington to do in Williamsburg. New elections were slated, and he would have to campaign in Fairfax County. So he returned to Mount Vernon, where he undertook some major home improvements. In happier times during the fall of 1773 he had initiated plans to extend the mansion on both wings, including a two-story banquet room on the north end and a study and a bedroom on the south end. Now, in the sweltering summer heat, he supervised and aided construction that progressed "better whilst I am present, than in my absence from the workmen."[12]

Washington's frustration remained, however, as did his support for a total trade embargo. Given Parliament's "regular, systematic plan formed to fix the right and principle of taxation upon us," he told his friend Bryan Fairfax (a moderate), Americans should "put our virtue and fortitude to the severest test." He continued to think in terms of economic warfare out of a belief that it promised hope of success without armed conflict. "I think we may do more than is generally believed, in respect to the non-importation scheme," he opined.[13]

On one measure, though, he refused to consent: withholding repayment of debt to Great Britain. "Whilst we are accusing others of injustice," he declared, "we should be just ourselves." Shortly after writing this letter, Washington presided over a gathering in Alexandria that resolved to send a public donation of £273 along with wheat and flour to the poor of Boston who were suffering under British punitive measures.[14]

Washington and Mason next crafted a list of principles to guide the coming assembly. The Fairfax Resolves, as they came to be called, were among the most radical in North America, but they reflected a consensus that consumer choice was among the most powerful expressions of both personal and popular will. Parliament, Washington and Mason explained, had "claimed and exercised the Power of regulating our Trade and Commerce, so as to restrain our importing from foreign Countrys, such Articles as they cou'd furnish Us with, of their own Growth or Manufacture, or exporting to foreign Countrys such Articles and Portions of our Produce, as Great Britain stood in Need of, for her own Consumption or Manufactures." This had once served a purpose, though "repugnant to the Principles of the Constitution." But its time had passed, particularly in view of Parliament's recent determination "to extort from Us our Money without our Consent," introducing "arbitrary Government" and reducing Americans to the status of "Slaves."[15]

The resolves proposed to reimburse the East India Company for tea destroyed in Boston Harbor because it constituted an "Invasion of private Property." However, Washington and Mason then demanded an almost complete embargo on imports from Great Britain, to be extended to exports as well if the British failed to mend their ways by November 1775. Nonimportation, Washington believed, would serve the dual purpose of helping to reduce American debt and punishing the British; he wanted to see how it would work before closing exports. The proposal struck at the heart of the colonial system.[16]

The 14th and 15th resolves, less well known today, were critically important. They addressed the question of American economic development, and how merchants and planters should behave in the current crisis. The language suggests they were largely authored by Washington. The 14th article resolved that every little jarring Interest and Dispute, which has ever happened between these Colonies, shou'd be buried in eternal Oblivion; that all Manner of Luxury and Extravagance ought imediatly to be laid aside, as totally inconsistent with the threatning and gloomy Prospect before us; that it is the indispensable Duty of all the Gentlemen and Men of Fortune to set Examples of Temperance, Fortitude, Frugality and Industry; and give every Encouragement in their Power, particularly by Subscriptions and Premiums, to the Improvement of Arts and Manufactures in America.

The 15th article prescribed that no merchants should take advantage of the embargo by price gouging but should continue to sell at the same prices, on pain that "if any Person shall sell such Goods on any other Terms than above expressed, that no Inhabitant of this Colony shou'd at any time, forever thereafter, deal with Him, his Agent, Factor, or Store keepers for any Commodity whatsoever."[17]

The Fairfax Resolves did not just constitute a reaction to British policies but promulgated Washington's still-developing vision of the economic future of what would become the United States: economic growth founded on self-sufficiency and the development of manufactures by men behaving with "Temperance, Fortitude, Frugality and Industry." The resolves were published across the country, and became the model for similar resolutions elsewhere. More than anything, they established Washington's Continental reputation as a visible figure in the—so far economic—rebellion. In this capacity he assumed the role of both political and business leader.[18]

Political maneuvering continued at a breakneck speed. Washington, who had been easily reelected in Fairfax, attended the Virginia Convention in Williamsburg from August 1 to 6. The delegates now met formally outside Dunmore's authority. The Convention duly approved the nonimportation agreement, while also calling for the development of domestic manufacturing and economic independence. The colonial bond was reaffirmed, but no attempt was made to petition the king. Washington was then elected as one of Virginia's seven delegates to the First Continental Congress, slated to meet in Philadelphia. Before leaving for Congress, Washington entertained a steady procession of Virginia merchants at Mount Vernon, lobbying them to stay firm in support of nonimportation.

In the First Continental Congress, which met in Philadelphia from September 5 to October 26, Washington—probably much to his surprise—filled a somewhat different role than he had before. Conducting himself carefully, he became known as a man of moderation and good sense. But whereas he had emphasized his role as a business leader in Virginia, on the national stage he was remembered as a military man who had been prominent in the French and Indian War.

His own thoughts had turned only briefly—back in 1769—to the possibility of armed conflict, and he still probably thought in terms of economic warfare. Prosperity, he firmly believed then as he would throughout his life, depended upon peace. No Americans anywhere, he assured a critic on October 9, had the desire "separately, or collectively, to set up for Independence." Rather, they sought by all reasonable means to have "the horrors of civil discord prevented."[19]

Others thought differently—if not on the question of independence, then on the likelihood of having to resort to armed conflict to secure their rights. People spoke of him now not just as a political or business figure but as a war "Hero." Adaptably, Washington went carefully with the political flow without being carried away by it. Though playing no major public role in the first Congress, he came reluctantly to recognize that solely economic warfare was no longer an option given the mood of the country and its leaders in Congress. Armed warfare, he knew by the time he departed, was a real possibility.

Washington returned to Fairfax to discover that in his absence the county had begun recruiting, training, and equipping militia. People expected him to help organize Virginia's militia, and he complied from a sense of duty, overseeing the establishment of several local county formations. But finance did not escape his mind. Ahead of many other county leaders, he faced the fact that military operations cost money. He and Mason assessed a tithe of three shillings on Fairfax inhabitants for support of the militia—shocking Dunmore, who remarked that "One County has already laid a capital tax of 3s."[20]

The Virginia Convention, meeting in March 1775 with Washington as a member, followed the example by urging local committees to collect funds for support of militia throughout the colony. Washington also served as a member of a committee "to prepare a Plan for the Encouragement of Arts & Manufactures in this Colony"; and although it was primarily tasked with promoting manufacture of munitions, he succeeded in diverting the committee's attention to discussion of promoting indigo, cotton, cloth, and linen. Thus did his mind remain on long-term economic issues even in the midst of preparations for conflict.[21]

For the first time in almost twenty years, Washington found himself unable to direct attention toward his own estate and its development and enrichment. Plans to visit his western lands had to go by the wayside, although he continued to work through intermediaries. In the brief interval between the closing of the Virginia Convention and his attendance at the Second Continental Congress, to which he had again been elected a delegate, Washington could devote only passing interest to his own affairs. War, politics, and nonimportation dominated discussion around the dinner table at Mount Vernon. As late as April 3, he implicitly recognized royal authority by writing an address to Lord Dunmore concerning the status of western land claims. By the time he set out on the ride to Philadelphia on May 4, however, armed conflict had already broken out in Massachusetts.

In Congress—where Washington wore his uniform not because he sought military leadership but in recognition of how his colleagues saw his role, and out of a sense of duty to perform whatever his country asked of him—he found himself deeply involved in military preparations. He understood the risks involved, but made an internal profession of faith that he reaffirmed to his brother John Augustine in a letter of March 25. Contemplating military command—in the militia—he commented that "it is my full intention to devote my Life & Fortune in the cause we are engaged in, if need be." But the prospect hardly made him joyful. Commenting to George William Fairfax on May 31 about the battles of Lexington and Concord, he sadly wrote: "Unhappy it is though to reflect that a Brother's Sword has been sheathed in a Brother's breast, and that, the once happy and peaceful plains of America are either to be drenched with Blood, or Inhabited by Slaves. Sad alternative! But can a virtuous Man hesitate in his choice?"[22]

Clearly there was no choice, for the die had been cast. From attempting to coordinate Continental acts of economic resistance but only local acts of military resistance, Congress now turned to the challenge of creating a

Continental Army to serve a confederated government in conflict with Great Britain. From there it was only a short step to appointing a national military leader. Washington did not lobby for the position, but realistically recognized that he would be the most obvious choice, and bowed his head to the prospect with an air of martyrdom. Congress made the choice on June 15, appointing Washington to lead the Continental Army in an armed conflict that he had neither wanted nor expected, but now accepted as a matter of cruel necessity.

---

ASKED TO EXPLAIN how his country had reached the point of war in June 1775, Washington might have struggled to respond coherently. Unaware of the larger social factors at play as Americans had developed a sense of shared economic interests and common identity over the previous decade, he likely felt baffled that matters had come to such a fateful pass. In 1774, he was still thinking entirely in terms of an all-out economic war to secure commercial freedom and allow for America's full development of its vast potential. His own interests certainly played a role in this. Future prosperity of the planter class, as he understood, depended on habits of frugality as well as industry aimed at developing economic self-sufficiency. By 1774 this was what he aimed at, and he thought it best for the country as well. Thus the prospect of an economic contest with Britain was both painful and cathartic.

Despite the changeover from tobacco to wheat and his bitter resentment of the Stamp Act, Washington had not broken completely with British merchants like Cary. He simply could not afford to, as not only luxury items but also a whole variety of vital manufactured goods were available only via import. His acquisitions through Cary included "A very best whole Hunter Whip, with a long silver Cap, engraved George Washington," along with china, cutlery, and fine clothing. Dressed too humbly, he would have cut a poor figure among his fellow planters however much he demonstrated his patriotism through dedication to homespun. He did, however, adopt a more modest style. Over time his shipments from Cary had come to include more equipment and tools, as well as plainer clothes. This change partly reflected his increasing maturity along with a determination to avoid waste. War would entail much greater adjustments.[23]

Military conflict threatened Washington's personal ruin as well as America's economic destruction. As he had learned during the French and Indian War, his prolonged absence from his estate was a recipe for its eventual degradation. Likewise, developing America economically would become more difficult in times of war. It is a measure both of Washington's realism and of his belief in the cause that he accepted the risk not just to participate in the war but to lead the army.

In both the first and second Congresses, Washington recognized that his vision of a purely economic contest was already outdated. Americans were determined to fight. Yet instead of standing against the popular militant tide, he accepted if not embraced it. His sense of personal and public virtue dictated that once he committed himself to the cause, he would have to see it through whatever the risks. But Washington, whether his fellow delegates recognized it or not, brought a peculiar and exceptionally valuable outlook to his task. Where others saw only soldiers and flags flying, he took the wider view. The key henceforth would be to fight the enemy while simultaneously laying the economic foundations of the war effort so that it could be carried on if necessary over a long period of time. Americans must not just defeat the British but establish a stable government and a civil society that would form the basis for future wealth and prosperity.

CHAPTER FOUR

# MONEY: THE SINEWS OF WAR

WASHINGTON WAS A PATRIOT WHO BELIEVED IN THE CAUSE yet carried himself with moderation and self-restraint. He was also an experienced soldier. As a Virginian, he represented one of the wealthiest and most strategically significant colonies. With all of these qualities at his command, he stood poised to unite the colonies in a concerted military effort. All of these considerations played a role in the congressional delegates' decision to appoint him commander in chief of the Continental Army in June 1775.

There was another factor, too, albeit often ignored: his personal wealth—what John Adams, in nominating Washington, called his "independent fortune." This self-sufficiency enabled him to decline a salary and devote himself to his duties without undue distraction. More important, his wealth was inextricably linked to his social and political standing. The George Washington of 1758 would never have been chosen, and not just because of his youth. Nor would a man who, like many Virginia gentlemen, lived a dissolute life or was mired in debt. Washington's resolution in the wake of the Stamp Act crisis to live within his means while aggressively building his fortune ideally situated him as a symbol of America's quest for economic freedom.[1]

Washington's personal motivations for leading the army were complex. There were limits to his ambition. He retained a desire for distinction all his life. The youthful yearning for military glory, however, had long faded. Washington engaged in Virginia's military preparations of 1774–1775 with energy

89

but without relish. He accepted command of the army in the same spirit. That Great Britain and the colonies were headed for a trial of strength and willpower he had no doubt—the showdown had been coming for a long time. Assuming that the trial would be solely economic in character, he had kept his eye on the long term: pondering the sale of his flour in London markets, for example, and petitioning Lord Dunmore about the status of his western lands even as Great Britain and the colonies tumbled desperately toward military confrontation.

Then, in the spring of 1775, armed conflict became a reality. Washington blamed the British for this state of affairs, but he also realized that his fellow Americans desired an armed struggle. Unlike congressional colleagues such as Patrick Henry and John Hancock, who were naïve in the ways of war, he felt no glee at the prospect. Washington had anticipated victory in a solely economic contest. He expressed no such confidence in the outcome of a military trial. War, he knew, might well wreck his personal estate. More than his life or his fortune, however, his reputation was on the line. His genuine fear of failure sparked doubts—similar, but on a much grander scale than those he had experienced during the French and Indian War. Believing that the colonies had no choice but to accept the war that had been foisted upon them, he nevertheless accepted the challenge and its attendant risks with sober determination.

Independence was not yet on the table when the war began. In New York on June 26, 1775, during a stop on his journey to take command of the army in Massachusetts, Washington told the Provincial Congress that "every Exertion of my worthy Colleagues & myself, will be equally extended to the re establishment of Peace & Harmony between the Mother Country and the Colonies" despite the "fatal, but necessary Operations of War." Even after the Declaration of Independence the following year, he looked forward to peace.[2]

Despite his military trappings—the fine uniform, the soldierly bearing—Washington hated war. He also believed that beneath the clash of arms the conflict was fundamentally economic in character, and that the nation's fiscal health was the yardstick of military success. This outlook was vital to his strategic vision. Keeping in mind that economic freedom and prosperity were the ultimate objectives, he sought to carry on the fight without undermining the foundations of future growth.

Winning the war, in other words, could not come at the price of losing the peace that followed. Building and maintaining a politically stable, democratic government would create a framework in which the economy could flourish. Conversely, establishing a functional economy and ensuring that it did not collapse under the strains of war would ensure stable government. The battlefield formed only one facet of a multidimensional war. Whatever his focus at any given moment, Washington strove always to keep the entire conflict fully in view.

This broad conception of the war made Washington's businesslike habits particularly valuable. His entrepreneurial outlook and intense interest in the worlds of business, commerce, and finance fed his drive to succeed as a general as well as a businessman. After years of working to expand his own estate, he came to think of the army and the fledgling United States as enterprises that he must both steward and develop. Used to thinking of Mount Vernon as a multilayered, multidimensional entity that both competed and collaborated with other diverse entities, he operated the Continental Army in much the same way.

Washington's astonishing skills as a military administrator—without which the army could not have survived—derived from his ability to visualize his entire command. Seeing that the health of the whole depended on the vitality of its parts, he demanded clear and strong internal chains of authority and lines of communication. He chose strong leaders and mandated thrift and efficiency. He knew how to motivate. Above all, he fed on details, the seemingly insignificant minutiae that were as vital to the army's survival as cells were to the human body. Likewise, Washington forged and worked ceaselessly to maintain ties with the outside entities—local and state governments, Congress, private contractors and financiers, foreign allies—upon which the army's prosperity depended. Finally, he combined vast responsibilities with an ability to think simultaneously in terms of military, political, and financial objectives. He understood how money ensured not just survival but future prosperity.

In his role as commander in chief, Washington's immediate sphere of control was the army. He was not civilian chief executive, or even a member of Congress, and so could not control economic policy on the national or local levels. He could influence those policies, however, and increasingly did so as the war progressed and his personal power solidified. Though respect for civilian authority was an overarching principle of his command, Washington was not above intervening in politics as circumstances dictated.

The weakness of the Confederation government, particularly in its inability to raise national revenue, worried him as the war went on. That in turn informed his military strategy. Contrary to legend, he did not seek to prolong the war in an effort to wear down the British will to win. Though some of his most experienced officers advocated guerrilla warfare, Washington explicitly rejected it because of the social, political, and especially economic dislocation it would produce. Instead, recognizing Great Britain's almost infinitely superior long-term economic resources (despite its heavy national debt) relative to America's fledgling economy, he persistently sought a quick military decision that would end the war and give the United States room to develop. That determination to end the war rapidly solidified as the conflict progressed.

---

AN AVALANCHE OF WORK smothered Washington almost from the moment he officially accepted his commission on June 16. Endless paperwork, interminable meetings, and—perhaps worst of all—alternately raucous or tear-soaked parties left the general scarcely able to breath, let alone think. On June 18 a crowd of delegates, dignitaries, and busybodies dragged him off to Vauxhall Tavern near Philadelphia, where he endured a grueling evening of dining, drinking, and small talk. A hearty toast to "the Commander in Chief of the American armies" capped the evening, followed by stifled sobs and an awkward silence that probably had Washington blushing and shuffling his feet. Back at his lodgings that evening—the door no doubt guarded by a scowling servant under orders to admit no one—the general composed a tender letter of farewell to Martha. "My unhappiness will flow, from the uneasiness I know you will feel at being left alone," he wrote. His own loneliness he would not admit, but it was profound. As the war progressed, he and Martha found separation so unendurable that she spent most of the war with him in camp.[3]

Beset though he was by worries and distractions, Washington devoted a good deal of his time to pondering money and finance. On June 19, 1775, in his first written commentary on the war effort, he told his friend Burwell Bassett with evident satisfaction that "Congress in Committee have consented to a Continental Currency, and have ordered two Million of Dollars to be struck for payment of the Troops, and other expenses arising from our defence." His initial confidence in Continental paper currency, issued in dollars under a bewildering variety of denominations and not backed by gold or silver, eventually proved unjustified. Few could have imagined in 1775 that within a few years $2 million in paper dollars would purchase a few horses or maybe a wagon. State bills of credit, which continued to be issued throughout the war, likewise proved hopelessly unstable. For everyday Americans, gold and silver in the form of coins issued by foreign governments would—when available—remain the exchange medium of choice.[4]

All that, though, lay in the future. In Washington's efforts to arrange the army, money took pride of place as a subject of concern before the number of troops called out or the identities of the officers appointed to command beneath him. He would come to learn that he could not simply leave problems of finance for the politicians to figure out, but that he had to apply pressure where needed to ensure that Congress and the states kept money flowing to the army.

After a ride of almost two weeks from Philadelphia, interrupted by stops to meet officials and receive public delegations, Washington arrived at Cambridge, Massachusetts, on July 2. He surveyed the mob-like army encamped there with a sense of shock. Ostensibly gathered to besiege the British in Boston, the militiamen seemed to lack both organization and purpose. Men floundered about in a sprawling, filthy shantytown, united in little else but their disdain for the British. Worst of all, they lacked a system. Officers—democratically elected on the basis of popularity rather than merit—and soldiers conducted themselves according to their immediate needs, without coordination or plan. With no organized system of procurement or distribution for everything from foodstuffs to ammunition, men plundered and stole from civilians or other soldiers to satisfy their needs. Waste was colossal. Instead of economizing, men squandered precious resources to no purpose, firing muskets off at random, mixing good food with spoiled, leaving powder and equipment out in the rain, and tossing aside soiled garments to rot, among other atrocities. Washington's annoyance did not solely reflect personal distaste. At this pace, he knew, the "army" had no staying power. It would probably dissolve in a matter of weeks.

In a foul mood, the commander in chief nevertheless wasted no time in angry speeches or displays. Instead, he stormed off to his desk and got to work. The first task as he saw it was to impose a system. He did so in much the same manner he had developed his estate—starting with the elemental building blocks and working upward from there. His goal was to create a military enterprise that was well-led, motivated, efficient, thrifty, and, as far as possible, self-sustaining. Orders flew off his desk demanding thorough and regular returns of men, clothing, equipment, and especially ordnance. Acquiring this knowledge would help him to assess fundamentals such as supply, needs, and costs. The process would also inculcate the same knowledge of needs and resources among his officers, and establish internal networks of communication and collaboration. But that was only a start. Without adequate resources, the army was doomed to wither and die no matter what Washington did. He therefore had to look first and foremost to the army's primary source of supply—the civil population—and to the means of procuring that supply—the fledgling national government, embodied in Congress.

Congress had already established a Continental currency and voted for $2 million to supply the army's needs. Getting that money to the army in a regular and efficient manner was another matter. To supply the army's immediate needs, Washington required a cache of ready money—a military chest. In his first letter to Congress of July 10, formally addressed to President John Hancock, the commander in chief wrote: "I find myself already much embarassed for Want of a military Chest—these Embarassments will increase every Day: I must therefore request that Money may be forwarded as soon as possible. The Want of this necessary Article, will I fear produce great Inconveniencies if not prevented by an early Attention."[5]

Congress complied, sending the general a supply of ready cash that he could draw upon for immediate needs. All too often over the years that followed, unfortunately, it seemed that the chest must have holes in its bottom.

Every day, Washington and his aides and secretaries had to plunder it not just to meet bills but to pay off Continental troops or tide over militia forces neglected by their states. When the chest ran empty, the general had no choice but to pester Congress with repeated and sometimes frantic reminders to send him funds as quickly as possible to prevent the army from breaking up. If that failed, he had to approach civilian lenders with apologetic requests to borrow funds to meet short-term needs. It was an embarrassing position for the commander in chief of the Continental Army, and one that would progressively reinforce his conviction in Congress's ineffectiveness.

Washington was throughout his life a fanatical account-keeper, and never more so than in a military capacity. Upon his appointment as commander in chief, he declined the salary of $500 per month that Congress offered to him, declaring that "as no pecuniary consideration could have tempted me to have accepted this Arduous emploiment at the expence of my domestik ease & happiness I do not wish to make any proffit from it: I will keep an exact Account of my expences; those I doubt not they will discharge & that is all I desire." John Adams exulted at the vision of "A Gentleman, of one of the first Fortunes, upon the Continent, leaving his delicious Retirement" and promising to "lay before Us, an exact account of his Expences, and not accept a shilling for Pay." Washington did, however, accept Congress's offer of a monthly allowance for his expenses, and for the wages and expenses of his "military family"—aides-de-camp, secretaries, and other support staff. He used the same allowance to pay for an extensive array of other needs, including headquarters maintenance, tack and saddle, entertaining dignitaries, paying couriers, and so forth.[6]

Transparency was another characteristic that served Washington well both in business and in the military life. Many of his acquaintances and business associates were in the habit of juggling accounts to obscure secret expenditures or investments—or, more often, to hide fiscal embarrassments. No one could ever justly accuse Washington of such deceits. Probity and openness, he knew, built the trust essential to establish and maintain personal credit. Ultimately it was what made profitable investments and business partnerships possible.

As commander in chief, Washington knew that his expenditures would sooner or later come under close scrutiny. His expense account book, usually maintained by his secretary Caleb Gibbs but always under the general's close supervision, was remarkably precise. Washington fretted about it throughout the war. In the spring of 1777, financier Robert Morris lent the general a few silver dollars to meet some trivial expense. Months passed, during which Washington marched his army around New Jersey and up and down the east coast, pursuing the British. In time, he forgot exactly how much Morris had lent him—a minor lapse that would hardly have troubled most people. In August, though, with a major battle against the British army looming just ahead, Washington could not stop worrying about those silver dollars and finally decided to write Morris—who was also busy with such insignificant business as helping to keep the Continental economy afloat—and beg for an exact accounting of how much he had lent him. "For want of the Sum," the general fretted, he could not balance his account. As he had anticipated, in later years some of his detractors—ignoring the many additional costs for his military family and other needs—would accuse Washington of purposefully overdrawing his expense account. In fact, there were few things he worked harder to keep correct.[7]

Economy was important both for its own sake and because of the need to project an appearance of frugality. Washington was careful to maintain a modest military household. Officers' wives—including Martha—were regularly present and set the example of economy and self-sufficiency by mending clothes and otherwise preventing wastage. Uniforms were clean and distinctive—visual rank distinctions being important to Washington— but not opulent. He preferred to have holes mended rather than make new purchases. Likewise, the general's table was ample but modest. In the account book Gibbs studiously jotted down purchases of commonplace viands such as turnips, potatoes, asparagus, eggs, cabbage, chicken, pork, and beef—along with occasional treats such as a piece of "smoak't venison" bought at Valley Forge in March 1778. The general's military family after all consisted of young men who, like him, worked and ate heartily. Other minor luxuries—such as berries and fish, which everyone knew the general adored—appeared on the table as gifts from local well-wishers. Washington nevertheless insisted that Gibbs strictly record the small tips he gave to the servants and children who brought these goodies.[8]

Like adolescents, the boys of Washington's family often disdained to eat their greens. The carnivorous propensities of his staff eventually went too far even for the general's taste, especially when he had to entertain visitors. In August 1779 at West Point, New York, he worried about how he was going to feed a group of refined women who had announced their impending arrival at headquarters:

> Since our arrival at this happy spot, we have had a Ham (sometimes a shoulder) of Bacon, to grace the head of the table—a piece of roast Beef adorns the foot—and, a small dish of Greens or Beans (almost imperceptable) decorates the center. When the Cook has a mind to cut a figure . . . we have two Beef-stake Pyes, or dishes of Crabs in addition, one on each side the center dish, dividing the space, & reducing the distance between dish & dish to about Six feet, which without them, would be near twelve a part—Of late, he has had the surprizing luck to discover, that apples will make pyes; and its a question if, amidst the violence of his efforts, we do not get one of apples instead of having both of Beef. If the ladies can put up with such entertainment, and will submit to partake of it on plates—once tin but now Iron—(not become so by the labor of scowering) I shall be happy to see them.

One necessity the general did not scrimp on was alcohol—wine, beer, cider, rum, and other beverages. He bought these in massive quantities, and often at his own expense. Drink had to be kept flowing freely, for social gatherings were frequent. In February 1780 Gibbs wrote "in haste" to assistant commissary John Chaloner: "We are out of Beer you will please send on a large Quantity as soon as possible."[9]

The point was not to put on an appearance of false poverty—that the general and his staff should enjoy a higher standard of living was fully expected—but to avoid intimations of an aristocratic lifestyle. During the Valley Forge winter of 1777–1778, British general William Howe in occupied Philadelphia notoriously threw grand banquets for his staff and dallied with mistresses. On May 17, 1778, on the day of his departure from North America, Howe

presided over an extravagant celebration that included a grand orchestra float-
ing down the Delaware River, a faux medieval costumed tournament, a tri-
umphal arch, and a sumptuous dinner among other entertainment. The price
tag amounted to "somewhat more than 4,000 guineas, that is about 25,000
dollars." Twelve days earlier, Washington had held a comparatively earthy and
far less expensive celebration for his own army to commemorate French intervention in the war. After huzzas and the discharge of cannon and muskets, the
men were given a special issue of rum and set loose to celebrate while officers
enjoyed a "profusion of fat meat, strong wine and other liquors" at tables set
up in the middle of camp. Washington shared the officers' toasts, and then
went off to mingle with the rum-swilling men in "mirth and rejoicing."[10]

Yet no amount of revelry could compensate for a lack of basic necessities—
especially pay. From the beginning and increasingly as the war went on, this
was in short supply. Sometimes Washington could meet officers' and soldiers' immediate needs by borrowing. Ultimately, though, he depended on
the states, either on their own behalf to pay militia or through Congress to pay
Continentals. Because of varying conditions in the individual states—from
resources to enemy occupation and the relative efficiency of government—
supply was never reliable. Washington asked Congress to appoint a paymaster
general, for there were limits to what he could manage on his own. Even after
the office was created and the first of many appointments to it made, however,
he still frequently had to intervene.

Again and again Washington had to address provincial councils and legislatures to keep troops paid, and he worked extensively with Congress as well.
Rather than leave decisions about rates and frequency of pay to Congressional
Committees, he instructed the delegates on how properly to recompense not
just officers and men but ancillary support staff such as commissaries and
wagon drivers. He even laid out standards for expense allowances, provisions,
clothing, and the like. The commander in chief's close attention to pay reflected his awareness—acquired first during the French and Indian War—of
the economic costs of service to soldiers, their families, and their communities.

So diligently did Washington labor that Congress could be forgiven for
sometimes thinking him capable of superhuman feats of administration. Because the delegates had made no provision for managing the army's accounts,

Washington spent much of the war handling them on his own. After six months' toil, he could no longer drudge in silence. On January 24, 1776, he wrote to Hancock that "It would be absolutely impossible for me to go into an examination of all the Accounts Incident to this Army, & the Vouchers appertaining to them, without devoting so large a portion of my time to the business, as might not only prove injurious, but fatal to It in other respects." Instead, he recommended "the absolute necessity of appointing fit & proper persons to Settle the accounts of this Army—to do it with precision, requires time, care & attention—the longer It is left undone, the more Intricate they will be—the more liable to error, & difficult to explain & rectify—As also the persons in whose hands they are, if disposed to take undue advantages, will be less subject to detection." Washington's points were both conscientious and incontrovertible. However, Congress considered his recommendation to form a select committee on forming a department of accounts—and, as would happen often, did nothing.[11]

Frequent nudges from Washington in the spring of 1776 finally provoked the congressional bureaucracy to budge, if only an inch or two. In April, the delegates voted to create a treasury department of accounts and the post of auditor general. This was all very well, but there remained one glaring problem: the auditor general would handle civilian government accounts, but no mechanism existed for auditing army accounts even though they took up a huge portion of public expenditures.

In New York City on July 11, 1776, with the British fleet hovering menacingly offshore and an invasion imminent, Washington decided that he had had enough. In a long letter oozing frustration, he wrote: "It is with unwillingness and pain I ever repeat a request after having once made It, or take the liberty of Enforcing any opinion of mine after It is once given, but as the establishing of some Office for auditing accounts is a matter of exceeding importance to the public Interest I would beg leave once more to call the attention of Congress to an appointment competent to the purposes." Doing so was essential for obvious reasons that Washington had shouted again and again into the congressional echo chamber—because he lacked the time to manage the accounts; because the lack of effective auditing invited corruption; and because "Accounts become perplexed and confused by long standing, and the errors therein not so discoverable as if they underwent an early revision and examination." Though he didn't say so to Hancock, all of these were lessons he had learned from having to audit the accounts of his own estate and others to which he had been appointed executor. This time, Congress finally responded by appointing auditors, giving Washington a little more time to prepare for battle.[12]

This incident encapsulated some of the challenges that Washington faced in maintaining amicable and efficient civil-military relations. Doing so was a matter of both political principle and practical necessity. Part of the army's duty was to defend and enforce civilian authority. While that authority was deeply flawed—as became increasingly apparent over the course of the war—it remained a primary building block for future prosperity. Despite Washington's Herculean (and sometimes Sisyphean) labors, Congress was far from irrelevant. Many of its delegates and presidents did yeomen's work to get the national finances in order and develop a functioning economy. But the body was hamstrung by its limitations in drawing money from states that were all too often dilatory.

State civilian officials such as Governor Jonathan Trumbull, Sr., of Connecticut accomplished much in support of the cause, but faced internal problems and divisions that made it difficult to coordinate effectively on a national level. It fell to Washington's lot to function as an informal chief executive, kind of an adviser-in-chief, who could mediate between states and Congress and help to coordinate policy. Some of the most important policy suggestions on financial matters small and large came from him, and he provided the impetus to push important measures through Congress. The creation of a War Office in 1776, for example—which Washington called "an event of great Importance" that "in all probability will be recorded as such in the Historic page," was largely his idea.[13]

Congress's many deficiencies included its inability to ensure that the army received essential supplies. Just like an estate, an army required a constant flow of food, drink, clothing, tools, building materials, and other items. It also needed things most estates could afford to do without, such as weapons and ordnance. And of course the army was much larger in terms of personnel than any estate, and it was more or less constantly on the move. Supplying these necessities involved procurement, transport, distribution—and especially payment. Congress created commissary departments to handle these duties, but over the war's course they were frequently rearranged (in close consultation with the commander in chief) while sometimes corrupt or incompetent officials came and went.

Washington insisted that commissaries provide him with careful accounts of their expenses. He also devoted considerable energy to ensuring that they performed their work efficiently. The fact that the army had to procure supplies directly from civilian local and state civil officials, and civilian mercantile firms, instead of relying on federal agencies or contractors, added another dimension to the general's never-ending work. He had to establish and maintain close personal relationships with civil officials, just as he would with any trading partner.

At the same time that he developed the means of procurement and supply, Washington modeled the army's internal processes on principles of economy, self-sufficiency, and even profit. He envisioned the army as less an agency of government than a vital entity in its own right. As such, it had to learn how to sustain itself. On August 7, 1775, he established regulations for the appointment of sutlers to each regiment "to supply the different Regiments with Necessaries . . . provided the public is not to be tax'd with any Expence by the Appointment." The sutlers could profit from their posts, but the commander in chief strictly enjoined them, in accordance with military regulations, not to attempt to "impose upon the Soldiers in the price of their goods."[14]

More broadly, Washington worked to promote self-sufficiency among the soldiers and to eliminate waste. He did so not just with a view to conserving army supplies and monetary resources, but also to provide "Saving to the publick." Because the army was such a major purchaser, resisting unnecessary expenditures would in time become a means of preventing the army from turning into too much of a catalyst for inflation—a fact of which Washington was fully aware. For similar reasons he sweated constantly over weeding out corruption from the army. He could not afford to delegate many details.[15]

Washington's army held no monopoly over Continental resources. Though it depended on civilians to provide it with supplies, it also competed with them for many of the same goods. The army also competed constantly with the British and even other American armies for scarce resources, just as Mount Vernon did with rival estates. Among the commander in chief's ongoing concerns was the problem of civilian trade with his army and with the enemy. He was aware that, in the last resort, the laws of economics trumped patriotism. Even the most well-meaning farmers and tradespeople produced and sold in accordance with their personal interests. A man seeking to feed his family and maintain his estate was more likely to listen to the hardy clink of British gold than to the feeble rustle of Continental scrip.

Still, Washington had weapons at hand. Though blessed with an already-established economy instead of having to invent one practically from scratch as the Americans did, the British fought the war in North America at the end of a desperately long supply chain. The British Isles might be resource-rich, but the king's army in North America was by comparison impoverished. With support from the home shores intermittent and inadequate, the British depended on their ability to procure resources in America. Here they faced an impossible conundrum: Seize supplies and alienate American civilians, or pay in gold and deplete their limited reserves?

Washington understood the competition for resources from both perspectives. Throughout the war he daily studied the shifting prices of goods in town and country, and measured them against the relative procurement abilities of the Continental and British armies. Outside Boston in 1775, for example, he ordered his intelligence agents to monitor provision prices in the besieged city, and expressed his satisfaction when they rose beyond the British army's purchasing power. He considered it one of his prime responsibilities to ensure that prices in British-held territory rose as high as possible while in American-held areas they remained relatively cheap. One of his means of doing so was to choke off routes of supply and trade.

The commander in chief never imagined that he would be able to reduce cities under British occupation—such as Boston, New York, and Philadelphia—to starvation. Indeed, he had no desire to do so—after all, if it came to that, American civilians would starve and not the British, who could simply seize what they needed. Rather, he hoped to place the British in an economic vise that kept them constantly at the cusp of having to decide whether to purchase supplies at exorbitant prices or confiscate them and infuriate (without actually starving) civilians.

Self-interest, as Washington knew, could work against the American cause just as much as it hurt the enemy. Price gouging particularly worried him. After observing prices of firewood, oats, and hay rising in the summer of 1775, he shared with the Massachusetts Council his fears that civilians were hoarding these commodities and creating "artificial Scarcity" to boost prices, with possibly "fatal" consequences for the cause. Though his opinions on price-fixing ebbed and flowed during the war depending on circumstances, on this occasion he demanded that the Council fix prices and force civilians to sell their goods if they refused to do so voluntarily. Mandatory sales were a last resort. While Washington was not averse to destroying civilian gristmills and manufactories near and within British lines—thus further driving up prices—he steadfastly refused to confiscate supplies from civilians. Morality informed this principle—but so did a conviction that he must do everything possible to uphold a functioning domestic commercial system.[16]

Property rights as Washington saw them were both a matter of principle and integral to a stable civil society. Protecting them was one of the reasons for which the war was being fought. With that in mind he not only insisted that his army respect private property rights but also used those rights as a motivating principle. On July 5, 1775, learning that some of his soldiers had plundered civilian property, he reminded every man in the army "that it is for the preservation of his own Rights, Liberty and Property, and those of his Fellow Countrymen, that he is now called into service: that it is unmanly and sully's the dignity of the great cause, in which we are all engaged, to violate that property, he is called to protect."[17]

Arriving in New York City the following year, Washington told his soldiers that "we come to protect; not to injure the property of any Man." An army that was raised to protect property but lived rapaciously off the land—as many eighteenth-century armies did—would have ruined the very cause it sought to protect. Even during the darkest moments of need, therefore, Washington resisted calls to confiscate property from civilians without ample and prompt financial recompense. Individual farmers who approached him with complaints of having been mistreated in this respect—as many did—found him willing to act forcefully on their behalf.[18]

Here as elsewhere Washington maintained the long view. He actively encouraged civilian manufacture for military purposes, for example, not just to keep his army supplied but to encourage the growth of American industry. On August 4, 1775, he sent Governor Jonathan Trumbull, Sr., of Connecticut a pattern for uniforms "both cheap & convenient," and asked him to purchase all available cloth and have "suitable Persons set to work to make it up" for supply to the army—incidentally helping the state to expand its fledgling textile industry. Washington offered similar encouragement to industries for the manufacture of iron, powder, ordnance, and equipment, urging John Augustine Washington to work to establish "a plenty of" those manufactories in Virginia.[19]

Self-interest, as the general knew, motivated production and innovation. Short-term recompense, especially as the real value of Continental currency declined, could offer only scant encouragement. Manufacturers and inventors were much more likely to be enticed by prospects of developing skills and enterprises that could flourish in the return to a civilian society after the war. He encouraged technical innovations for purely military purposes, such as inventor John Macpherson's plan to develop explosive torpedoes that would "destroy every ministerial armed vessel in North America" or David Bushnell's various infernal machines that included the notorious submarine *Turtle*. In the same spirit he would promote civilian inventions after the war had ended. America did not just need solutions to specific individual problems—it needed innovators.[20]

---

WASHINGTON'S VARIED DUTIES would have been more than enough to occupy or overwhelm most generals. But military administration made up only a portion of the commander in chief's overall scope. His belief that the contest with Great Britain was essentially economic in character despite the clash of arms motivated his vigilance about the international aspects of wartime trade and supply. On August 4, 1775, the commander in chief wrote to Rhode Island governor Nicholas Cooke about the possibility of outfitting ships to procure powder supplies from Bermuda—whose inhabitants Washington imagined as "well disposed" to the American cause—in exchange for provisions. The general even went to the point of formally inviting Bermudans to develop this trade.[21]

Bigger game lay across the Atlantic. Washington was not the only American with his eye on France, but he was among the first to seek the development of trade with this potential ally. He began with a scheme to import gunpowder from Bayonne in September 1775, and followed with fostering contracts for essential supplies such as cloth and even a variety of long-denied luxury items. He sought to handle some of these imports directly or through Congress, but in most cases he encouraged venturesome American merchants to handle the import trade. The remarkable thing was not that trade with France developed but that Washington recognized the need so quickly and acted to promote it instead of waiting for civilians to take the lead.

Washington could not take credit for the explosion of overseas imports that followed, especially after French intervention in 1778. Luminaries such as Benjamin Franklin, along with scores of now-forgotten American merchants, were primarily responsible for this, leaving Washington in the role of an interested spectator. Mounting debt did, however, concern him as the war approached its conclusion. Nor did he view exports as an unmitigated benefit, especially when they threatened to deprive the country of vital resources needed by the army. On June 9, 1776, he wrote commissary general Joseph Trumbull: "I am informed, that several Merchants are about to purchase Salt Pork for Exportation; and I would recommend it to you to apply immediately to the [Connecticut] Provincial Congress, to take some Measures to prevent them, as there is not only a Probability that it may fall into the Hands of the Enemy, but we may 'ere long experience the Want of it ourselves." The state halted the export as he demanded.[22]

Just as it had been before the war, trade was a means of carrying on the economic contest with Great Britain. Interfering with British trade and supply to its North American army was a first step. In the summer of 1775, Washington hired a fleet of Massachusetts schooners at Continental expense to operate as privateers off New England. Dubbed "Washington's Navy," this force continued to act under his direct authority—and outside the purview of the nascent Continental Navy—until 1777. Over the course of its escapades the little privateer fleet captured fifty-five prizes—hardly a crippling blow to the British, but an inspiration to other American privateers throughout North America. This naval venture was remarkable enough for a man who was expected to concentrate his energies on land affairs; but he also invested in the arming and equipage of privateers both to aid the cause and to generate personal income. On July 1, 1777, Washington invested several hundred pounds of Virginia currency in the privateer *General Washington,* which operated successfully throughout the war, even in European waters.

Washington was willing to be ruthless when it came to ratcheting up the pressure on British maritime trade and supply. In the spring of 1779, Bermuda—specifically its slaves—faced famine because of the ongoing trade embargo with the United States, and the island's representatives petitioned Congress to allow them to purchase provisions from American merchants. Agreeing to their request seemed the profitable and humane thing to do—but Washington was unalterably opposed. Writing to then-president John Jay, he argued that refusing to help alleviate the famine would "throw many additional mouths" upon the already overburdened British supply system. "They will not and cannot," he wrote, "let their people starve." Fortunately for the island's suffering slaves, this was one of Washington's few suggestions that Congress—at French urging—ignored.[23]

---

THE GENIUS OF WASHINGTON'S WARTIME LEADERSHIP would become apparent only with time. In the summer of 1775, it seemed that his efforts to reform the army at Cambridge were only producing more confusion. Orders descended from headquarters with studied regularity, but the commander in chief had to repeat them frequently as officers and soldiers struggled to understand their roles. Administrative solutions generated an almost infinite array of practical problems, leading men to besiege headquarters with queries and laments. At times Washington may have felt like the manager of a complaints department in some ambiguous government agency. He had to put administrative troubles out of his mind, however, as he pondered how to squeeze the British out of Boston.

Scanning British positions through his telescope, the general could not help noting the enemy's isolation. The city sheltered sixteen thousand civilians and six thousand soldiers on a small peninsula. Their only connection to the mainland was via a narrow neck blocked by Washington's troops. Geography made the task seem straightforward. Like a hangman, he could simply tighten the noose. To that end, he planned initially to "cut off all Communication between their Troops and the Country" and "prevent them from penetrating into the Country with Fire and Sword." With thousands of soldiers, sailors, and civilians compressed within the city, competing for the same resources, Washington thought that "the whole Force of Great Britain in the Town and Harbour of Boston, can answer no other end than to sink her under the disgrace and weight of the expence." Seeking to drive provision prices in Boston beyond endurance, he ordered his men to drive livestock out of reach and interdicted sea lanes with privateers. Intelligence reports told him that the strategy seemed to be working.[24]

Time was the biggest enemy. As summer faded to autumn, the British tightened their belts and prepared for a long contest. Poring over reports at a headquarters desk that at any given time groaned under sheaves of paper, Washington marveled at the enemy's endurance. The exorbitant costs of maintaining the Boston garrison did not seem to weaken their determination to resist. So far, the impact of the war on the British national economy—which Washington always monitored closely—seemed insignificant. News of the defeats at Lexington and Concord, he noted, had only caused stocks in London to tumble briefly by about 1.5 percent. British and royalist newspapers, which he scanned line by line, continued to boast remorselessly—almost as if the colonials, rather than their adversaries, were trapped on a tiny peninsula.

"The inactive state we lye in is exceedingly disagreeable," the general wrote in frustration to his brother John Augustine, "especially as we can see no end to it, having had no advices lately from Great Britain to form a judgment upon." Instead of worrying about their accounts, the enemy seemed smugly to assume that the colonists would pay for it all in the end: "The expence of this one would think must soon tire them were it not that they intend to fix all the Expence of this War upon the Colonies—if they can I suppose we shall add." By contrast, the Americans seemed to lack resilience. Supply shortages caused officials to throw up their hands in helpless consternation while soldiers and militiamen were quick to plunder or desert. Not for the first time and certainly not for the last, Washington worried about the economic burden of carrying on the conflict over the long term. The cause, he knew, was frail. It would not take much to snuff it out.[25]

Worried more than he would admit but disdaining to formulate strategy on the basis of vague prognostications, Washington decided (as no one in Congress or the army had done so far) to determine just how much Americans were paying to keep their army in the field. In October he ordered commissary general Joseph Trumbull and quartermaster general Thomas Mifflin to estimate how much it would cost just to feed and house his army of twenty-two thousand men through May 1776. Their response: over $730,000 in Continental dollars.

Pay was another matter entirely. Per month on average, the commander in chief reported to Congress in December, expenses for pay were $275,000. But this was not a steady expenditure. On Christmas Day of 1775, with the first Continental Army about to be dissolved and an entirely new one formed under a one-year term of enlistment, Washington demanded a report of how much it would cost to discharge pay arrearages for the old army and advance a month's pay to the new. He learned that this transaction alone would cost a staggering $927,429.

The $2 million that Congress had authorized at the beginning of the war now looked paltry. Instead of facing up to the probability of having to commit over the long term, however, Congress insisted on authorizing money only in inadequate dribs and drabs. This forced Washington both to continue pestering the delegates for funds in increasingly large amounts and to formulate a short-term strategy based on ending the war quickly. Neither he nor Congress knew if the country could bear the cost for long.

Much of the money that Congress authorized either was issued inefficiently or disappeared before reaching its intended target. Corrupt officials plucked some of the money to line their own pockets. Other funds evaporated under the care of incompetent handlers, or because of the absence of skilled accountants. And not just public but private funds went to waste.

Patriot propagandists liked to portray Americans as a people united, eager to sacrifice self-interest for the good of the whole. In 1775 many Patriot leaders were deluded by this image into thinking that the goodness of their cause sufficed in and of itself to ensure victory. Washington disagreed. As an experienced businessman, he suspected that some of his countrymen would take advantage of wartime conditions for their personal profit. Even so, he was amazed and outraged at the extent of the problem.

Laziness, incompetence, and corruption in army and civilian financial administration were bad enough. Worse was pernicious public speculation, such as forestalling and stock jobbing, which artificially inflated prices and increased market volatility. Such practices did not just weaken the army, the states, and the government but undercut the entire economy. No topic brought Washington closer to apoplexy. To his friend and secretary Joseph Reed he wrote on November 28:

> Such a dearth of Publick Spirit, & want of Virtue; such stock job-bing, and fertility in all the low Arts to obtain advantages, of one kind or another, in this great change of Military arrangement I never saw before, and pray God I may never be Witness to again. what will be the ultimate end of these Manouvres is beyond my Scan—I tremble at the prospect. . . . [C]ould I have foreseen what I have, & am like to experience, no consideration upon Earth should have induced me to accept this Command.[26]

However much he rued it, however, Washington was an astute enough observer of human behavior—particularly in an aspiring but still unformed capitalist society—to understand that he could not just wish away this kind of behavior. It must be either endured or preempted by ending the war. If it surged out of control, it could leave the country an economic basket case.

The best solution, it seemed, was to push for an immediate and decisive victory—both to overawe the British and to convince the American people that their privations would not last for long. "The State of Inactivity, in which this Army has lain for some Time," Washington informed Hancock, "by no means corresponds with my Wishes, by some decisive Stroke to relieve my Country from the heavy Expence, its Subsistence must create." Delivering a "decisive Stroke" was easier said than done. Supplies—especially powder—were scarce, the troops poorly trained, the British well-entrenched, and the army's general officers balky. Washington nevertheless repeatedly convened councils of war to consider attacking Boston in order to avoid the "Expence" of maintaining the army through the winter; but each time, the council rejected his proposals. In desperation, he asked Congress to let him burn the enemy out by means of an incendiary bombardment. The delegates sensibly refused.[27]

While Washington simmered at Cambridge, the war took an ominous new turn. On the afternoon of October 17, 1775, four British warships anchored off Falmouth, Massachusetts—now Portland, Maine. The British commander sent an emissary ashore warning the inhabitants to evacuate as he was under orders to set the town ablaze. When a committee from the town asked why, he curtly informed them that every New England seaport was about to be destroyed—and New York as well. The next morning, the ships opened fire and part of the town burst into flames. A British landing party came ashore to finish the job. Four hundred buildings were burned to ashes, leaving more than a thousand men, women, and children homeless with the winter on the horizon.

This brazen act of terrorism was meant to shock and awe—and in that it succeeded. Washington publicly denounced the "desolation and misery" wrought by "ministerial vengeance," but dread inwardly enveloped him as he contemplated the future. Although the British did not immediately carry out their threat of torching the entire seacoast, he expected them to begin doing so at any time. "The Ministry have begun the Destruction of our Sea Port Towns," he announced, ordering local militias to take defensive measures that he knew would be useless.[28]

The prospect of enemy warships penetrating the very waterways that he had promoted as avenues of commerce haunted Washington's mind with images of Alexandria and Mount Vernon in flames. He urged Virginia to block "the Navigation of the Potomack without loss of time; conceiving, that at an Expence, not amounting to one tenth of the damage which the Estates [like his] on that River may sustain in the course of next Summer, such obstructions may be laid as to prevent any Armed Vessell from passing." The tax burden would be heavy, but he for one was willing to pay his share.[29]

The horror and rage that gripped America in the aftermath of the burning of Falmouth were comparable in some respects to the aftermath of 9/11.

Apocalyptic visions abounded. An all-out scorched earth campaign by the British Navy would inflict almost inconceivable human misery, leaving many thousands of people homeless, and leading inevitably to disease and starvation. The economic dislocation would be catastrophic. Even if the American people managed to fight on to victory—by no means a sure thing, since soldiers might hesitate to take the field when their families were starving—their commerce would be destroyed. Rebuilding would take years, maybe decades (Falmouth did not approach recovery until the end of the century). The prospect did not weaken Washington's will to seek victory. It did, however, reinforce his conviction that the war must be ended quickly, before war's ravages destroyed the country.

British attacks on the principle of private property infuriated Washington and eventually transformed his attitude toward the Revolution. In the summer and early autumn of 1775, independence was still an abstract idea. He did not embrace it immediately. When further major attacks did not immediately materialize after Falmouth, the general briefly indulged the luxury of imagining it as an aberration never to be repeated. After the burning of Norfolk, Virginia, on January 1, 1776, however, he became a full-fledged advocate of independence. The destruction began when British ships opened fire on the town and landing parties came ashore to set certain Patriot-owned buildings ablaze. Patriot gangs finished the job by torching Loyalist property in revenge, and flames spread across the entire town. Unaware of the details, Washington assumed that Norfolk was the dreaded next step in a British campaign against American property and commerce. In reaction, he began for the first time to speak of "the Propriety of a Seperation" from Great Britain. In breaching the sacred principle of private property *in a war against its own citizens,* the ministry had renounced its right to govern. For Americans, it was no longer an option but a necessity to "shake off all Connexions with a State So unjust, & unnatural."[30]

With the attacks on Falmouth and Norfolk giving him both a gritty determination and a greater sense of urgency, Washington commenced his final campaign for the liberation of Boston. On January 1, even as Norfolk erupted in flames, the commander in chief began assembling a new army. The new troops were a motley bunch, scarcely better than those he had encountered the previous summer; but the general promptly set about whipping them and their officers into shape. Blizzards of paper blended with winter snowstorms as Washington's military bureaucracy heaved into motion, and parade grounds echoed to the sounds of shouting officers and drilling soldiers.

By February the army was only marginally improved, but Washington decided that he had seen enough. Remarking that "no oppertunity can present itself earlier than my wishes," he announced himself ready to assault Boston. His generals remained skeptical, and once again rebuffed his proposal to launch an all-out attack. They did, however, suggest placing artillery on Dorchester Heights overlooking the city. Maybe that would be enough to drive the British out. Washington quickly agreed. On the night of March 4–5, his men industriously hauled cannon that had been captured at Fort Ticonderoga atop the heights. Washington looked forward hopefully to a British assault and bloody repulse, but the enemy refused to oblige and instead evacuated the city.[31]

The commander in chief was crestfallen. He had anticipated that a battle with heavy British casualties would speed the end of the war. Thoughts of the haul of booty left behind in the city helped to boost his spirits for a time. He expected to find £30,000–40,000 worth of stores, equipment, and British property and ordered his commissaries to prepare precise returns of material that it could "turn to the public advantage." In this he was not disappointed. However, his hopes that "we shall be able to collect some hard Money from the Inhabitants of Boston" were dashed because "the posessors of it, are not of Late accustomed to a paper Currency, and keep their Gold & Silver Close."[32]

––––––––––––

The wages of victory were sweet, but the contest had only begun. The British might or might not continue their campaign of destruction on the seacoast, but their forces would certainly return, and civilian privations would increase. The main thing was to maintain unity. "Every person should be active in some department or other, without paying too much attention to private Interest," Washington told John Augustine on March 31. "It is a great stake we are playing for, and sure we are of winning if the Cards are well managed—Inactivity in some—disaffection in others—and timidity in many, may hurt the Cause; nothing else can, for Unanimity will carry us through triumphantly in spite of every exertion of Great Britain, if link'd together in one indissoluble Band."[33]

Boston and Cambridge were hives of activity in March and April as troops assembled their gear and ox-drawn wagons heaped with supplies lumbered down the mud-choked roads leading south from the city. Washington fussily oversaw these preparations to shift the army to New York, but could not help noticing civilians carrying on business as if Massachusetts were still a British colony. Old associations died hard. There, in the harbor, stood British warships surrounded by a small fleet of civilian boats placidly selling foodstuffs and supplies. Furious, Washington stalked off to headquarters and scrawled or dictated a message demanding that the civilian authorities make a choice. "We are to consider ourselves either in a state of Peace or War with Great Britain," he told them. "If the former why are our Ports shut up—Our Trade destroyed—Our property siezed—Our Towns burnt, and our worthy and valuable Citizens led into Captivity & suffering the most cruel hardships?" He followed this up with a proclamation on April 29 decreeing that anyone trading with the British would be treated as an enemy to the rights of the colonies.[34]

Army expenses continued to lay heavy on the general's mind as he rode south to New York with his mud-stained entourage. Careless financial management, he knew, could undermine military success. Although the country's purse strings lay beyond Washington's grasp, his efforts to tighten up military administration had a national impact. Before he arrived in the city, the New York Provincial Congress had contracted with merchant Abraham Livingston to supply army provisions at 10d. 1/2 per ration. Looking over the contract after arriving in Manhattan, Washington thought the price seemed high and demanded an investigation into alternate possibilities. Continental commissary Joseph Trumbull, it turned out, could provision the troops at 8d. 1/3 per ration. "The difference is immense," Washington informed Congress, "as it will amount to no less than two hundred Pounds per Day for 20,000 Men." Livingston relinquished his contract and the army purchased provisions at the lower rate. Over the following weeks Washington inspected every corner of army operations, administration, and supply to root out waste and impose thrift. He even mandated that his soldiers would have to repair their weapons—except in case of "unavoidable accidents"—at their own expense. His mother would have been proud.[35]

The cumulative importance of these relatively inglorious measures—all but forgotten today—in boosting the country's financial endurance would become apparent over time, but the arrival in New York Harbor of a massive enemy fleet bearing more than twenty thousand British and German troops in June and July posed more immediate dangers. Within days—weeks at the most—the Americans could expect to face a life-or-death struggle for arguably their most important city and commercial hub. The soldiers were hardly prepared for it despite months of training and preparation. A German officer on shipboard chuckled to see Americans strutting about in old-fashioned Spanish outfits or sporting "wretched farmers costume" and carrying their equipment in cloth sacks. Teenage Continentals and militiamen toyed with and often broke their weapons and other accoutrements—the wastage was astonishing. Grimly observing such antics, the commander in chief lamented that "we are not, either in Men, or Arms prepared for" the "bloody Summer" ahead.[36]

The unpreparedness if not incompetence of his men was among the least of Washington's worries. One of his first acts upon arriving in the city had been to drive off livestock and destroy or secure all provisions stores within range of the enemy, giving civilians chits for reimbursing their losses. Loyalist sentiment in the region was strong, however, and civilians actively traded with the enemy fleet. Washington furiously pushed forward defensive preparations, and exhorted his troops to embrace the Declaration of Independence that he had read to them on July 9. As the summer wore on, however, so did his impatience. British troops occupied Staten Island against only token American resistance. And the ever-hovering problem of finance continued to plague him. On August 19, just before the British landed to attack his forces on Long Island, he wrote worriedly to his cousin and farm manager Lund Washington about "the enormous expence" that the war was imposing on both America and Great Britain. The collapse of one, he thought, entailed the ruin of both and an impoverished future that he did not care to contemplate.[37]

The storm broke—literally and figuratively—on the night of August 21, as a raging tempest pelted the harbor with rain and lightning that killed three American officers. The next morning fifteen thousand British and German troops crossed over from Staten Island to Long Island. With battle imminent, Washington exhorted his troops to "Remember that you are Freemen, fighting for the blessings of Liberty." Fine words could not shore up weak and poorly prepared defenses, however, and on August 27 the enemy stormed and easily broke the American positions on Gowanus Heights. Fortunately for Washington and the American cause, British general William Howe hesitated to follow up his victory and left the last-ditch American fortifications on Brooklyn Heights unchallenged. Washington availed himself of the opportunity to withdraw his forces to Manhattan on the night of August 29–30. Two more weeks of dithering followed before the Americans began withdrawing from the lower part of the island, where they might easily have been cut off and destroyed. They pulled back just in time, for a British landing at Kip's Bay on September 15 routed the American defenders. Looking on horrorstruck, Washington spurred his horse into a suicidal direct assault on the advancing enemy before his aides held him back. Fortunately the British failed to push inshore aggressively, giving the Americans and their despairing commander time to escape.[38]

Depressed and considering resignation, Washington temporarily forgot some of the principles he was fighting to defend. After leaving Manhattan he asked Congress for permission to burn the city in order to make it uncomfortable if not untenable for the victorious enemy. The delegates refused. Days later, however, torch-bearing incendiaries dispersed through the city, setting much of it alight. Their identity was never ascertained, but it is plausible to suppose that they might have been acting under the orders of a commander in chief who thought he and the country had nothing left to lose. Whatever its cause, the conflagration had next to no impact on the British but resulted in severe civilian hardship and long-term economic dislocation that affected the entire region. Washington eventually learned about the fire's impact on his countrymen, and would never again advocate policies that contradicted his hopes of emerging from the war with an intact civil society and infrastructure.

As the army limped north from Kip's Bay and continued its slow evacuation of Manhattan, it seemed little more than a miserable remnant. The men still showed surprising pluck at times and inflicted a number of minor reverses on the cautiously pursuing enemy. Still, Washington knew that what remained of the army of 1776 would not outlast the year, even if it survived defeat in the field. The next force he led into the field had to enlist for substantially more than one year—preferably for the war's duration—in order to give the general and his officers time to meld it into a competent fighting formation with the strength to ride out reverses and maintain pressure on the enemy. As he pondered how to get the point across to a Congress still remote from the realities of warfare, Washington understood that elemental questions came into play. Why did men fight? Would they sacrifice their prosperity for principles? For well-to-do Patriots who never had to scrounge for their bread, it was easy to demand that men live on ideals alone. Nurtured on this belief, delegates simply could not understand why such good and well-motivated men as the American Continentals continued to lose.

Washington exploded the delegates' long-cherished fantasies in a remarkable letter to Congress on September 25. Tell the common soldier to subsist on patriotism, he demanded; the man would respond "that his pay will not support him, and he cannot ruin himself and Family to serve his Country, when every member of the community is equally Interested and benefitted by his Labours." The general admonished Patriots to face the elemental truth that if they were to have any hope of victory, those willing to fight on "Principles of disinterestedness" were "no more than a drop in the Ocean." The country could no longer fight the war with short-term armies and militias—or finance it in penny packets. The investment in manpower and resources had to be total. "This contest is not likely to be the Work of a day," Washington declared; "the War must be carried on systematically." An army must be established "upon a permanent footing." And for that—men needed pay.[39]

Patriot leaders had been used to thinking of pay as a detail, or at best as an ugly necessity almost too sordid to discuss. That was one reason why the states, and Congress, continued to fund the war so haphazardly. Propaganda berated British and German soldiers as mercenaries who fought for lucre; to admit that Americans needed money as well, if only to feed their families, seemed to subvert the very concept of righteous revolt. This belief in the supremacy of altruism was naïve but tenacious. It was also corrosive, gnawing away at the vitals of the American war effort.

Washington's ruthless explosion of impractical idealism at this pivotal point of the war was both timely and essential, and constitutes one of his most outstanding contributions to independence. He argued his case logically, drawing on his incisive understanding, bred of experience in war and business, of what motivates men—and especially leaders of men. Nothing, he explained, was more important than "giving your Officers good pay." This would "induce Gentlemen, and Men of Character to engage," ensuring that they would be motivated both by "Principles of honour, and a spirit of enterprize." Moreover, Washington insisted—outraging some delegates' egalitarian principles—that officers must not receive just subsistence pay but "such allowances as will enable them to live like, and support the Characters of Gentlemen; and not be driven by a scanty pittance to the low, & dirty arts which many of them practice to filch the Public." Paying the man who fought for you was not corrupt, but a way of *preventing* corruption. Moreover, it was a *moral* contract. "Something is due," Washington argued, "to the Man who puts his life in his hand—hazards his health—& forsakes the Sweets of domestic enjoyments."[40]

Calling for officers and men to be paid was all very well—where would the money come from? For this Washington could offer no prescription. Though he had begun to recognize the inefficiency of a confederated government that left national funding wholly dependent on the whims of the states, there was nothing he could do to reform it. He could and did, however, assure the delegates that an army established for the duration of the war was significantly more economical than the system of militia and short-term enlistments that had so far prevailed. Getting this point across was challenging, but Washington pulled it off. Military explanations would have left the delegates unmoved. The general's arguments based on financial prudence, however, forced them to take heed.

Washington's contempt for the militia—what he called a "destructive, expensive, disorderly Mob"—is well known. Less well recognized is his emphasis on the second point—its wastefulness. Put simply, the militia system failed the cost-benefit test. Civilian leaders deluded themselves into thinking that militia not only obviated the dangers of a standing army taking over the country but also saved money. Not so, Washington pointed out. "Certain I am," he told Hancock, "that it would be cheaper to keep 50 or 100,000 Men in constant pay than to depend upon half the number, and supply the other half occasionally by Militia."[41]

The system's costs were enormous. Since most militiamen were farmers and simple manufacturers, and since the military campaigning season coincided with the spring planting and fall harvest, calling them out almost always resulted in "farming & manufactures in a manner suspended," with resulting economic dislocation. Moreover, the time militiamen spent "in pay before and after they are in Camp, Assembling & Marching—the waste of Ammunition—the consumption of Stores, which in spite of every Resolution, & requisition of Congress they must be furnished with, or sent home—added to other incidental expences consequent upon their coming, and conduct in Camp, surpasses all Idea; and destroys every kind of regularity & œconomy which you could establish among fixed and Settled Troops; and will in my opinion prove (if the scheme is adhered to) the Ruin of our Cause."[42]

Washington was not the first American to recognize or even act upon the fact that money motivated men to enlist. Even as he wrote his letter to Congress, states desperate to fill up their enlistment quotas bribed potential recruits with additional bounties of up to twenty shillings per month. The upshot of what Washington called these "fatal & mistaken" policies was to create bidding wars as privates from Massachusetts, for example, demanded the same bounties that their counterparts received in Connecticut. Left unchecked, state bounties would send inflation spiraling out of control and lead to fiscal disaster. Washington's intervention played a crucial role in leading Congress to crack down on the practice.[43]

In place of ad hoc measures and state bidding wars, Washington offered a national system—one that could endure for the war but also be adjusted by Congress as circumstances dictated. His plan for a long-term army establishment was long not just on justifications but on specifics as well. To it he appended a detailed plan of proposed pay rates broken down by rank. The delegates hesitated, but after some further prodding Washington got his wish.

From 1777 onward, men enlisted in the army for three years or the duration of the war, and they and their officers were granted adequate if not extravagant rates of pay. Though not immediate, the military ramifications of this decision—made in large part for economic reasons laid out by the commander in chief—would be dramatic.

---

DISASTERS IN THE FIELD overshadowed legislative victories in the fall and winter of 1776. Exploding out of Manhattan into New Jersey, British forces rumbled victoriously toward the Delaware River, driving all before them. Washington's army shriveled to a dismal rump, withdrawing into Pennsylvania in a series of small detachments. On December 12, confessedly unable to cope with the crisis, Congress granted the commander in chief substantial short-term powers to manage national affairs in its absence. The body then dissolved. For the next few months, Washington would essentially run the country on his own.

The general foresaw both military challenges and economic hardships ahead as his country crumbled around him. "I think the game will be pretty well up," he told Lund on December 17, "as from disaffection, and want of spirit & fortitude, the Inhabitants instead of resistance, are offering Submission, & taking protections from Genl Howe in Jersey." He did not "apprehend half so much danger from Howes Army, as from the disaffection of the three States of New York, Jersey & Pensylvania." These were no mere complaints, but practical observations made on the basis of experience. New Jersey militiamen "either from fear or disaffection, almost to a man, refused to turn out." Pennsylvanians, reeling from financial privations and despairing of victory, "I am told exult at the Approach of the Enemy and our late Misfortunes."[44]

None of Washington's wartime experiences traumatized him so much as these. Motivating men to enlist and fight was a challenge. Convincing them just to carry on the struggle and not to make terms with the enemy was both vital and exponentially more difficult. Patriots and Loyalists talked tough, but for the most part they were not fixed categories. Fanatics aside, Washington understood that each person at every moment had to make a moral decision based on circumstances. And everyone had a breaking point. A firm patriot at one moment might at the next find his farm wrecked and his family starving and decide to treat with the enemy. Call him a traitor if you would; but the needs of survival established a basic human calculus.

The "Treachery and defection of those, who stood foremost in the Opposition, while Fortune smiled upon us, make me fearful that many more will follow their Example," the general worried. "By using their Influence with some, and working upon the Fears of others," he thought they might "extend the Circle so as to take in whole Towns, Counties, nay Provinces." As individuals and in the aggregate, people would come to terms with whatever power offered them financial security and prosperity: the same considerations that had driven revolution could drive reconciliation. In December 1776, it seemed that Washington's army and the whole assembly of Patriot leaders in and out of Congress could offer the American people only ruin. Why, then, should they continue the struggle?[45]

Men like Tom Paine spoke of hope, and to some degree enkindled it. By the fall of 1776, though, talk was cheap. Actually restoring hope—real, physical hope—was Washington's business. He could not reform the government, or command the economy. Though he could establish long-term plans for a stable army, these would do nothing to turn the tables in the short term. With his current army down to a few thousand scraggly men, he could not even dream of inflicting a militarily significant defeat on the British army. His early aspirations for a decisive stroke to end the war were by now long out of view. What he could do, however, was to use his small force as a tangible (as opposed to a rhetorical) symbol of hope to restore public confidence. "I am certain that the Defection of the people in the lower part of Jersey," he told one of his generals on December 18, "has been as much owing to the want of an Army to look the Enemy in the Face, as to any other Cause." Trenton's genesis lay in this observation.[46]

By December 20 Washington had assembled six thousand men, enough to strike what he hoped would be a "lucky blow" sufficient to "raise the spirits of the People, which are quite sunk by our late misfortunes." No American general ever worked harder to cobble together such a tiny force for such an important mission. After a secret nighttime council of war on December 22,

Washington and his officers decided to launch a daring attack across the Delaware River against a German outpost at Trenton. On Christmas Eve, seemingly "much depressed" as he contemplated the stakes for which he was playing, the general penned the sentinels' passwords for the following evening: Victory or Death. Twenty-four hours later he led his troops through a swirling snowstorm down to the river.[47]

Thoughts of money did nothing to inspire the men who clutched freezing fingers to the oars and gunwales of the Durham boats that crossed the Delaware, and who left bloody footprints in the snow on the road to Trenton on Christmas night, 1776. Visions of liberty may or may not have flitted across their minds. Without question, the shivering Continentals brooded about their families and what would happen to them if Washington's mad attack failed. That attack's improbable success against all odds inspired and continues to inspire millions. For the men of '76, however, victory could not drive hard realities from their minds. As the Hessian prisoners captured at Trenton shuffled off, the Continentals unanimously determined either to go home as their enlistments expired or to be paid overtime—*ample* overtime.

Though distressed by their reluctance, Washington sympathized with them too much to be angry. Other men would bring to camp the hard currency that kept the soldiers in service and set them on the road to Princeton in January 1777—a campaign that would eventually rout the British from New Jersey. It was Washington, though, who identified the need for cash and argued that his men should receive it as both a prerequisite and a right. Podium Patriots spoke of abstract principles. When Washington addressed his men, by contrast, he warned them of the "ravage and a deprivation of property" that they could expect from the British if they failed to resist. This simultaneous recognition of and appeal to their livelihoods established the terms of a contract between commander and soldiers that would endure for the remainder of the war. They were his to be led—and he was their advocate.[48]

---

THE TRENTON-PRINCETON CAMPAIGN ended with the British pulling back to New Brunswick and the Continental Army filing into winter camp at

Morristown, New Jersey. There the work of building an army began anew. Washington spent long daytime and evening hours hunched over his desk, poring over reports and drawing up schemata for army arrangement. Around him bustled a platoon of secretaries and aides-de-camp. One of them, twenty-year-old Alexander Hamilton, displayed record-keeping skills almost as impressive as his ability to attract women. A steady stream of visitors, from humble farmers walking hat-in-hand to somber delegates, and from privates to generals, ensured that the commander in chief had little opportunity to relax. This time, though, Washington could look on his work with some expectation of permanence. The administrative framework that he established would remain in place until the enemy called it quits.

Still acting under the extraordinary powers granted him by Congress—which expired after six months—Washington appointed commissaries and other military administrators, recruited and arranged units, and reformed regulations at will without having to seek approval from civilian committees. Congress would approve all of his measures retroactively. Only time, though, could undo the traumas of the previous winter. While the army had undergone many trials, American civilians had arguably suffered more. And their woes continued. New York City's loss and partial destruction dealt a severe blow to surrounding counties that had depended upon it for commerce and trade. Lower New York and much of New Jersey still reeled from the ravages of the previous autumn, when enemy troops had seized supplies, burned or looted farms, and committed widespread murder and rape.

Areas spared of fighting were also hard hit. Export industries in both agriculture and manufacturing withered along with others, such as the New England fisheries, which were dependent upon free navigation. Congress had opened trade with the nations of Continental Europe and their colonies, but these markets were excruciatingly slow to develop under the dual pressures of the British blockade and the collapse (until privateering got well under way) of American shipbuilding. On top of this came the dramatic and continuing rise in military expenditures with its consequent increase in taxation. While few were actually starving, hardships were intense and widespread.

Civil distress had a tangible impact on military affairs. For one thing, recruiting lagged well behind expectations. Washington had correctly identified pay as a pivotal factor in retaining officers and attracting recruits. In times of trial, however, men instinctively preferred to stay home to tend to farms, businesses, and families. Pay rates and bounties could be elevated, but by how much?

The instability of Continental scrip complicated the problem. Civilians nervously hoarded hard money in preference to both state and Continental paper currency, severely undercutting the dollar. And though Congress had established a Continental Loan Office "to restore the Credit of the Continental Currency," its credit had collapsed with the catastrophes of the previous fall and no long-term fix seemed possible. This left Washington and the civil authorities facing yet another conundrum: Pay officers and men more, further driving inflation? Or, hold firm and watch them stay away or resign in droves (as many did) because their pay could not defray their expenditures let alone support their families?[49]

Piling injury upon injury, the canny British began a campaign to destabilize American finances by surreptitiously distributing counterfeit currency. Despite the death penalty for counterfeiters, this problem would continue unabated. Moreover, the British exploited pay shortages and depreciation to bribe troops into deserting and turning over their arms in return for hard currency or bounty lands.

Washington could do little to hold back the inflationary tide except to issue and enforce regulations that generally addressed symptoms rather than causes. He could also lecture anyone who would listen about root principles. In May 1777, one of his generals reported news of an American officer who had been caught passing off counterfeit money to recruits while pilfering the genuine article. "Money is the sinews of War," Washington wrote in response. "That in which we are engaged is a just One, and we have no means of carrying it on, but by the Continental or State Notes. Whoever attempts to destroy their credit, particularly that of those, emitted by the United States, is a flagitious Offender & should forfeit his life, to satisfie the demands of public justice." Alarmed as British counterfeiting grew increasingly widespread, he exhorted Congress: "Nothing therefore has a greater claim to the close attention of Congress, than the Counteraction of this part of their diabolical Scheme—every thing depends upon it." He and the delegates knew, however, that they were practically powerless to halt the practice.[50]

THE ARMY THAT CONDUCTED the summer and autumn campaign of 1777 was better organized than any that had preceded it, but still unstable. Recruiting had finally picked up in the late spring. Training, however, remained incomplete and supplies such as ordnance and clothing were lacking. Worse, although Washington had labored heroically to establish an efficient military administration, he had of necessity to rely upon untested men to fill important offices. Some of these would turn out to be incompetent or corrupt.

Washington had to work with the tools at hand, however, and as the British army launched an inconclusive spring campaign in New Jersey and then boarded ships for an undisclosed destination in July, he had no choice but to take the field. For a month he marched his army back and forth in brutal summer heat until the British landed at Head of Elk, Maryland, on August 25 and commenced their march on Philadelphia. Washington drove his force south to intercept them, but suffered a severe defeat at Brandywine on September 11. The British forces, commanded by General Howe, occupied Philadelphia on September 26 and then beat off an American surprise attack at Germantown on October 4. Over the weeks that followed, Washington tried and ultimately failed to hold on to a series of forts along the Delaware River that would have made it difficult if not impossible for the British to keep the city supplied. December found Washington and his army at Whitemarsh, Pennsylvania, reeling from a series of defeats and wondering where they would spend the winter.

In seizing Philadelphia, Howe had hoped to exploit what he thought was a vast undercurrent of loyalism in the mid-Atlantic and to reassert royal control over the region. He would have done better to think, as Washington did, of how to appeal to American civilians' self-interest. The winter of 1777–1778 would demonstrate once again that while some civilians were too patriotic to regard their pocketbooks, many—enough to have made a difference if the British had made a concerted effort to reach them—were not. For them, the decision of whether to side with Loyalists or Patriots boiled down to survival—or, less dramatically but just as fundamentally, to a choice between mere subsistence versus profit. It was a war not just of hearts and minds, but of stomachs.

Facing these realities, Washington spent less time worrying about his military defeats than he did about money. By this point he and his staff and field officers were all stridently warning that currency depreciation demanded desperate measures—including military action—to restore public credit before the economy collapsed. "The Depreciation of the Currency of these States, Points out the Immediate necessity of giving the enemy Battle," said General "Mad" Anthony Wayne to a chorus of approval from many of Washington's deputies. Calmer heads, such as Henry Knox, advised the commander in chief that although inflation had become dangerous, measures that the states had taken to raise taxes still might hold it back, obviating the need for "some desperate attack." Washington to some extent agreed, writing of "the indispensable necessity of a Tax for the purpose of sinking the Paper money" and advocating targeted price regulations. Still, though, he believed (as Trenton had taught him) that the army's actions played an important role in maintaining public credit. This belief would set him on the road to Valley Forge.[51]

There were two basic options for the winter camp of 1777–1778. The first—and by far the most popular with officers and men—was to retire to a settled location such as York, Pennsylvania. There the army could recuperate and train at leisure, with the troops well sheltered, amply supplied (utilizing already-established routes of communication and commerce), safe from enemy attack, and able to gather their strength for the coming campaign. The most obvious disadvantage of that option was that it would leave the British secure and in control of Philadelphia's mid-Atlantic commerce. The second option was to choose a location closer—but not too close—to the city, from which the Continental Army could pressure the enemy and contest control of the surrounding region. In that case, though, the Americans would have to construct their own shelter, forge new lines of communication and supply, and keep on guard against British attack.

Washington was not initially predisposed toward either option, and polled his officers on their opinions. They were divided; but the man the commander in chief trusted most had no doubts as to the wisest course. In choosing an encampment, General Nathanael Greene told Washington on December 1 that "an appearance should be kept up as much as possible of besieging the enemy, not only to cover the country but to preserve the credit of our currency which will always rise and fall as our army appears superiour or inferior to the enemy." Greene recommended Valley Forge, and Washington, ever the businessman, agreed.[52]

Valley Forge typically conjures up images of cold, squalor, and hope-lessness. Shortly after arriving in camp, many of the soldiers assembled to raucously protest the fetid meat the commissaries had seen fit to feed them. Hooting like owls and cawing like crows, they hinted that the commissaries might join them after a course of tarring and feathering. The men were pla-cated with promises, for a time; but as the protest suggested, none of them were going to sit around in the slush and simply endure their misery. Valley Forge was in fact perhaps the most active winter encampment of the entire war.

The encampment's two primary and obviously interrelated themes were supply and commerce. Supplying the soldiers was of course a priority. Wash-ington visibly worked himself almost to exhaustion on their behalf. To do so, however, he had both to develop efficient systems of procurement and distribution and to compete effectively for resources. Confiscation was not an option. This meant that the army had to convince civilians that it was in their interest, both ideologically and financially, to supply the army. Success in establishing commerce with civilians would improve public credit and thereby strengthen Continental currency.

A parallel objective in the competition for civilian commerce was to exclude the British from the market. This could only partly be achieved militarily—by using cavalry and militia to interdict supply lines. Legal coer-cion could also only have a marginal effect, given the limited reach of military and civil justice at the border of two contesting armies. Civilians would have to be convinced that it was not in their interest ideologically or financially to trade with the British. The contest for hearts and minds was elementally a struggle for commerce.

Ensuring supply to the American army boiled down, first and foremost, to establishing effective military administration. Major shortages of food, clothing, and other essentials, owing to the corruption and ineffectiveness of individuals as well as organization inefficiencies, induced Washington to conduct a major overhaul of army administration. He carried out the lion's share of this work on his own, developing detailed plans and passing them on to Congress for execution. His forty-one-page letter of January 29, 1778, to a Congressional Committee on army reform must have astonished the delegates with its detailed, top-to-bottom prescriptions. Once again he zeroed in on pay as a prerequisite for improvement. "Besides feeding and cloathing a soldier well," Washington wrote, "nothing is of greater importance than paying him with punctuality." By February, thanks to Congress's inherent difficulties in raising funds from the states and disbursing them to the army, pay was on average at least three months in arrears.[53]

Washington vehemently protested but could not solve this problem, the causes of which lay beyond his purview. He could and did, however, reaffirm the old mantras of economy and self-sufficiency. Total self-sufficiency was of course out of the question. The commander in chief nevertheless issued careful instructions to the troops for constructing log huts, making soap, bartering hides for dressed leather to make shoes, and practicing other daily economies to reduce expense. He trumpeted "a new fashion which I think will save Cloth—be made up quicker and cheaper and yet be more warm and convenient to the Soldier." He promoted industriousness by creating "Laboratory Companies" made up of convalescent soldiers for the manufacture of ordnance and stores, and ordered each army division to establish a "Travelling Forge" for the repair of weapons and equipment. Even Washington's oft-cited proscriptions against gambling had less to do with moral abhorrence (after all, he had often gambled himself) than with a conviction that the money "Squander'd" in the process could have been devoted to necessities.[54]

Administrative reforms and economies dovetailed with Washington's objectives in the contest for civilian commerce. His first steps in this realm were repressive, as he demanded "immediate & Coercive Measures" by civil and military authority to halt civilian trade with Philadelphia. He also sent troops to steal or break millstones at gristmills near the city to shut down flour production. But these were only stopgaps.[55]

More positively, Washington established Valley Forge as a hub of commerce resembling in some aspects a small city. After a series of close consultations with local farmers and tradespeople to determine supply, demand, and, above all, fair prices, he opened a "public market" at the camp where civilians could sell or trade their wares directly with the army. By the late winter and early spring of 1778 it had become an active and profitable concern, jammed on market days with milling crowds of soldiers and civilians who established a free intercourse of mutual interest.[56]

Here and in transactions taking place further in the country, Washington insisted on the use of Continental currency and forbade confiscations that would "have the most pernicious consequence . . . spreading disaffection—jealousy & fear in the people." That the bills of credit his agents provided were honored by Congress only after long delays—ironically further injuring public credit—was not Washington's fault. He did his best, as everyone knew, to treat civilians fairly, and encouraged farmers and tradespeople not just to subsist but to profit.[57]

Market forces, Washington hoped, would operate of their own accord for the army's and the public's benefit. Only in exceptional cases did he countenance state intervention in the manufacture of ordnance and other necessities, as for example when he learned that an important lead mine in the Allegheny foothills had been infested by squatters who impeded its production. "The Mine ought or may at least for the present," he suggested to the Pennsylvania government, "be seized by, and belong to the State . . . that private persons who without right may have sat down on that reserved Tract [may not] be admitted to make a monopoly of the Mine."[58]

The general likewise hoped that free commerce would of itself suffice to "fix a value . . . upon that [paper currency] which is to be the medium of our internal commerce, and the support of the War." Unfortunately, the same price-gouging practices that had appeared earlier in the war emerged at Valley Forge with redoubled force. Their first appearance left him baffled. While asking Congress to find a solution, he confessed that "I know not how it is to be effected." Finally, he asked the states to institute price-fixing measures to circumscribe the avarice of greedy farmers and imposed controls on sutlers seeking to market their wares in camp.[59]

Washington knew that such policies would be ineffective over the long term. In November 1777 Congress asked the New England states to appoint commissioners "to regulate and ascertain the price of labour, manufactures, internal produce, and commodities imported from foreign parts, military stores excepted." Most states complied, but the measure backfired; for by keeping prices artificially low it created a dangerous scarcity of meat as farmers refused to sell their livestock. Seeing this, Washington pressured Congress and the states to ease off, and most of the price-fixing measures were repealed.[60]

The ugly truth was that nothing Washington or the civil authorities did could make the money problem go away. The states had endemic problems of their own, while Congress's attempts to raise money without printing it were sometimes almost comical in their futility. Continental lotteries, established in hopes of raising revenue at the distant prospect of substantial reward, were without exception miserable failures as sales stayed low and the government lost rather than earned money. Rail though he did against speculation that debased the Continental currency, Washington could understand and even empathize with civilians' continuing reluctance to trust paper money.

The general was of course not immune to the immutable laws of self-interest. In instructions to Mount Vernon's farm manager, his cousin Lund Washington, the commander in chief urged him to discretely invest wealth in land and hard currency while avoiding paper. Like the army, the estate at Mount Vernon was a significant part but still just a part of a larger whole. The sputtering economy could not be repaired without the implementation of national measures that were ultimately dependent on peace. Measures such as opening a market at Valley Forge could create a community of interest and help to build public credit, but not permanently establish it. Until then, just getting by was an accomplishment in and of itself.

The Continental Army emerged from Valley Forge in the spring of 1778 stronger than it had entered. There were many reasons for this, including the dedicated hard work of Washington and his officers, and the heroic perseverance of his men. Fundamentally, though, in winning the contest of supply and commerce the army had also secured victory in the battle for hearts and minds.

The British, who had relied in large part on overseas supply, had failed to establish the kind of extensive civilian commerce that might have generated sympathy or outright Loyalist sentiment. Instead, they had relied on their (increasingly limited) supplies of hard currency to entice civilian trade—partially curtailed anyway thanks to American military interdiction—and confiscated without recompense what they could not purchase. General Howe's dream of an upswell in pro-British feeling never materialized. This was not so much because his army lacked the means to impose military control but because it and the loyalists who supported it failed to emerge with the mass of the population as partners rather than adversaries.

Washington, by contrast, operated within a system that respected private property while pushing commercial intercourse that encouraged legitimate profit. His communications with local officials, farmers, and tradesmen demonstrated his acknowledgment of civil authority. It was in thousands of everyday individual transactions, though—from commissaries purchasing grain from farmers, to soldiers haggling with vendors over turnips and camp kettles in the Valley Forge market—that established the army as a partner to civil society in the common struggle against British imperial domination. Valley Forge cemented Washington's leadership among the soldiers, who came to love him for his attention to the fundamental details that determined whether they lived or died. It also established a vital bond between soldier and civilians. The bond would be tested, but thanks to Washington it would never break.

CHAPTER FIVE

# VICTORY WITHOUT PEACE

NEWS OF FRENCH INTERVENTION IN THE SPRING OF 1778 generated a wave—all too fleeting, alas—of popular joy. Americans dreamed of the arrival of a French army that would drive the British from the continent while the French Navy routed them from the high seas. Washington's official camp celebration, with its parades and artillery salutes, was intended to reinforce that impression. His immediate hopes, though, were economic. Most obviously, the United States could look forward to an influx of French loans and supplies. But Washington also rejoiced at receiving "a clear proof of the intention of France to encourage and protect our trade" with the West Indies and Europe, and looked forward to the boost that public confidence would give to Continental currency. "The favorable news from Europe," he wrote optimistically on May 15, "has already begun to produce a visable effect on the value of paper money . . . that . . . will extend its influence and reduce the price of horses and every other article." Meanwhile, he expected the British to find it increasingly expensive to carry on a struggle that now extended beyond North America to the West Indies, Europe, and even Asia.[1]

With three years of war under his belt Washington had learned a great deal about the limits of patriotism, and he incorporated these lessons in his revised strategic vision for victory. He summed up his approach in a letter of April 21 to Virginia planter John Banister:

Men may speculate as they will—they may talk of patriotism—they
may draw a few examples from ancient story of great atchievements
performed by it's influence; but, whoever builds upon it, as a sufficient basis, for conducting a long and bloody War, will find themselves deceived in the end. We must take the passions of Men, as
nature has given them, and those principles as a guide, which are
generally the rule of action. I do not mean to exclude altogether the
idea of patriotism. I know it exists, and I know it has done much in
the present contest. But I will venture to assert, that a great and lasting War can never be supported on this principle alone—It must be
aided by a prospect of interest or some reward. For a time it may, of
itself, push men to action—to bear much—to encounter difficulties;
but it will not endure unassisted by interest.[2]

This was no declaration of cynicism, or recognition if not endorsement of self-
ishness. That is not what Washington meant by "interest." Instead, he pointed
to the basic human calculus of expense and reward. Patriots and Loyalists, he
believed, were not born but created by virtue of their experiences and per-
ceived interests. The categories were not rigid but ever-changing. Today's popular war against British rule might well have become tomorrow's revolt against
Congress if personal sacrifices for independence seemed to go for naught.

Even French intervention, then, might avail nothing if the American people lost the sense that they had a personal stake in success, and lost confidence
in victory. "Men are naturally fond of peace," he told Banister, and there were
clear signs "that the people of America, are pretty generally weary of the present war." Many of them doubtless would be willing to come to an "accommodation" with the enemy "rather than persevere in a contest for independance."[3]

With that in mind, it was essential to place the army upon "a substantial
footing"—as a means not just of securing victory in the field but of encouraging the people. "This will conduce," he wrote, "to inspire the Country with
confidence [and] enable those at the head of affairs to consult the public honor
and interest, notwithstanding the defection of some and temporary inconsis-
tancy and irresolution of others, who may desire to compromise the dispute."
At the same time, and more important, it was essential to educate the people

that their personal interests lay in "Nothing short of Independence"—not least because independence held forth the prospect of "unrestricted commerce."[4]

Currency was the bellwether of public confidence. Building confidence strengthened the currency and vice versa. After 1778, this knowledge increasingly defined Washington's military strategy. In June 1778, British forces evacuated Philadelphia and marched in sweltering heat across New Jersey with the Continental Army in their tracks. No one told Washington that he had to attack the British—the prospects for cutting them off were almost nil—but he did so anyway. The Battle of Monmouth on June 28 was essentially a draw, but in its aftermath Washington and his officers did everything in their power to spin it as an important victory. They did so partly to reinforce the commander in chief's authority, but primarily to inspire public confidence.

Afterward, the British hunkered down in New York City and refused to engage militarily with the Americans on a large scale in the mid-Atlantic region, although the threat that they would do so—particularly up the Hudson toward West Point—always hovered overhead. The following months passed for Washington in grinding frustration. Ennui, he feared, could inflict as much harm as outright defeat, perhaps even more so—eroding confidence and endangering the economy, and thus independence, in the long run. Troubling financial signs reinforced his fears as the currency once again neared total collapse.

To Washington it seemed likely that time, despite French intervention, would work against American prospects for independence. "Can the Enemy prosecute the War?" he asked his friend Gouverneur Morris on October 4, 1778:

Can *we* carry on the War much longer? certainly No; unless some measures can be devised, and speedily executed, to restore the credit of our Currency—restrain Extortion—and punish Forestallers. Without these can be effected, what funds can stand the present Expences of the Army? And what Officer can bear the weight of prices, that every necessary article is now got to? A Rat, in the shape of a Horse, is not to be bought at this time for less than £200—A Saddle under Thirty or forty—Boots twenty—and Shoes and other

articles in like proportion! How is it possible therefore for Officers
to stand this, without an Increase of pay? And how is it possible to
advance their pay, when Flour is selling (at different places) from five
to fifteen pounds pr Ct—Hay from ten to thirty pounds pr Tunn—
and Beef & other essentials in this proportion. The true point of
light then, in which to place, & consider this matter, is not simply
whether G. Britain can carry on the War, but whose Finances (theirs
or ours) is most likely to fail.[5]

Washington was not the only one concerned that financial ruin would herald
total defeat. Up to now Congress—still stubbornly thinking in the short
term despite the commander in chief's warnings—had attempted to curry
popular support for the war effort by keeping the tax burden light. In
December 1778, however, the delegates voted to enact a new war tax of
$15 million. This, President of Congress Henry Laurens informed Wash-
ington, would hopefully return "many of us to first principles from which
we have been too long wandering." Though "almost intolerable," he expected
the tax to "rouse & animate our fellow Citizens" by forcing them to economize and eliminate waste and showing "the necessity for consolidating our
strength, as well as the impropriety & danger of new expensive Military
enterprizes." Of course, it might also convince them that the war was too
expensive to continue.[6]

    French financial aid, both Laurens and Washington recognized, was a
double-edged sword. "I warned my friends against the danger of Mortgaging
these States to foreign powers," Laurens wrote. "Every Million of Livres you
borrow implies a pledge of your Lands." Washington agreed, arguing that
loans should be kept to a minimum and that even French military aid should
be welcomed with care. It was for this reason among others that he rejected
in 1779 a proposal for a prohibitively expensive Franco-American invasion of
Canada. Almost instinctively, he returned to the old mantra he had learned in
childhood. Economize, economize, economize, he proclaimed: "retrenching
our Expences and adopting a general system of Oeconomy which may give
success to the plans of Finance Congress have in contemplation and perhaps
enable them to do something effectual for the releif of public Credit and for

restoring the Value of our Currency. . . . The most uniform principle of Oeco-nomy should pervade every department."[7]

But nothing seemed to work. By the spring of 1779, inflation once again clutched the economy in its grips. "Speculation—peculation—engrossing—forestalling—with all their concomitants, afford too many melancholy proofs of the decay of public virtue," Washington wrote to Massachusetts Patriot James Warren on March 31; "and too glaring instances of its being the inter-est & desire of too many, who would wish to be thought friends, to continue the War." There was nothing wrong with honest profit; but rampant specu-lation in pursuit of "a little dirty pelf" out of a "lust of gain" was among the most "monstrous evils" imaginable. "Let vigorous measures be adopted," he begged Warren, "not to limit the price of articles—for this I conceive is inconsistent with the very nature of things, & impracticable in itself—but to punish speculators—forestallers—& extortioners—and above all—to sink the money by heavy Taxes—To promote public & private Œconomy—[and to] encourage Manufactures."[8]

A crushing sense of helplessness engulfed Washington as he watched the currency continue to plunge despite his exhortations. By May 1779 he feared that economically speaking "our affairs are irretrievably lost," and that "a gen-eral Crash of all things" was imminent. But what could he do? The British remained firmly ensconced in New York City, and despite pinprick raids that summer at Stony Point and Paulus Hook—symbolic actions specifically de-signed to refocus public energy on the war effort—there seemed little prospect of rooting them out. Washington nevertheless determined to try.[9]

Heavily fortified by land and sea and easily reinforced, New York was next to impregnable. Even if successful, an American assault on it would entail almost unimaginably heavy casualties. Why, then, was Washington so determined to attack it? Was his aggressiveness born of impatience or some sort of mental imbalance? In fact, from his perspective the focus on New York was completely rational. The collapse of the Continental currency—shored up only by massive French and eventually Dutch loans that might reduce the United States to debt slavery if allowed to continue for long—augured in Washington's view a total paralysis of the war effort, forcing the army to concentrate solely on survival. This in turn would undermine popular support of the war, leading in a viciously spiraling circle to further economic dislocation, unrest, civilian commerce with the enemy leading to the development of pernicious communities of interest, and total defeat.

Washington did not want to risk everything on a single throw of the dice—he feared that he would be *compelled* to do so. For the remainder of 1779 and into 1780, as the British launched a crushingly successful campaign to conquer the South, and as Washington's army reeled from mutinies brought on by pay shortages and economic distress, he set the groundwork for an assault that would decide everything in one stroke. The moment appeared to have arrived in the fall of 1779, when a French fleet seemed prepared to anchor off New York City. Washington eagerly mobilized his entire army for an imminent assault on the British entrenchments. When the fleet failed to materialize, he had to go back to biding his time. Still, though, he was prepared to resume the operation in an instant—whether from opportunity or out of final desperation.

---

THE YEAR 1781 DID NOT DAWN HAPPILY. At Morristown on New Year's Day, troops of the Pennsylvania line rose up in mutiny. The men were orderly on the whole, but snarled ominously that if their demands for immediate relief were not met, they would push their quarrel with Congress at the point of the bayonet. They then marched to Princeton and made menacing gestures toward Philadelphia. Washington bought them off with honorable discharges and furloughs, only to face another mutiny by New Jersey troops a few weeks later. Alarmed that disaffection was metastasizing throughout the army, he put this revolt down brutally, rounding up the mutineers and forcing the men to execute their ringleaders.

The root causes of disaffection nevertheless remained, and they were predominantly financial. Pay, as usual, was badly in arrears; but that hardly mattered since it was worthless anyway. A horse cost $150,000, almost four times what it had cost a year earlier. Literate soldiers read letters from home telling tales of devastated farms and businesses, and of suffering wives and children. Illiterate soldiers fed on a rumor mill that warned of wholesale economic collapse and eventual starvation.

Washington was under no illusions about the probable outcome of this miserable state of affairs. At Valley Forge, he had labored hard to establish a community of commerce between the army and the civilian population—a community that left the British on the outside looking in. Now, despairing civilians were not only selling provisions to the British in New York City on a scale never seen before—they were also turning their long-cherished hoards of hard specie over to the British in exchange for desperately needed consumer goods such as clothing and household supplies.

This dangerous—and humiliating—commerce, Washington warned, "serves to drain us of our Provisions and Specie removes the barrier between us and the enemy, corrupt[s] the morals of our people by a lucrative traffic and by degrees weaken[s] the opposition." Shattering the American system that Washington and others had labored so hard to create, it established new bonds of interest with an erstwhile enemy that might, over time, begin to look like a friend. "Men of all descriptions are now indiscriminately engaging in" commerce with the British, Washington anxiously observed, "Whig, Tory, Speculator. By its being practiced by those of the latter class, in a manner with impunity, Men who, two or three years ago, would have shuddered at the idea of such connexions now pursue it with avidity and reconcile it to themselves (in which their profits plead powerfully) upon a principle of equality, with the Tory."[10]

Congress, finally, was doing more than just talk. Early in 1781 the delegates proposed to create ministers for war, foreign affairs, and finance. Some suggested Alexander Hamilton, whose talents "as a financier" had become well known, for the latter office, and Washington extolled his "probity and Sterling virtue." In February, though, the delegates tapped Philadelphia financier Robert Morris. A successful businessman who had earned a small fortune from privateering, Morris had provided important financial support to Congress and the Continental Army in the winter of 1776–1777. He was also a fervent supporter of free-market advocates who decried Congress's many ad hoc restrictive measures, such as price-fixing, to shore up the Continental currency.[11]

After taking the oath of office in June, Morris and a talented team that he assembled attempted to tackle the nation's many economic problems and in particular to restore its currency. So much damage had already been done that his task was largely hopeless. Nevertheless, by securing more French loans, extending his own personal credit, creating a system of in-kind taxes that allowed farmers to fulfill their obligations to the government with goods rather than specie, and establishing the Bank of North America that advanced perhaps $1 million in loans to the government, Morris was at least able to prevent things from getting much worse.

Washington could not afford to wait and see what Morris could accomplish. Up until now his army had been paralyzed, from both lack of opportunity to smite the British and lack of funding. Enemy advances continued in the South despite hopeful signs at places like Cowpens and Guilford Courthouse. Virginia had now entered firmly in the enemy's crosshairs. In the winter of 1780–1781, the traitor Benedict Arnold, sporting a general's commission in the British army after attempting to betray West Point the previous September, conducted raids along the Virginia coast. He sacked Richmond, occupied Portsmouth, and in April torched warehouses full of tobacco at Petersburg. The blow to Virginia's economy was severe and might have become crippling.

Nor was Mount Vernon safe. In April the British warship *Savage* appeared in the Potomac below the estate. Soldiers from the ship had already landed on the Maryland side, torching a number of estates there. With plumes of smoke rising high into the sky above the river, the British captain sent a message to Lund Washington promising him to expect the same treatment unless he provided the ship with "a large supply of provisions." Lund hesitated, whereupon the ship drew closer to shore and the threat was repeated. Terrified, Lund boarded the ship carrying some cooked chicken for the British tars' enjoyment. The captain praised George Washington's character and promised that he would never "entertain the idea of taking the smallest measure offensive to so illustrious a character as the General." Now charmed, Lund returned onshore and sent the British a large supply of livestock and other supplies. The warship then departed, carrying with it seventeen of Washington's slaves who had taken the opportunity to escape. News of the affair sent George into a rage, though by then there was little he could do but chastise Lund—a catharsis he indulged in freely if fruitlessly. The net effect was to renew the commander in chief's determination to end the war quickly.[12]

The means to force a showdown now seemed at hand. In July 1780, a French army under the Comte de Rochambeau had landed at Newport, Rhode Island. Washington conferred with the French general repeatedly and, in a conference at Wethersfield, Connecticut, on May 22, 1781, thought he had convinced him to collaborate in an attack on New York City. An approaching French fleet was supposed to cooperate by blockading the city. On August 14, though, Washington learned that the French fleet under Admiral de Grasse was instead heading for the Chesapeake, where it would bottle up a British force under Lord Cornwallis at Yorktown.

At any other time Washington might have hesitated to change his plans on the spur of the moment, but "Matters having now come to a crisis" he promptly decided to throw the Franco-American army in motion toward Virginia. If this was the only way to force the decision that could end the war before the economy collapsed, so be it. A timely infusion of funds from Morris helped to provide the means. After a long march characterized by impressive logistic efficiency, a troubling and all-too-brief visit to the now run-down estate at Mount Vernon, and a surprisingly short siege, Cornwallis surrendered on October 19.[13]

Wine flowed freely at headquarters as American and French officers celebrated the victory, and Washington was the dubious recipient of a hearty series of kisses from the French admiral that left him blushing "like a coy damsel." He had no way of knowing, though, whether Yorktown was indeed the decisive war-ending victory that he had so avidly sought. The general repeatedly warned his army and Congress about the need to maintain vigilance, but to his chagrin nobody seemed to take him very seriously.[14]

The following months were anticlimactic, and as 1781 turned into 1782 and again into 1783, Washington's anxiety increased. Peace negotiations had begun in Paris, but as they continued, the American economy and government seemed to be falling apart at the seams. Back in 1778, the commander in chief had proclaimed the essential need for "Congress to be replete with the first characters in every State." But by 1783 those "first characters" were gone, leaving behind an assembly of mediocrities who could get nothing done. Congress's inability to raise funds, thanks to deep financial woes and the recalcitrance of the states, left officers' pay up to $5 million in arrears and their families pauperized. The delegates could not agree on means to address this, or on a pension establishment that would allow servicemen to get back on their feet after the war. "We have borne all that men can bear," the officers protested; "our property is expended—our property is expended—our private resources are at an end." By March they were on the verge of leading the army out of its camp at Newburgh, New York, and marching on Congress.[15]

Washington's speech to his officers at Newburgh on March 15, 1783, is one of the great moments in American history. He delivered it with trembling hands, and famously punctuated it by donning spectacles that hearkened back to the years that he had labored to feed and clothe his men and keep them in the field. His message was simple: now was not the time to sacrifice all that they had worked for when peace was in view. True, the army—the government—the economy—had held together by a thread. But they had held. The war had been brutal. Families, as the officers knew too well, had been impoverished. At places like Falmouth and Richmond, much property had been destroyed. But for the most part it had been a limited war. Though weak, the civil polity was alive and stable. With peace, there would be something to build on, a hope for prosperity—not, though, if the country collapsed internally just as it arrived at the threshold of achieving its dream. He asked his officers, then, to "express your utmost horror and detestation of the Man who wishes, under any specious pretences, to overturn the liberties of our Country, and who wickedly attempts to open the flood Gates of Civil discord, and deluge our rising Empire in Blood."[16]

Washington's success in dissuading his officers from rebellion at Newburgh, gaining the necessary time that helped the United States to pull through to the September 1783 Treaty of Paris, was a magnificent accomplishment. Before resigning, though, he left behind one more great public legacy. This was his circular to the state governors of June 8, 1783. In it he expressed the perhaps naïve hope that the nation's diverse civilian leaders would unite in a vision for the United States in which its people would grow "respectable and prosperous." The human and natural resources necessary for America's well-being already existed in abundance. So did the enlightened principles necessary for "the unbounded extension of Commerce." To establish conditions conducive for natural growth, though, political leaders needed to adhere to four principles: a government "under one Federal Head," a "Sacred regard to Public Justice," a military "Peace Establishment," and a spirit of national unity in which individuals would "make those mutual concessions which are requisite to the general prosperity."[17]

Economic considerations underpinned all of these principles. It was only in a unified government, Washington wrote, that "our Independence is acknowledged, that our power can be regarded, or our Credit supported among Foreign Nations." Public justice meant above all that the states rendered "compleat justice to all the Public Creditors." All debts domestic and foreign, he insisted, must be scrupulously honored—including those to the men of the army. The alternative was "a National Bankruptcy, with all its deplorable consequences." The military stood as "the Palladium of our security" under which free commerce could thrive. Finally, in advocating an undivided public spirit in which individuals would make sacrifices for the "interest of the Community," Washington enshrined the principle of limited taxation, necessary not just for the survival of the government but for the public welfare.[18]

Washington's understanding of the economic underpinnings of the war effort had informed his military leadership. As commander in chief he had set an example of probity and thrift, and by his intelligence, hard work, and ability to identify effective deputies he had ensured that the army ran efficiently. Washington's diligence in this regard probably saved the country many millions of dollars. And while he could not solve the country's economic problems, he did help to alleviate them. He did so in part by advising and consulting with Congress, and partly by working—if only symbolically—at critical moments such as Trenton to restore confidence and shore up public credit.

The community of commerce that Washington built between army and civilians simultaneously helped to unify American society and rebuff British efforts to undermine the war effort. Most important, Washington's sense that the true threat to American independence was not external military pressure but internal collapse led him to conduct military operations in a way that ensured that a functioning civil society would emerge from the war. Much work remained to be done if the plant of national prosperity was to grow. Nothing would have been possible, though, had Washington not helped to sow and lovingly nurture the seed.

CHAPTER SIX

# AN ESTATE GROWS,
# A NATION STUMBLES

MOUNT VERNON DELIVERED AN INSPIRING WELCOME TO
Washington as he returned there on Christmas Eve, 1783, a day after resigning
his commission at Annapolis. Enfolded by the warm embraces of Martha and
her grandchildren, he could finally sit back and—for a moment—put his feet
to the fire. Outside snowflakes began to fall, and soon the entire estate was
encased in white. From the cupola or the piazza, both built in 1774, he could
scan the frozen Potomac and imagine how it might look in the spring when
the fish began to jump, and when ships filled with goods once again sailed to
and from Alexandria. Riding about the estate, he could ease his weary mind
with thoughts of spring planting, and of the fertility locked in the frozen soil.
Soon, though, Washington's critical eye caught hold of the defects that had
distressed him during a brief layover on the road to Yorktown in 1781: peeling
paint, rotten wood, dilapidated outbuildings, broken tools, disordered gardens
and fields—all the wages of neglect.

He had expected something like this. Before leaving to take command
of the army in June 1775, Washington had attempted to set his personal
affairs in order. He prepared a will, outlining its tenets with Martha and
telling her proudly that his debt was "trifling." Managing the estate in his
absence would prove a thornier problem. Martha was a capable woman but
not prepared to administer a large estate, and the demands of wartime would
keep her almost as busy as her husband and often with him in camp. The

logical choice to keep the estate running in the master's absence was his cousin Lund Washington. Lund had served as George's business manager for a decade before the war began, but his authority had been limited because of the master's proclivity for micromanagement. From a position that bore little autonomy, Lund now found himself, practically speaking, expected to conduct day-to-day business on his own. Moderately capable but no genius, he would struggle to measure up to George's high standards. In truth, George was under no illusions that his expectations would be met.[1]

Having appointed Lund to take charge in his absence, and then gone off to manage the army, George struggled to let go. In August 1775 he wrote Lund about the mismanagement of a large gristmill that he had under construction on a tract in Fayette County, Pennsylvania, fretting that the machinery "& my whole money" would be "totally lost." He told his cousin to shut down the Mount Vernon gristmill, as with the ports closed "all Mill business will probably be at an end for a while." In the meantime Lund should keep wheat "in the Straw, or otherwise for greater Security." On the other hand, George ordered that "Spinning should go forward with all possible dispatch, as we shall have nothing else to depend upon if these disputes continue another year." He demanded regular reports from his manager all through the war, and commented on each in detail. George also dispensed advice to family members on how to handle wartime conditions—for example, telling his brother Samuel not to proceed with his planned purchase of a gristmill in the uncertain wartime market.[2]

The general's initial instructions to his farm manager masked the reality that neither he nor anyone else had any idea what to expect from the approaching struggle. As the hoped-for short war turned into a protracted conflict, and particularly as paper currency began to depreciate, Washington recognized the need for stern decisions to preserve his fortune. At first he resorted to stopgap measures. He raised rent prices on his property to keep up with inflation, while public-spiritedly telling Lund that he should accept payments in paper money "with chearfulness," although in careful relation to its true value.[3]

As paper became increasingly unsafe, however, George turned to an old standby: land. Writing on May 26, 1778, to his stepson John Parke Custis—

who had reached his majority and was expected to handle the Custis properties despite his poor business sense—Washington urged him not to unload any territory. Any money that Custis received for it, the general warned, would "melt like Snow before a hot Sun" unless immediately reinvested. It was better to purchase land than to sell it. "Lands are permanent—rising fast in value—and will be very dear when our Independancy is established, and the Importance of America better known," he wrote—at which time "the heaviness of our taxes, the rage for getting quit of, and realizing paper money must cease, and Men & measures will resume a more reasonable tone." Until then, Washington intended to acquire land "at (almost) any price," and urged his stepson to do the same.[4]

Prudence was essential all the same. For example, Washington admonished Custis against "the evil tendency of paying compound Interest." "I presume you are not unacquainted," he continued, "with the fact of £12,000 at compound Interest amounting to upwards of £48,000 in twenty four years—Reason therefore must convince you that unless you avert the evil by a deposit of the like Sum in the loan Office—and there hold it sacred to the purpose of accumulating Interest in the proportion you pay, that you will have abundant cause to repent it." Even patriotic considerations should not override pragmatism—for though Washington denounced speculation, he had no quibble with taking elementary precautions. As inflation grew he conceded that Custis should discreetly conduct transactions in hard currency rather than paper, even though in the aggregate such transactions contributed to depreciation.[5]

Though the general was at that moment exhorting Congress and the states to do everything possible to buttress the currency, he told Custis privately that he doubted "whether it is in the power of an Individual to check this evil when Congress, & the several Assemblys are found unequal to the task." Washington told his stepson "Not to require, or contract for the actual payment in Specie, but to keep this as much out of sight as possible in common cases." Meanwhile, he instructed Lund to barter slaves—"whom I every day long more & more to get clear of"—for land; and told him to sell everything around the estate "that is not essentially necessary," placing the proceeds, along with those from the sale of flour, in the Continental Loan Office.[6]

Lund helped facilitate two land purchases during the war, one of 480 acres in 1779 and another of 118 acres in 1783, bringing the whole Mount Vernon tract to just over 7,100 acres. He spent most of his time, though, trying to keep the estate and household functioning. At the beginning of the war George had informed Lund that since he would be receiving no salary as commander in chief, "it becomes necessary therefore for me to be saving at home," and so urged him to practice "the greatest Oeconomy and frugality" in household management. The only nonessential expense he countenanced was charity—to the tune of up to £50 yearly. "Let the Hospitality of the House, with respect to the Poor, be kept up," he wrote. "Let no one go hungry away."[7]

With the general directing from a distance, Lund oversaw the completion of some minor home improvements, and the gristmill (after a brief hiatus at George's command), fisheries, and other industries continued to operate. But the wear and tear was substantial. A stable burned down and was not replaced, numerous slaves absconded during the British raids on Virginia of 1781, and shingles and planking decayed on the house and outbuildings. The mansion house's interior grew dingy, certainly not presentable for distinguished guests. Further afield, Lund was powerless to prevent depredations to the general's lands in western Pennsylvania and the Ohio region. In 1775 alone, Native Americans inflicted £1,568 worth of damage to improvements and crops on Washington's Ohio lands.

All of this was repairable. But the damage to Washington's personal fortune done by currency depreciation was profound and continued after 1783. During and after the war, the general's many debtors paid him off in depreciated paper money at, he complained, "Six pence to the pound." Some instances were especially egregious. Gilbert Simpson, the feckless manager of Washington's Fayette County property, deliberately waited until September 1784 to pay off the money he owed for debts and damages, knowing that he was giving the general worthless currency. Simpson lived at a safe distance from Washington's legendary temper; but proximity failed to restrain others willing to defraud the Father of His Country. In personal business, as Washington came to realize, his fame counted for little against fraudsters who may have targeted him out of awareness that his public profile prevented him from taking private retribution.[8]

Profits from the gristmill and other estate industries did no more than allow the estate to tread water. Lund's limitations as a man of business further complicated matters. At best, he was an indifferent account-keeper; his messy record-keeping forced the general to spend many days at his desk in 1784 trying to sort out his tangled finances. And though George's prescience in sinking his fortune in land rather than paper, and in placing money in the Continental Loan Office, sheltered him somewhat from the nation's tumultuous finances, Lund neglected to collect rents from tenant lands either in paper or "in kind" (in the form of produce and other goods).

After he returned to Mount Vernon, Washington aggressively sought to collect back rents and to secure new tenants for his lands in Pennsylvania and Ohio, but without much success. Throughout the 1780s he would remain asset-rich but chronically cash-poor, forcing him to such expedients as selling off Bank of England stock inherited from the Custis estate in order to meet immediate demands. The same depreciation weakened the public securities he held and the "interest of the money I lent to the Public in the day of its distress."[9]

Bringing order to this mess at a time when the nation's financial future remained uncertain was challenging, and the strain on Washington's accounts increased exponentially almost the moment he walked through his door. Martha and her grandchildren had to be fed and clothed, along with Lund, and soon George Augustine Washington and his fiancée Fanny Bassett (Martha's niece) took up residence at the estate. George did not hesitate to fulfill family obligations. Every day, though, flocks of visitors—some mere curiosity-seekers—tried his patience and lightened his pocketbook. Hospitality demanded that they should be fed and quartered, along with their horses and servants. Worse, they guzzled his beer and emptied his wine cellar. Washington also had to provide financial support to his mother, who had embarrassed him in 1781 by attempting to petition the Virginia legislature for emergency aid—implying that her son was neglecting her. Well-intentioned members of Congress suggested providing him with a federal allowance to defray his postwar expenses, but he refused to accept public money.

The challenges were great, but they were Washington's own even though they eventually forced him to borrow, thus reviving the specter of debt that he once thought banished. On March 4, 1789—just a month before he took the oath of office as president of the United States—Washington had "to do what I never expected to be reduced to the necessity of doing—that is, to borrow money upon interest." He borrowed £500 in Virginia currency from merchant Richard Conway, repaying £649 8s 4d including interest just over a year later.[10]

Adopting a spirit of retrenchment would have been forgivable under the circumstances. Yet, though tired and overburdened, Washington continued thinking big—even at the cost of drawing heavily on his capital. He began with his mansion house, setting measures in place to complete the improvements he had begun before the war. Inspired by the Anglo-Palladian architectural styles of his day, which hearkened back to classical Greek and Roman concepts, Washington nearly doubled the house's size over the years that followed. When he finished there were new, matching wings to the north and south facades, and a large new porch along the full length (ninety-four feet) of the east front. He also installed a new Venetian window on the north wing and put the finishing touches to the cupola surmounted by a weathervane. Topping it all off was a new main entrance.

Washington demanded that all of this work be carried out not just precisely but according to the most modern techniques—specifying, for example, that stucco work be done according to methods outlined in Benjamin Higgins's *Experiments and Observations on Cements* (1780), which Washington had purchased for his library. Outside, he remodeled the landscape in a way that complemented the new mansion house and adhered to the naturalistic ideas fashionable in Europe. New features included a bowling green framed by serpentine paths, garden walls that blended into the landscape, and planting—a lot of planting. Washington carefully supervised trees, shrubs, and flower gardens to fit the new design, conceived to make a man-made landscape look natural; built a greenhouse; and relocated outbuildings. This work alone, including refurbishing and redesigning the mansion house and the surrounding landscape, took four years.

Amid his ambitious plans for Mount Vernon, Washington prepared to return his estate and its various ventures to profitability. He understood that a reversion to prerevolutionary business as usual was unrealistic. After eight years of war, the world was a far different place. Conditions of finance and trade had changed. So had agriculture. As spring coaxed the land into wakefulness and farming began anew, he rode over his plantations and found them, as he had feared, in states of stagnation. They functioned, to be sure—crops were sown, grew, and were harvested—but an air of inefficiency hovered above them, making Washington regret having stayed "so long in the ruinous mode of farming, which we are in." Overseers planted crops without careful regard to soil conditions or the dictates of the market, and utilized decades-old plows and other implements for sowing and harvesting. Change was essential.[11]

Facing similar circumstances, many of Washington's friends in the Virginia gentry invested in "get rich quick" schemes to return them to the heady, spendthrift days they had enjoyed before the war. "Light Horse" Harry Lee, who like Washington had inherited a large fortune from a good marriage, was a case in point. Lee never saw an investment opportunity he didn't like. Rather than build his wealth methodically, he speculated and gambled at every turn. He entered into some of these ventures, such as the Potomac and Dismal Swamp companies, side by side with Washington. But while Lee focused his energy and much of his fortune on these gambles, eventually bringing his estate to ruin, Washington regarded high-risk investments as sidelights, and never essential to his fortune. The basis for his financial health was, and would always be, land.

The concept of a bold farmer-entrepreneur seems foreign to the twenty-first century, but it describes Washington's business character. Land was not just a place to invest wealth away from unsteady markets but a stage for experiment and innovation. As in so many other areas of his life, Washington restructured his farming activities with a methodical mind and tremendous energy.

First, the old had to go. By 1785, Lund was ready to leave and start his own farming operation. Washington decided to seek his replacement from the global epicenter of agricultural innovation: Great Britain. Now in the first throes of an Industrial Revolution, Great Britain had already emerged from an Agricultural Revolution. The latter, as Washington probably sensed, had to a great degree fed the former by releasing a vast agricultural labor force that could now be fed cheaply while devoting its strength to manufacturing. A good British farm manager would bring Mount Vernon firmly in line with the best agricultural practices and potentially enable Washington to experiment with new modes of manufacturing.

Thinking big entailed uniting personal profits with national interests. In addition to improving his own farming, Washington hoped to promote a universal overhaul of American agriculture. As he wrote to Charles Carter on January 20, 1788, the system of farming "now in general practice (if it can be called a system) is beyond description ruinous to our lands." Small farmers and even well-educated planters heavily tilled their land with tobacco or other crops and, when it was exhausted, simply abandoned it to clear more. Ignoring elementary methods of soil conservation, they let topsoil wash away and the land erode. Farmers also neglected new technologies, preferring to stick with age-old methods.[12]

What the country needed, Washington believed, was "a *course* of experiments by intelligent and observant farmers; who will combine things and circumstances together—Theoretical opinions should have no share in the determination." Such "ought to be the pursuit of every farmer. On this ground every experiment is a treasure—and the authors of them valuable members of Society." If the curious visitors who constantly peeped over his shoulders taught Washington anything, it was that he had the power to improve popular practices by setting a positive example.[13]

Washington's English friends proved invaluable assistants to his efforts. None of them was closer to him than George William Fairfax, husband of Washington's youthful love Sally Fairfax. George William and Sally had moved from Virginia to England in 1773 after inheriting an estate there, but despite years of war they had stayed in touch with their old friends. On June 30, 1785, Washington wrote Fairfax that "as I believe no Country has carried the improvement of Land & the benefits of Agriculture to greater perfection than England, I have asked myself frequently of late, whether a thorough bred *practical* English Farmer, from a part of England where Husbandry seems to be best understood & is most advantageously practiced, could not be obtain'd?" He continued: "When I speak of a knowing Farmer, I mean one who understands the best course of Crops; how to plough—to sow—to mow—to hedge—to Ditch & above all, Midas like, one who can convert every thing he touches into manure, as the first transmutation towards Gold."[14]

The bonds of friendship held true. Fairfax industriously sounded out his connections around Bath in Gloucestershire and discovered that the leading gentleman farmers of the region were eager to assist Washington, whom they held in high esteem. On the recommendation of one of them, Fairfax dispatched to Virginia a talented farm manager named James Bloxham, who "will answer any Persons purpose, as a hard working Servant, capable of Ploughing, Sowing, Hedging, Ditching, Shearing, Mulling and Brewing for a family, particularly attentive to Stock, and not inferior to any Man . . . in Thatching of Houses and Barns." Bloxham transplanted his family to Virginia and, after initially turning up his nose at the Americans' backward farming practices, worked alongside Washington for four productive years. More important, through the Bath Agricultural Society, Fairfax put Washington in touch with Arthur Young, perhaps the leading farmer-philosopher in Great Britain.[15]

Born in London in 1741 to a respectable middle-class family of small means, Young was to become a symbol of scientific self-improvement and self-sufficiency. He was a complex man, described by one perplexed biographer as "whimsical, pathetic, enthusiastic, despairing, a born optimist." As a youth he received a middling education and was attracted to writing, publishing a number of pamphlets and attempting to start a periodical magazine that drew the attention of Samuel Johnson (who advised him to abandon the venture as "you will lose a great deal of money by it").[16]

As Johnson predicted, none of this sufficed to earn Young a living. His father invested £400 in an attempt to make young Arthur a mercantile accountant, but the money was wasted. After his father died, debt-ridden, in 1759, Arthur went to live with his mother on an 80-acre farm—a paltry endeavor compared to the estate that Washington commanded at the same time on the other side of the Atlantic. After an aimless youth spent dabbling in the humanities, Young faced the future with fear and trembling. "I found myself in a situation as truly helpless and forlorn as could well be imagined," he later remembered, "without profession, business, or pursuit. . . . I had no more idea of farming than of physic or divinity."[17]

With no choice but to make the best of it, Young applied himself to learn. His farm prospered with moderate success, and within a few years he was able to transition to a more extensive estate in Hertfordshire. There he conducted "a great number of experiments" in agriculture. Young's genius expressed itself not through farming, however, but in his skill as a communicator. Despite a deep depression that plagued him all his life, Young loved both to learn from others and to share with the world every bit of the knowledge he acquired.[18]

Young also delighted in travel. In 1767, he published "Farmer's Letters," based on his experiments and information gathered from neighbors. Now debt-free and with some disposable income, he toured the north, south, and east of England, gleaning knowledge from the most innovative agriculturalists he could find and publishing what he learned in a series of pamphlets and books. These works, he admitted in his otherwise savagely self-deprecating memoirs, "excited the agricultural spirit which has since rendered Britain so famous." They did so because they made known "to the world the exertions of many capital cultivators and in various parts of the kingdom" along with those of "common farmers . . . whose operation wanted only to be known to be admired."[19]

By the time Washington got to know Young, the Englishman had become a celebrity throughout Europe. He conducted and published accounts of tours of agriculture and industry in Ireland and France, and continued to gather information from England and Scotland. In 1784, he revisited the dream that Samuel Johnson had helped scuttle—publishing a periodical. This time, the periodical was no literary magazine but a work with a purpose that appealed to the entrepreneurial spirit so prevalent in the Great Britain of his day. Titled the *Annals of Agriculture,* it was hailed by contemporaries as "a work of great merit as a repository of enthusiastic and valuable information on the agriculture of this and other kingdoms." In recognition of his achievements, he would be appointed in 1793 as secretary to the British Board of Agriculture. His fame cemented and his fortune established, Young never farmed again; but he was consulted on all the most important matters of his day in both agriculture and manufacturing.[20]

Young was more than an agriculturalist, or a classifier of information. He was a nationalist whose views on the foundations for national prosperity found willing ears on both sides of the Atlantic. In reflecting on the "good of the State," Young wrote in 1770 that the object was not simply to make people well-clothed, fed, and housed. Rather, there was an "aggregate interest . . .

George Washington as a young surveyor. *Library of Congress*

Virginia governor Robert Dinwiddie (1693–1770) helped to establish George Washington's career, first by establishing his career as a surveyor and then by appointing him to military office. *National Portrait Gallery*

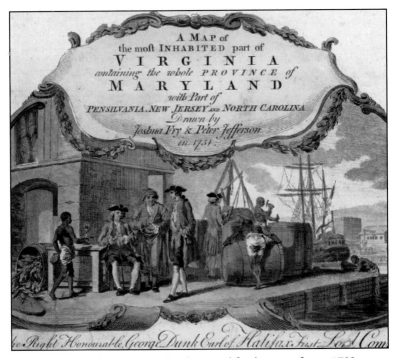

Tobacco hogsheads being inspected and prepared for shipment, from a 1755 map. Tobacco was both the source of Washington's wealth and an obstacle to his future prosperity. *From the 1755 Fry-Jefferson map at the Library of Congress; detail in the lower right.*

Martha Dandridge Custis, a wealthy widow, brought more than just money to her marriage with George Washington in 1759. Over the course of their long, loving relationship she proved a steady partner and an able estate manager during her husband's long absences from home. *From an engraving by J. Cheney & J. G. Kellogg in Sparkes, Jered, "The Life of George Washington," Boston: Tappen & Dennet 1843, "The Cooper Collections of American History"*

Robert Morris (1734–1806), who as American Superintendent of Finance after 1781 helped to stave off financial collapse in the waning years of the Revolutionary War. *Painting by Robert Edge Pine*

Arthur Young (1741–1820), English agricultural innovator and George Washington's collaborator. *National Portrait Gallery*

Alexander Hamilton, who as US Secretary of the Treasury from 1789–1795 both implemented and helped to define Washington's economic policies. *Bureau of Engraving and Printing*

| 1788 | | | | | | |
|---|---|---|---|---|---|---|
| | | Amount brought over | 269 | 568 | 15 | 6¼ |
| July | 10 | By 6 Packs of Playing Cards | | 0 | 8 | 0 |
| | | By the Freight of two Harrows from Philadelphia | | 0 | 4 | 0 |
| | 10 | By Joseph Davenport p.d him on acc.t of wages | 258 | 8 | 6 | 9 |
| | 24 | By Thomas Mahony p.d him on acc.t of wages | 275 | 6 | 0 | 0 |
| Aug.t | 1 | By John Sullivan p.d him for digging & walling a well | | 3 | 0 | 9 |
| | | By Mess.rs Peterson & Taylor p.d them on acc.t of Scantling &c | 266 | 52 | 13 | 9½ |
| | | By Major Geo. A. Washington p.d to John O'Conner on his acc.t for surveying land | 261 | 4 | 3 | 0 |
| | 2 | By Colo. Chas. Carter sent to him by Mr. John Bassett for the cost of repairing the Tomb of Mrs. Dandridge & Francis | | 1 | 10 | 0 |
| | | By William Gray p.d him on acc.t of weaving | 263 | 1 | 16 | 0 |
| | 3 | By Doct.r Jam.s Craik p.d him | | 30 | 0 | 0 |
| | 5 | By the Potomack Comp.y for expences in attending a meeting of the directors in Alexandria the 4 & 5 inst. | 232 | 0 | 15 | 0 |
| | 9 | By Mrs. Washington | | 5 | 0 | 0 |
| | 15 | By Thomas Green p.d him on acc.t of wages | 252 | 4 | 0 | 0 |
| | 22 | By Mess.rs Geo: Law. Washington p.d to Mess.rs Peter & Ingraham on their acc.t | 250 | 27 | 0 | 0 |
| | | By ditto p.d R. Wightman for making their Cloathes | 250 | 5 | 27 |
| | | By ditto p.d for trimmings for making Cloathes for them | 250 | 0 | 4 | 5 |
| | | By a Cutting knife 2/ fig blue 7/. 2 Grofs Corks 5/ | | 0 | 7 | 0 |
| | 28 | By Mr. Porter p.d him for a box of Lemons | | 2 | 2 | 0 |
| | | By Charity | | 0 | 2 | 6 |
| Sept.r | 1 | By William Gray p.d him for weaving | 263 | 2 | 0 | 0 |
| | 6 | By Mess.rs Peter & Ingraham sent them to pay the freight of Goods from Philadelphia | | 1 | 7 | 7 |
| | 7 | By Hezekiah Fairfax p.d him on acc.t | 260 | 15 | 10 | 0 |
| | | By 2 gall.s of Honey b.t of Negt. | | 0 | 10 | 0 |
| | 13 | By Mess.rs Peterson & Taylor p.d to Hans Orman by their order the Balance due to him, amounting to | 266 | 30 | 11 | 11½ |
| | 21 | By J.P. Franklin (Geo. Smallwoods agent) p.d him by John Fairfax for 14 Lambs b.t of him this fall | | 1 | 4 | 0 |
| | 22 | By John Fairfax p.d him on acc.t of wages | 260 | 10 | 14 | 10½ |
| | | Amount carried forward to Folio | 275 | 797 | 7 | 9 |

Meticulous account-keeping, which George Washington practiced throughout his life as in this record from 1788, was an essential element of his prosperity. *Library of Congress*

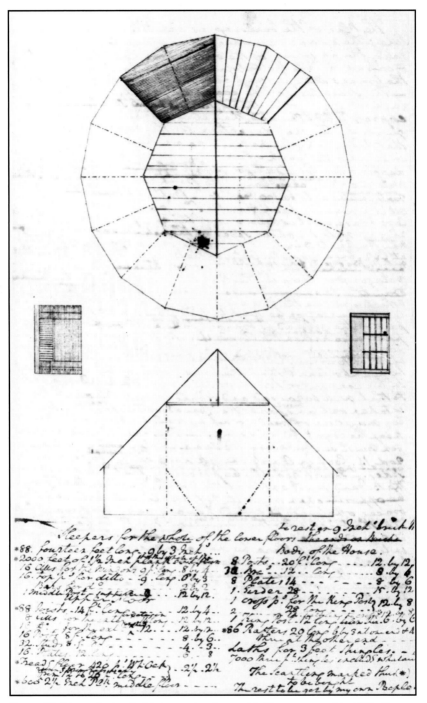

George Washington's plan for his innovative sixteen-sided barn, prepared in 1792. *Reproduced in* The Papers of George Washington Presidential Series, *11:279; original in Library of Congress*

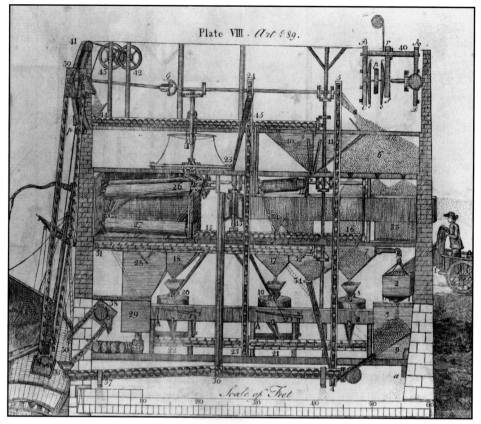

Milling designs patented by the American inventor Oliver Evans formed the basis for Washington's Mount Vernon gristmill and other highly productive eighteenth-century operations. *From* The Young Mill-wright and Miller's Guide, *by Oliver Evans, 1795*

Washington inspects the Mount Vernon harvest, an 1851 painting by Junius Brutus Stearns. Slavery operated through coercion, removing any positive incentive for industry. Washington eventually came to view it as both morally reprehensible and economically counterproductive. *Virginia Museum of Fine Arts*

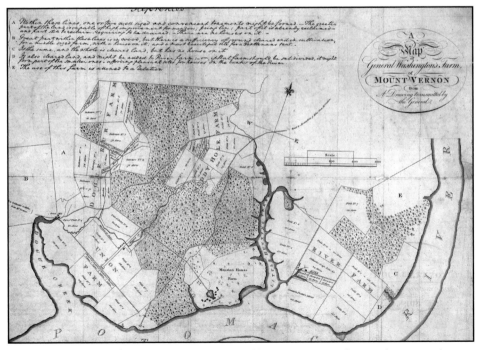

George Washington's meticulously drawn 1793 map of his Mount Vernon farms with notes on their contents. *Reproduced in* The Papers of George Washington Retirement Series, *4:460–61; original in Henry E. Huntington Library, San Marino, California*

which consists of two kinds, first, the support of internal government and national works; and secondly, the power of the nation relative to her neighbours." These aggregate interests, he explained, were "but other names for the public revenue; it is that which sets in motion the whole machine of government. Thus, the general wealth of the kingdom must not only be sufficient for the private ease and affluence of individuals, but also for the levying [of] all those taxes which form the public revenue." For effective taxation, of course, there must be an ample and ever-growing national wealth. Young was clear on where that wealth came from: "Both public and private wealth can arise only from three sources, agriculture, manufactures, and commerce. . . . Agriculture much exceeds both the others; it is even the foundation of their principal branches."[21]

This was not a clarion call for an eternal nation of farmers but a statement of facts. Washington thought the same way. As he wrote to another farmer in 1788: "Every improvement in husbandry should be gratefully received and peculiarly fostered in this Country, not only as promoting the interest and lessening the labor of the farmer, but as advancing our respectability in a national point of view; for, in the present state of America, our welfare and prosperity depend upon the cultivation of our lands and turning the produce of them to the best advantage."[22]

Young's understanding of the foundations of national prosperity had led him to predict, as early as 1759, the probable causes of a break with the colonies: "The thing that breeds a jealousy between Britain and her colonies is not power, but manufactures, in which they interfere with one another and as the people increase, their manufactures and the necessity for them, must increase likewise; which will be the first cause of a rupture between this nation and her colonies, if ever such a thing should happen." In this he and Washington could agree. They also shared a vision for America's future. In 1768, Young looked forward to how "those regions, which now are boundless forests, wastes, and wilds, will one day be peopled with flourishing cities, and adorned with beautiful cultivation; and possessing in all their brilliancy the arts, the sciences, and all the consequences of luxury and empire." By 1786, even if the concept of "empire" in America had changed, the vision of prosperity remained.[23]

Inevitably for two men who thought so much alike, Washington and Young hit it off. Opening their correspondence on January 7, 1786, Young praised Washington's example in retiring "from the head of a victorious army to the amusements of agriculture" and promised as a "brother farmer" to send him "men, cattle, tools, seeds, or any thing else that may add to your rural amusement." Probably more to Washington's taste, Young enclosed the first four volumes of his *Annals of Agriculture,* and promised to send more as they were published. Not only did Washington accept this gift—he had thirty-one volumes of the *Annals* along with several of Young's other works in his library at the time of his death—he perused them carefully, extracting passages of particular interest that he collected in separate notebooks.[24]

Washington responded to Young's missive enthusiastically. "The system of Agriculture . . . which is in use in this part of the United States, is as unproductive to the practitioners as it is ruinous to the landholders," he wrote. "Yet it is pertinaciously adhered to. To forsake it; to pursue a course of husbandry which is altogether different & new to the gazing multitude, ever averse to novelty in matters of this sort, & much attached to their old customs, requires resolution; and without a good practical guide, may be dangerous. . . . Your annals shall be this guide." If his fellow American farmers largely fit the conservative historical stereotype of that profession, Washington broke the mold. He also gladly took up Young's offer to provide material assistance, requesting "Two of the simplest, & best constructed Plows" along with large quantities of cabbage, turnip, herb, grass, and clover seeds—for all of which his English agent would pay handsomely.[25]

The *Annals* introduced Washington to a wealth of new and ever-expanding knowledge. Through them he developed a new "system" of agriculture that he adapted regularly as methods evolved. Because his fame placed him constantly in the public eye, he also sought to set an example for his countrymen in entrepreneurial farming, encouraging the economic transformation of the young United States. Soil fertility was central to the "new husbandry" the *Annals* advocated. To conserve it, crops were rotated for longer. To enrich it, the draft animals that powered plowing, sowing, harvesting, and grinding would provide manure. Above all, using this natural fertilizer effectively—and allowing for the vagaries of climate, soil quality, and other factors—required vigorous experimentation.[26]

The entrepreneurial mindset entailed a focus on both self-improvement and public duty. In the absence of a National Board of Agriculture—for which he would advocate, unsuccessfully, during his presidency—Washington believed that he and other wealthy farmers must take on the risks associated with experimentation in order to instruct their resource-poor countrymen. "Experiments must be made," he wrote to another inventive American farmer in 1788, "and the practice (of such of them as are useful) must be introduced by Gentlemen who have leisure and abilities to devise and wherewithal to hazard something. The common farmer will not depart from the *old* road 'till the *new* one is made so plain and easy that he is sure it cannot be mistaken, and that it will lead him directly to his object. It is right perhaps it should be so—for new ways are thorny and require time for amelioration."[27]

The search for quality fertilizer merged with mechanical innovations. In August 1785, a friend in the Philadelphia agricultural society, knowing of Washington's professed interest in raising river mud for use as manure, informed him of inventor Arthur Donaldson's "Hippopotamus." This machine, a precursor to the clamshell dredge, had been employed successfully in Philadelphia for clearing the docks and removing wartime underwater log obstructions. Washington was fascinated. "The bed of the Potomac before my door," he wrote, "contains an inexhaustable fund of manure; and, if I could adopt an easy, simple, and expeditious method of raising, and taking it to the Land, that it may be converted to useful purposes." He secured a model of the machine from Donaldson and, in early November 1785, ventured out on the Potomac in a small borrowed scow (and no doubt wearing an old suit) to raise sloppy lumps of river mud. He carried the stuff back to test it on his farms, promising Donaldson that if the fertilizer was productive he would purchase the Hippopotamus if it wasn't too expensive. Dissatisfied with the experiment, or with the price, Washington never bought the machine—but he kept looking.[28]

The *Annals* inspired a transformation in the farms at Mount Vernon and Washington's other landholdings. After study he adopted a seven-year crop-rotation plan for wheat, corn, and potatoes. These and a constantly changing array of experimental crops with seeds imported from other parts of the United States and overseas were laid out according to precise plans depending on soil quality, labor efficiency, and other considerations. Young's plow was used as a basis for new designs that were implemented, improved, and, when necessary, discarded. The livestock on which the estate's livelihood depended also were managed differently, with better penning, superior fodder, and careful breeding to improve the animals' bloodlines.

Washington constructed new barns, service buildings, and yards on his various farms so that they were located for maximum efficiency. These included a "dung repository" that he finished in 1787 according to an original design that was the first of its kind in the United States. He also had a new ice house built according to an innovative plan developed, oddly enough, by Philadelphia financier Robert Morris. Yet more ambitiously, Washington constructed three barn complexes, two of them according to English models inspired by the *Annals* and a third following a design entirely his own.[29]

All of this extensive and expensive work required careful record-keeping and account management. Fortunately, these were among Washington's strengths. He demanded extremely detailed reports of every activity at Mount Vernon and his other estates. He took complete inventories of animals and equipment at each farm, and prepared a thorough census of the slaves—which he would update periodically. He also took "notes and observations" on his farming activities. Toward the end of 1785 he initiated the practice of preparing weekly "farm reports," and beginning in April 1786 he turned the job over to his succession of farm managers (though still maintaining close personal oversight of the reports' preparation). Every Saturday he would assemble his farm overseers and demand from them detailed accounts of how many slaves and other workers toiled on each and every field, their respective duties, and, most importantly, the outcome of their labors. He also tabulated the births, illnesses, and deaths of his livestock, a practice he would continue weekly until the end of his life.[30]

MOUNT VERNON'S MOST WELCOME VISITOR wasn't human. His name was Royal Gift, a magnificent Spanish jackass sent by King Charles III of Spain. Washington accepted him ecstatically. For many years he had been interested in breeding mules. A cross between donkeys and horses, mules were stronger, more durable, and longer-lived than most horses and made excellent draft animals. The best donkey stock was in Spain, but the king preempted Washington's attempt to purchase them by sending two as an act of royal benevolence. One was lost at sea; the other was Royal Gift. Studying the animal and finding him well up to expectations, Washington set him to work making baby mules and donkeys. At times the jack, as befitted his race, was stubborn in the performance of his duties, prompting Washington to remark that "he follows what one may suppose to be the example of his late royal Master, who cannot, tho' past his grand climacterick, perform seldomer, or with more Majestic solemnity, than he does. However, I am not without hope, that when he becomes a little better acquainted with republican enjoyments, he will amend his manners, and fall into a better & more expeditious mode of doing business." In time, Royal Gift took to his duties with gusto sufficient for Washington to sell his services and send him on a breeding trip to South Carolina. Mount Vernon, meanwhile, became the residence of dozens of Royal Gift's hard-working descendants.[31]

Other animals being bred for profit at Mount Vernon in the postwar period included sheep, hogs, cattle, and even deer. In 1785, Washington purchased a magnificent Arabian horse named Magnolio for £500. His hope was to profit by selling the stallion's services at stud, but the earnings disappointed him. Enter the gullible Harry Lee. In 1788, after a dinner at Mount Vernon where the wine flowed freely, Washington and Lee struck up a deal exchanging the horse for 5,000 acres of Kentucky land that Lee had recently received as a bequest. Lee sent Magnolio to a relative in South Carolina, who promptly lost him at cards. Washington kept the lands, which were valued at £1,000 in the 1790s, in his possession and passed them on to his heirs.

He also passed on a boisterous kennel full of dogs of all varieties. In 1785 Lafayette sent him several French hounds by way of John Quincy Adams for breeding, even though "English dogs are so much in fashion Here that the King who likes to Ride fast Has no French Hounds, which, says He, are Very Slow." Washington also possessed a greyhound appropriately named Cornwallis. Although an Irish friend supplied him with information about Irish wolfhounds and mastiffs, however, Washington decided they were too expensive. Instead he focused on domestic hounds, receiving in September 1787 a lovable shipment that included "Droner, a black & white dog with spots"; "Doxy—black or rather dark brown & white"; "Dutchess—mostly White & large"; "Dublin—a young dog brown & white"; and "Rover . . . with a black Spott on his Rump."[32]

When not tending his mules or frolicking with his hounds, Washington kept busy with an abundance of small gadgets and innovations. These included a "Potatoe Machine" for separating the tubers that an inventive planter had built on a nearby estate. Always, Washington had some purpose in mind—usually saving labor, cutting costs, and boosting productivity. In the fields he tested a variety of implements including a barrel plow attached to a harrow that deposited seeds automatically as it moved. People and animals worked more efficiently with easy access to water, so he had pumps installed at Mount Vernon and his Alexandria property even though most southern farms and estates still relied on wells. He also closely followed developments in water desalinization technologies, although none of them proved economical for his estate.[33]

On evening walks, Washington could not help noticing the dozens of candles burning in slave huts and mansion house windows. His accounts recorded how thousands of them were expended every year. Washington wondered: Were imported New England spermaceti candles or generic tallow candles more economical? After a chilly and frustrating morning foxhunt in December 1785—his French hounds had lagged behind, too lazy to take up the chase—he lit one of each type of candle side by side. Nine hours later, the far more expensive spermaceti had fizzled while the tallow still burned merrily. There would be no more candle imports from Boston.

Wheat production remained vital, so Washington inspected the process from top to bottom in a search for efficiencies. He zeroed in on threshing. Up to this time, wheat threshing in America was almost medieval in character. Some farmers had their servants and slaves flail the wheat by hand. Others laid the wheat in circles and let horses walk over it to separate the kernels. What these techniques shared in common was dependency on the weather and inefficiency. They left the grain jumbled and filthy, requiring gathering, further separation, and cleaning by hand.

In the autumn of 1787, studying Young's *Annals,* Washington learned about a threshing machine developed by the English inventor William Winlaw. He plied Young for more information, but although Young described reports of the machine as "too vague to be satisfactory," Washington (then president) went to Manhattan's Murray Hill in January 1790 to visit Friedrich, the Baron von Poellnitz, who had one of them. Washington spent the day watching the machine clack away, studying all its components, and calculating labor efficiency. He concluded that "Upon the whole it appears to be an easier, more expeditious and much cleaner way of getting out Grain than by the usual mode of threshing; and vastly to be preferred to treading, which is hurtful to horses, filthy to the Wheat." It was imperfect and still somewhat labor-intensive, but Washington used it as a basis for improvement.[34]

Though immersed in his duties as president and harassed by a "constant succession of company," Washington forged ahead with plans to revolutionize the threshing process at Mount Vernon. He began gathering building materials in the summer of 1791, and in October 1792 he drafted detailed architectural plans. He spent the next three years—as often as he could escape his presidential duties—supervising the building's construction. The resultant sixteen-sided barn, completed in 1795 and the first of its kind in the United States, was a remarkably innovative structure. Outside it was neatly symmetrical—Washington had worried lest it betray "a very aukward look." But it was inside that the important business took place. There, protected from the weather, horses trotted in a placid, never-ending circle, breaking out the wheat as grain kernels fell through the slotted floor boards into storage bins located in the building's base. The process was clean, efficient, and carried on whatever the weather.[35]

The final point of grain production was the gristmill. Washington had renovated this facility in the 1770s, and it had operated efficiently. But twenty years was a long time in the life of a mill, and by 1791 it badly needed repair. In keeping with his ambitious scheme for the Mount Vernon estate, Washington did not just patch up the facility but entirely redesigned it. His inspiration for the new design was, to his pleasure and preference, domestic. In Delaware, young inventor Oliver Evans—a self-made man without financial backing who had previously generated improvements in textile machinery—had been working since 1783 to develop a fully automated gristmill. He had an experimental model running in 1785 and secured state patents in 1787 to protect his further innovations. His ideas caught on slowly, however, and it was not until 1789 that local sales in Maryland and Delaware spurred their further development. In 1790, he secured US Patent No. 3 for his invention. Washington, by then president but with his ears constantly to the ground for technological improvements that could save labor and increase productivity, took notice.

Now recognized as the first fully automated continuous production process—a central feature of the Industrial Revolution—the automated mill was a radical innovation. Washington was among the first to adopt it. In the summer of 1791, he sent his millwright to view an Evans mill constructed on Occoquan Creek about ten miles from Mount Vernon. Impressed by what he learned, Washington purchased the rights to the design, and in the autumn of 1791 Evans's brothers oversaw its installation in the gristmill at Mount Vernon.

The mill's first operations must have amazed the president. Instead of the older, labor-intensive system that ground by a series of separate (and unsanitary) processes, Evans's mill operated in a fully integrated manner. Water powered everything: moving grain through the mill and grinding, drying, sifting, and storing it via a combined system of elevators, chutes, and other devices. As at the sixteen-sided barn, no significant human intervention was required, except for standard maintenance and repairs to the machinery. Washington later purchased a copy of Evans's *The Young Mill-Wright and Miller's Guide* (1795) and, until the end of his life, remained in contact with the brilliant but somewhat ornery inventor, seeking advice on millers and improvements. After some adjustments to the millrace to improve the water flow, the new mill operated productively well into the nineteenth century. Meanwhile—thanks in part to Washington's example—Evans's system revolutionized milling in the United States. With his innovations adopted everywhere, the total value of flour production in America increased twentyfold by the beginning of the new century, making it a leading national industry.

Americans took notice of Washington's improvements. Some visited Mount Vernon to observe and share ideas, or to trade experimental seeds, plows, and other items. The president also joined agricultural societies from Philadelphia to South Carolina and, through them, shared ideas on how to improve American farming. These societies, to which Washington contributed funds, ran prize-essay contests and raised money to import British farmers and build experimental farms. Writing to State Justice William Drayton after being elected an honorary member of the South Carolina Agricultural Society on March 25, 1786, Washington "wished that every State in the Union would establish a Society similar to this; & that these Societies would correspond with, & fully & regularly impart to each other, the result of the experiments actually made in husbandry, together with such other useful discoveries as have stood, or are likely to stand the test of investigation."[36]

Washington increasingly thought of himself as an American Arthur Young, spreading knowledge across the nation and serving as a beacon for improvement. His prestige made this possible. As his friend and comrade Benjamin Lincoln wrote to him on September 24, 1788: "The share your Excellency holds in the affections of the people, and the unlimited confidence they place in your integrety and judgment, gives you an elevated stand among them which no other man can or probably ever will command."[37]

With this mindset Washington provided financial support and counsel to educational institutions such as the Alexandria Academy. His intentions were only partly charitable. Over time he had come to believe that educated citizens were indispensable to an ordered civil society. He had also become convinced that the poor could be transformed into productive contributors to American material prosperity. As he wrote the trustees of the academy on December 17, 1785, in giving them a donation of £1,000 in state currency he sought to promote "that kind of education which would be most extensively useful to people of the lower class of citizens, viz.—reading, writing & arithmetic, so as to fit them for mechanical purposes."[38]

Students in multiple fields looked up to Washington as a patron, not just because of his prominence but because of his known interest in experimentation and the expansion of knowledge. One such was John Leigh, a medical student at the University of Edinburgh who dedicated to Washington his 1786 book, *An Experimental Inquiry into the Properties of Opium, and Its Effects on Living Subjects: With Observations on Its History, Preparations and Uses.* Washington gratefully accepted a copy of the book from Leigh and kept it in his library, remarking that "I should always wish to encourage every useful and beneficial performance as much as is in my power."[39]

The problem of slavery increasingly bedeviled Washington in both its economic and moral dimensions. Slave labor was integral to production on his primary properties just as it was to other large plantations in the South. He had long taken this for granted, relying on ostensibly free slave labor as one of many cost-cutting devices. By the early years of the Revolution, however, Washington started speaking of his hope to "get clear" of slaveholding. Seeing blacks fight for American freedom during the war may have influenced this change of heart. Economic considerations certainly played a role. Put simply, he began thinking of slaves as a drag on his profits as they intermarried and their numbers increased.[40]

By the 1780s, Washington had a substantial surplus labor force. Other planters dealt with the problem by selling off the slaves with scant regard for their status as human beings; and Washington initially did so, too. By 1786, however, he found it "against my own inclination . . . to hurt the feelings of those unhappy people by a separation of man and wife, or of families." Although he sold small numbers of slaves individually thereafter, for the most part he simply kept them on at increasing cost, although he nurtured hopes (never realized) of settling slave families on his western lands.[41]

Prone as he was to nationalize his personal challenges, Washington began to view slavery as an American problem. In the long term, he thought that its immorality and inherent inefficiency would divide the nation and drag down the South. "I never mean," he wrote on September 9, 1786, "(unless some particular circumstances should compel me to it) to possess another slave by purchase; it being among my first wishes to see some plan adopted, by the legislature by which slavery in this Country may be abolished by slow, sure, & imperceptable degrees." How that plan would be implemented or even what it would look like, however, he had as yet no idea.[42]

The challenge of building national prosperity boiled down in Washington's mind to the conflict between freedom and dependency. As a form of dependency, slavery constituted a burden. So did the nation's continuing economic reliance on Great Britain. Though commerce and trade were theoretically now open to the entire world, in practice the United States—like other postcolonial nations throughout history—subsisted almost entirely on trade with its former overlord. Freeing America from the remnants of the colonial system, he believed, would follow in part from the improvement of domestic manufacture and industry.

Washington was not the only American who thought that way, but as the most prominent figure of his era, his actions affected public opinion. Promoters of various manufacturing schemes often approached him in the knowledge that his support could help determine their future success. One of them was Englishman Edmund Clegg, who told Washington in April 1784 of his plan to promote textile manufacture, including silk weaving, in America using new machinery. Limited by time and discriminatingly cautious by nature, Washington left some applicants—including Clegg—hanging. Others initially benefited from his favor, only to see their schemes bog down in hapless national and state legislatures.

French textile manufacturer Gilles de Lavallée, who had constructed looms in New England on the strength of recommendations from Thomas Jefferson and Benjamin Franklin, approached Washington in late 1786 with a plan to expand cotton manufacture to Virginia. Washington interrupted his Christmas Day festivities to forward the idea to the governor of Virginia, Edmund Randolph. "To promote industry and œconomy, and to encourage manufactures, is certainly consistent with that sound policy which ought to actuate every State," he told the governor. "There are times too, which call loudly for the exercise of these virtues; and the present, in my humble opinion, may be accounted a fit one for the adoption of them in this Commonwealth." The governor and delegates declined to take up the proposal, however, and so Lavallée returned to Europe, griping that "no establishment of European manufacture can succeed" in America.[43]

In choosing which schemes to support and which to ignore, Washington preferred those that simultaneously fostered domestic manufacture and advanced his own interests. One such was an idea by English noblewoman Selena Hastings, Countess of Huntingdon, to settle thousands of British Methodists on the American frontier. At first glance the countess's scheme looked solely religious in nature. The Methodists were supposed not just to improve the land upon which they settled but to convert Native Americans to Christianity and better their living conditions by introducing them to British methods of farming and manufacture. Her friend Sir James Jay—brother of John Jay and the wily inventor of foolproof invisible ink for use in espionage—saw in her proposal an opportunity to circumvent British regulations prohibiting the export of their industrial secrets.

In 1750 and 1774, Parliament had decreed severe restrictions not only on the export of new innovations in silk, wool, and cotton manufacturing but also on the emigration of artisans skilled in these new technologies. These kept the innovations of men such as Richard Arkwright in cotton manufacturing largely out of the American market and reinforced—as they were intended to do—America's subservient economic position. As Jay told Washington, the countess's proposal to export skilled British artisans *en masse* for a missionary endeavor offered a heaven-sent opportunity to obtain the workers and technologies America craved. Jay informed Washington that he was "much induced to promote it . . . for the opportunity it would afford of getting over a number of Mechanics & Manufacturers, and establishing several useful Manufactures in the Country. . . . Should the Plan be adopted and vigorously pursued, it would soon prove very beneficial to our Country. It would soon lessen the importation of several Articles from Europe. In a few years, it would not only put a stop to the importation of such articles, but enable us to export them."[44]

Washington responded excitedly. "I highly approve" of the measure, he told Jay, and offered his "best endeavours" in support, including writing to the current president of Congress, Richard Henry Lee, on their behalf. The idea "has humanity & charity for its object," he explained to Lee, "and may, as I conceive, be made subservient to valuable political purposes." The biggest problem as he saw it was that the states generally did not have appropriate frontier land at their disposal to cede for the project. Washington therefore suggested that the Confederation government should designate land for the scheme—preferably in the Ohio region, where he incidentally held land and still nurtured hopes of commerce and improvement.[45]

Offering a "dernier resort," Washington slyly sent the countess a newspaper advertisement seeking settlers for Washington's own lands on the Ohio and Kanawha Rivers. They were both "convenient" to the Native Americans, he suggested, and would soon be opened up by his projects to extend navigation and commerce along the Potomac and James Rivers—"by means of which the produce of the settlers on these Lands of mine, will come easily & cheaply to market." Unfortunately, expecting support from the Confederation Congress was like leaning on a broken reed. The delegates quashed the project on the basis that it would be irresponsible to import large numbers of "religious people" who "were remarkable in the late war for an unanimous and bitter enmity to the American cause, and as such might form a dangerous settlement." Rebuffed, the countess abandoned her project.[46]

If Congress and the states could not always think or act big, Washington— a prominent but still private citizen—could at least concentrate on the underpinnings of future prosperity. So it was with domestic manufacture. When it came to standard consumer products, he made a point of buying American. "We have already been too long subject to British prejudices," he wrote Lafayette on January 29, 1789. "I use no porter or cheese in my family, but such as is made in America—both those articles may now be purchased of an excellent quality."[47]

Beer was typical of many consumables. Before the war, Washington had mostly imported the beverage from Great Britain. Now, stung by his prewar disappointments—and perhaps haunted by memories of those sadly plundered beer casks he had opened back in the summer of 1762— Washington favored domestic brewers. His favorite, Robert Hare, Jr., of Philadelphia, supplied Washington during the Confederation years and the presidency. After participating in Philadelphia's grand Fourth of July procession of 1788, Washington teasingly asked merchant Clement Biddle to procure him "a groce of Mr Hairs best bottled Porter if the price of it is not much enhanced by the copius droughts you took of it at the late Procession." Later, after an accidental fire destroyed Hare's brewery, Washington hedged his bets against an ensuing beer shortage by hoarding a cache for his personal use, telling his secretary "to lay in a pretty good Stock of his, or some other Porter." He also exploited the postwar boom in domestic beer production by growing a crop of barley specifically for sale to brewers. In 1786, he purchased from Baltimore brewer Thomas Peters a special machine designed for cleaning barley for production.[48]

In his quest to promote American prosperity, Washington fervently advocated peace. Free trade and commerce, stifled under the colonial system and shut down almost entirely during the war, looked to flourish in an atmosphere of international amity. The United States would become for the world both a land of opportunity and a refuge. Pondering war in a letter to his friend and biographer David Humphreys on July 25, 1785, Washington wrote: "My first wish is, to see this plague to Mankind banished from the Earth; & the Sons & daughters of this World employed in more pleasing & innocent amusements than in preparing implements, & exercising them for the destruction of the human race. Rather than quarrel about territory, let the poor, the needy, & oppressed of the Earth; and those who want Land, resort to the fertile plains of our Western Country, to the second Land of promise, & there dwell in peace, fulfilling the first & great Commandment."[49]

Free trade and commerce could not only enrich but also bind the world together. "As the member of an infant-empire, as a Philanthropist by character, and . . . as a Citizen of the great republic of humanity at large," Washington wrote to Lafayette on August 15, 1786, "I cannot avoid reflecting with pleasure on the probable influence that commerce may here after have on human manners & society in general. On these occasions I consider how mankind may be connected like one great family in fraternal ties—I endulge a fond, perhaps an enthusiastic idea . . . that the period is not very remote when the benefits of a liberal & free commerce will, pretty generally, succeed to the devastations & horrors of war."[50]

Like many of his countrymen, in the war's immediate aftermath Washington looked to develop a flourishing commerce with France. It was, economically speaking, an undiscovered country despite its years of alliance with the United States. By contrast, years of familiarity with the British had generated wellsprings of resentment if not outright contempt. Writing to Lafayette in 1786, Washington rebuked the "supine stupidity" of British policies that restricted trade with the United States, while France by contrast seemed "by the invitations it is giving to stretch forth the friendly hand to invite them into its Ports." Great Britain, he complained, "arrogantly expects we will sell our produce whereever we can find a Market & bring the money to purchase goods from her; I know that she vainly hopes to retain what share she pleases in our trade, in consequence of our prejudices in favor of her fashions & manufactures; but these are illusions which will vanish & disappoint her, as the dreams of conquest have already done."[51]

From what he had seen—which was actually quite little—Washington thought that French manufactured goods were superior to their British equivalents. He daydreamed of a system of in-kind exchange—for the United States remained money-poor and was now deeply in debt—of American "timber, fish, oil, wheat, Tobacco, rice, Indigo &c." for French finished goods. Down the road, as the American economy recovered and shed its debt burden, trade with the nations of Europe headed by France would become more equitable. "However unimportant America may be considered at present, & however Britain may affect to despise her trade," Washington predicted, "there will assuredly come a day when this country will have some weight in the scale of Empires."[52]

An opportunity to set this dream on the road to reality occurred in January 1788 with the arrival of Eléanor-François-Elie, comte de Moustier, the French minister to the United States. Moustier contacted Washington and James Madison on the subject of developing trade between the two countries, asking for advice on the products upon which this commerce might subsist. Washington characteristically studied the proposal at length and responded in precise detail. Reiterating that the trade should at first be conducted in kind since the United States was cash-poor and did not want to build debt through a credit system, he proposed likely "articles of importation, directly from France," such as cloth, glass, assorted fripperies, wine, brandy, fruit, and printed goods. Sugar, coffee, molasses, and rum could be imported from French colonies. In return, the United States could provide mostly raw produce and unfinished items such as tobacco, grain, flour, fish, furs, lumber, coal, and livestock; but American shipbuilders might also get to work on constructing vessels for the French Navy. Changing American consumer habits—as for example in their increasing preference for French brandy and wine over rum—appeared to augur France's displacement of Great Britain as America's primary trading partner.[53]

Shipping was of course indispensable for commerce. Washington therefore avidly promoted the development of an American shipbuilding industry to end the colonial-era reliance on British carriers. The expansion of this industry would promote the establishment of a favorable balance of trade. "The Maritime Genius of this Country is now steering our Vessels in every ocean; to the East Indias, the North-west Coasts of America and the extremities of the Globe," he rhapsodized in his letter to Moustier. "I have the best evidence that the scale of commerce, so long against us, is beginning to turn in our favour, and that (as a new thing in our new world) the amount of exports from one State, last year, exceeded that of the imports, more than 230,000 Pounds."[54]

Security was essential if this process was to continue. Unfortunately, even as North America settled into calm, distant war drums echoed over the Atlantic. These led Washington to fear that instead of a peaceful world in which "all restrictions of trade would vanish . . . we must go in the old way disputing—& now & then fighting, until the Globe itself is dissolved." With that in view—and always hoping against global dissolution—it behooved the nation even in times of peace to take steps to protect its commerce in case of war.[55]

On May 1, 1783, Washington had composed his "Sentiments on a Peace Establishment," which he sent to Hamilton in his capacity as chair of a Congressional Committee on the subject. In it, he argued for the creation of a small standing army and a navy. His primary object was the protection of internal and external commerce rather than repelling foreign invasion, which he rightly considered unlikely. For that reason he prioritized "preparations for building and equipping a Navy, without which, in case of War we could [not] protect our Commerce."[56]

Likewise, Washington argued for small fresh-water flotillas and frontier garrisons not simply to overawe Native Americans or fend off incursions from British Canada but to protect and foster "National Intercourse and Traffic" with the Native Americans and "to protect the Peltry and Fur Trade." Military posts, though useful, would in the long run be less valuable to security than the westward migration of European settlers "who, under proper Regulations and establishments of Civil Government, would make a hardy and industrious race of Settlers on that Frontier; and who, by forming a barrier against the Indians, would give great security to the Infant settlement."[57]

For Washington, then, the peacetime military served chiefly as a guarantor and even facilitator of commercial expansion. Unfortunately, though he proposed an army of only three thousand men alongside a small fleet, Congress ignored him. The army was dissolved at the war's end, and the national "flotilla" amounted to a mere collection of paper boats. The results during the Confederation period were as he could have predicted. The frontier remained unstable—the British, in violation of the peace terms, continued to occupy posts on American territory and encouraged Native American depredations—and the United States was helpless to resist armed enemies on the high seas.

Among these were the "barbarians" of the "piratical states" of North Africa, who raided American merchantmen and enslaved their crews with impunity. The raiders even preyed on European vessels when they could, despite the efforts of European navies; but the Americans could do nothing at all except pay them off with humiliating and expensive ransoms. How was it possible, Washington asked Lafayette on August 15, 1786, "in such an enlightened, in such a liberal age" for such things to take place? "Would to Heaven we had a navy able to reform those enimies to mankind, or crush them into nonexistence." But a navy did not yet exist—and even as president, Washington would have to pay off the pirates.[58]

Weightier considerations were at stake regarding American commerce with Great Britain, France, and the nations of northern Europe, as well as with the West Indies and Asia. Washington probably read Adam Smith's wildly popular *Wealth of Nations* (1776) and advocated free but not entirely unregulated trade. He believed that both its continuing freedom and its profitability—to merchants as well as to the nation at large—depended on the existence of a regulating power, or mechanism. For that, Americans needed a peaceful world as well as a stable national government. "From Trade our Citizens *will not* be restrained," he wrote to Jefferson on March 29, 1784, "and therefore it behoves us to place it in the most convenient channels, under proper regulation." To

James Warren on October 7, 1785, he elaborated that "this, any more than other matters of national concern cannot be done by thirteen heads, differently constructed; The necessity therefore of a controuling power is obvious, and why it should be with-held is beyond comprehension."[59]

The Confederation government fell short in its efforts to both protect and regulate commerce. In the spring of 1785, some delegates proposed to alter the Articles of Confederation to give Congress "the sole and exclusive right . . . of regulating the trade of the States, as well with foreign Nations, as with each other, and of laying such imposts and duties upon imports and exports as may be necessary for the purpose." Their idea was to allow the states to present a united front in potential tariff wars with other countries, particularly Great Britain. Southern delegates, though, worried that giving Congress these powers would benefit New Englanders at their expense.[60]

As debates continued that summer, Washington's former secretary James McHenry wrote to him on the assumption that as a Virginian he would side with the southerners. He must have been taken aback at the general's angry reply. "I can foresee no evil greater, than disunion," Washington wrote; "than those unreasonable jealousies . . . which are continually poisoning our minds, and filling them with imaginary evils, to the prevention of real ones. . . . I do not know that we can enter a War of Imposts with G. Britain, or any other foreign Power, but we are certain that this War has been waged against us by the former, *professedly,* upon a belief that we never could unite in opposition to it. . . . Our Trade in all points of view is as essential to G.B., as hers is to us—and she will exchange it upon reciprocal & liberal terms, if an advantage is not to be obtained." Washington also argued in favor of breaking British dominance of the carrying trade by reducing imports, and by uniting the states in the cause of American navigation through the development of a mercantile fleet. His opinions were disregarded, though, and the regulatory proposal foundered.[61]

---

Disappointments such as these did not immediately shatter Washington's confidence in the potential of developing American commerce even under a weak system of government. His pulse rose especially when he looked to the west and cherished dreams dating from his youth. In the last days of peace before Lexington and Concord, Washington had scrambled to amass large landholdings along the Ohio and Kanawha Rivers. During the war these tracts had remained wild if not badly managed or plundered. Their potential still shone brightly, however, and he yearned to develop it.

Others felt the same. Jefferson, Madison, and Harry Lee all were involved to some extent in pushing western schemes, and backed Potomac navigation as the best means toward their realization. Ever the dreamer, Jefferson imagined the development of a bucolic western wonderland secure from infection by eastern decadence. Lee enticed Madison into joining with him in some speculative ventures designed to reap quick profit by developing trading settlements along the Potomac.

Washington's ideas were broader and more tough-minded. Before pursuing any large venture, he liked to inspect it in person and from all angles. To that end he took yet another western journey in the late summer and autumn of 1784. On the way he stopped at the town of Bath (now Berkeley Springs) to observe, to his "very great satisfaction," a mechanical self-propelled boat invented by the "ingenious" James Rumsey. Actually two boats connected by a paddle wheel, the contraption used the current's rush through the wheel to operate poles that pushed it upstream. Agog with visions that the boat could be "turned to the greatest possible utility in inland Navigation," Washington provided Rumsey with a certificate of approval.[62]

Hopeful thoughts about Rumsey's contraption buoyed Washington as he pushed on to tour his sadly run-down "Washington's Bottom" tract, with its dilapidated gristmill, along the Youghiogheny River near what is now Perryopolis, Pennsylvania. Continuing, he explored more landholdings at Miller's Run southwest of Pittsburgh before turning back to follow the old Braddock Road to Virginia. On the last day of his 680-mile journey home, Washington ate breakfast by candlelight, mounted his horse, and rode through driving rain to reach Mount Vernon just before nightfall.

Retiring to his study, Washington pulled out the diary he had carefully kept during the journey and filled several pages with his final observations. The ruin of his Pennsylvania lands he bitterly lamented. Overall, though, he felt "well pleased" at the journey, for it had renewed his faith in the west's potential and the prospects for developing its navigation. Tracing in detail the routes and distances for waterborne travel (preferably via fleets of magnificent Rumsey boats) and portages, Washington imagined traders carrying furs, agricultural produce, and eastern manufactures to and from the frontier, enriching legions of investors from Virginia and Maryland. The United States itself would profit. "The more the Country is explored," he wrote in a letter to Richard Henry Lee, "the more it will rise in estimation—consequently greater will the revenue be, to the Union." The government could reserve "for special Sale, all Mines, Minerals & Salt Springs in the general grants of land, from the United States"—a controlled process that would also dissuade roving prospectors from antagonizing the Native Americans.[63]

Penetrating the interior would create a new community of commerce such as Washington had worked to build during the war, but this time on a national scale, pulling east and west together by applying "the cement of interest to bind all parts of it together, by one indissolvable band." Just as the ties of interest had separated Americans from British in wartime, so would working "to fix the Trade of the Western Country to our Markets" entice westerners away from forging "commercial connections" with "foreigners" such as the British and Spanish. Developing western, specifically Potomac, navigation would promote commerce, which in turn would build national unity. Congress's refusal to approve a military force to protect such commerce remained a problem, but Washington was hopeful that the ties of interest would trump conflict.[64]

Such was the vision; and in advancing it Washington set the tone for the whole country. His national argument for western navigation was not, as Joel Achenbach has argued, a mere front that "absolved him of any charge of self-interest." Washington actually made no real distinction between the two. If his personal interest served to promote national prosperity, so did the good of the nation also work to Washington's benefit. Ideally, he believed that self-interest did not divide but united communities.[65]

That others felt the same way became abundantly clear after Washington became president of the "Patowmack Company" in May 1785 and investors contributed almost £38,000 in the venture on top of his contribution of £2,400. Investors likewise imitated his interest in the James River Company formed in 1785, and in the Dismal Swamp Company that predated the war and continued to push plans for draining and developing that land. Washington eagerly endorsed a project to settle the former swampland with a coterie of skilled German immigrants. And while the Mississippi Company had gone defunct in 1770, his continued interest in the prospect of inland commerce helped inspire a popular drive to push the Spaniards to grant free navigation of that waterway—a drive that would come to fruition during Washington's presidency despite his reservations about insisting too vehemently on it during the Confederation. Whatever his private motivations may or may not have been, many Americans clearly viewed Washington's interests as synonymous with their own, and with those of the nation.

THE END OF THE REVOLUTIONARY WAR reduced Washington to the status of a private gentleman with no political standing. As with his investments, however, when he spoke on the economy, people listened even if they did not always agree or obey. His continuing concerns over the currency were a case in point. With the terms of the Articles of Confederation still in force, both states and the national government remained empowered to issue unbacked paper bills of credit while large amounts of hard currency of all types remained in circulation. The fiscal chaos that resulted troubled many including Thomas Jefferson, who in May 1785 drew up a proposal for the regular coinage of gold, silver, and copper currency. Washington called the measure "indispensably necessary" and predicted that "Without a Coinage . . . a Man must travel with a pair of money scales in his pocket, or run the risque of receiving gold at one fourth more by Count, than weight." Prodded in part by Washington's lobbying, Congress contemplated establishing a mint for this purpose. Although nothing came of it immediately, the efforts of Jefferson, Washington, and many others ensured that the currency problem dwelt foremost in the minds of those who assembled in 1787 for the Constitutional Convention.[66]

The nation's fiscal difficulties helped lead men like Washington to advocate political change. Without a smoothly running—and safe—civil society that could operate without threat of disruption from without or within, the economy would never flourish. Only a stable authority that could gather revenue and protect and promote national prosperity would suffice. Unfortunately, the Confederation government was not up to the task.

Writing to Benjamin Harrison on January 18, 1784, Washington decried the "disinclination of the individual States to yield competent powers to Congress for the Foederal Government" and warned that this "will, if there is not a change in the system, be our downfall as a Nation." He succeeded for a time in suppressing his doubts. "This is an abounding Country," he wrote Irishman Edward Newenham on June 10, 1784, "& it is as fine as it is extensive. With a little political wisdom it may become equally populous & happy. . . . We have indeed so plain a road before us, that it must be worse than ignorance if we miss it."[67]

Later that same year, though, on December 5, Washington complained to Henry Knox that "our foederal Government is a name without substance: No State is longer bound by its edicts, than it suits *present* purposes, without looking to the consequences. How then can we fail in a little time, becoming the sport of European politics, & the victims of our own folly?" The absence of a system of revenue gathering both mirrored and fed the lack of a stable national currency. This in turn contributed to the erosion of public credit. On February 15, 1786, Congress adopted the report of a committee on the General Revenue, warning that "whilst Congress are denied the means of satisfying those engagements which they have constitutionally entered into for the common benefit of the Union, they hold it their duty to warn their Constituents that the most fatal evils will inevitably flow from a breach of public faith, pledged by solemn contract, and a violation of those principles of justice, which are the only solid basis of the honor and prosperity of Nations." On its own, though, a warning changed nothing.[68]

Shays' Rebellion of 1786 in Massachusetts catalyzed change. Entangled in unpaid war debts, Congress desperately levied requisitions for specie on the states. This in turn forced states to impose painful taxation—payable in scarce specie—on their citizens. Massachusetts, conflating its obligations to the national government with its own war debts, hit its taxpayers particularly hard, and in the west they revolted. The rebellion was crushed easily. Still, it foretold an era of unrest that unsettled men like Washington. To Knox he wrote on December 26: "I feel . . . infinitely more than I can express to you, for the disorders which have arisen in these states. Good God! who besides a tory could have foreseen, or a Briton predicted them! . . . notwithstanding the boasted virtue of America, we are far gone in every thing ignoble & bad." To Harry Lee he wrote: "I am mortified beyond expression whenever I view the clouds which have spread over the brightest morn that ever dawned upon any Country." And to Madison he foretold "anarchy" on the near horizon. In concordance with other signs of fiscal and political instability, Shays' Rebellion wrecked the visions of peace and prosperity that had so recently beguiled Washington, who suspected that Great Britain would foment and exploit America's problems to reduce it to social and economic prostration. From a cautious desire to amend the Constitution, he grew almost desperate for a convention that would replace it entirely.[69]

When Madison urged Washington to lead the Virginia delegation to the Constitutional Convention in Philadelphia, however, he demurred. His reasons for doing so were no less sincere than those that had made him balk at accepting the office of commander in chief, or those that would make him hesitate to become president of the United States. Reluctance to reenter public life arose both from his desire to focus on his own personal interests, such as the Patowmack Company, and from a fear that failure would stain his public reputation. Madison was persistent, though, and Governor Edmund Randolph added his voice by urging Washington to "rescue America from the impending Ruin." National interests mirrored his own, after all; Washington accepted.[70]

In Philadelphia, Washington presided over the convention but remained in the background, more an arbiter than a participant. Outside Independence Hall, though, he occupied his time visiting educational institutions, the botanical gardens, and innovative farms and estates. On July 22, 1787, he rode to the Spring Mill estate along the Schuylkill River in Montgomery County, where he inspected French émigré Pierre Legaux's experimental vineyard and bee hives. Washington and his entourage—which included several convention delegates—"found great delight" in the operations and offered their "highest approbation" for the hives. Before departing, the general—who also reputedly took a little time out to go fishing in the Schuylkill—encouraged Legaux "to bring the Culture of the Vine to perfection in this Country." His discoveries elsewhere included Benjamin Franklin's "Mangle" for pressing clothes and table cloths—a device that, as Washington noted in his diary, was "well calculated for Table cloths & such Articles as have not pleats & irregular foldings and would be very useful in all large families." The public followed his movements closely. Consciously or not, he was making the symbolic case for learning, innovation, and domestic manufacture.[71]

Washington played a more active if less public role in the debate for ratification in Virginia. Preferring not to campaign openly for ratification, he worked behind the scenes, writing letters to the dramatis personae of Virginia's ratifying convention as well as those of other states. His opinions also found voice through intermediaries. In Virginia the most prominent opponents to ratification were George Mason, Richard Henry Lee, Edmund Randolph, and Patrick Henry. That their views were diametrically opposed to Washington's concepts of the relative measures of liberty and prosperity became apparent during the debates. On June 5, 1788, Henry thundered: "You are not to inquire how your trade may be increased, nor how you are to become a great and powerful people, but how your liberties can be secured; for liberty ought to be the direct end of your government." Harry Lee, who took it upon himself to challenge the famed orator, argued to the contrary that prosperity, guaranteed by a government that ensured fiscal stability and public order, was the bedrock of liberty.[72]

In the end, of course, the arguments in favor of Constitutional government won out. Washington did not consider the new political order to be perfect. The road ahead was rife with challenge. But it was also ripe with opportunity. With a government finally empowered to impose taxes, to establish a national currency, to ensure the public "harmony and accommodation . . . most essentially requisite to our public prosperity," to foster and protect national and international commerce, and, most importantly, to establish a strategy and a system for a truly national economy, the future held hope. To "promoting & rendering permanent the national prosperity" he would henceforth devote himself. "This," he declared in looking forward to his duties as president, "should be my great—my only aim." The road from intention to execution, he would soon learn, was bumpy and full of blind curves.[73]

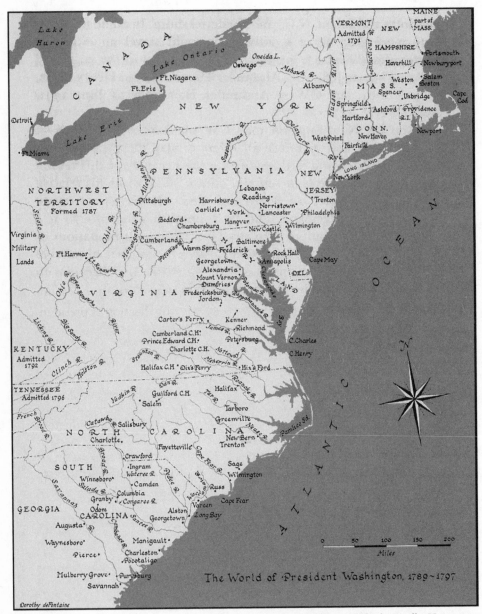

The World of President Washington, 1789~1797

Dorothy deFontaine

Donald Jackson and Dorothy Twohig, eds., *The Diaries of George Washington* (Charlottesville: University Press of Virginia, 1976–1979), 6:97.

CHAPTER SEVEN

# BUILDING A NATIONAL ECONOMY: WASHINGTON'S FIRST TERM

IF WASHINGTON EVER HAD A SLEEPLESS NIGHT IT WAS THAT of April 15, 1789. On the previous day Charles Thompson, secretary of Congress, had arrived at Mount Vernon to inform him of his election as president of the United States. The news was not unexpected. Anticipating the heavy expenses that would attend assumption of high public office—for which he of course refused to accept a salary—Washington had been struggling for months to get his personal finances in order. It was a frustrating process, for though his assets were substantial he remained cash-poor thanks to continuing expenditures, weak crops, and an unstable currency that dissuaded him from selling land to raise funds. In January he had borrowed £500 in state currency at 6 percent interest—the first and last such transaction of his life. As he stepped into his carriage at ten o'clock on the morning of April 16, the president-elect's mind was "oppressed with more anxious and painful sensations than I have words to express" as he contemplated leaving his "peaceful abode for an Ocean of difficulties."[1]

Willfully banishing self-doubt—a mental discipline he had practiced until it became a habit—Washington pondered the nation's future. The crowds he encountered on his journey focused his priorities. In Baltimore, the city's leading citizens exhorted the new president to place the "public credit on the most solid foundation" and expressed hopes that "under the administration of a Washington the useful and ingenious arts of peace, the agriculture, commerce, and manufactures of the United States will be duly favored and improved." In Wilmington, the Delaware Society for Promoting Domestic Manufactures threw a party and addressed him along the same lines, prompting Washington to respond that "The promotion of domestic manufactures will, in my conception, be among the first consequences which may naturally be expected to flow from an energetic government. . . . I propose to demonstrate the sincerity of my opinion on this subject, by the uniformity of my practice, in giving a decided preference to the produce and fabrics of America." In Philadelphia, Trenton, and finally New York City, the tone was the same—pomp and celebration alongside a hard-headed commitment to business.[2]

Public praise improved Washington's mood, helping him to recover the optimism he had felt in the wake of ratification. With the Constitution in place, he believed that Americans' native talents would come to the fore in building an industrious "Land of freedom." The government's role was to establish the conditions conducive to prosperity. The people—rich and poor, native and immigrant—would create the wealth. "I really believe that there never was so much labour and economy to be found before in the country as at the present moment," he had written to Lafayette on June 18, 1788. "If they persist in the habits they are acquiring, the good effects will soon be distinguishable." The process was already under way. The people, Washington told Jefferson on August 31, 1788, "are emerging from the gulf of dissipation & debt into which they had precipitated themselves at the close of the war. Œconomy & industry are evidently gaining ground. Not only Agriculture, but even Manufactures are much more attended to than formerly."[3]

Always keen on symbolism, Washington had long pondered how he should appear at his inauguration. In January 1789, he read a newspaper ad by the Hartford Woolen Manufactory. The firm's owners, who had served under him as commissaries during the war, encouraged Americans to wear suits made from their fabrics, such as "Congress Brown," as an act of patriotism. As a "PASSION for encouraging American manufactures has at last, become fashionable in some parts of our country," one of their promoters declared, the president, vice president, and members of Congress "should all be clothed in complete suits of American manufactured cloth" on inauguration day.[4]

Washington caught the trend and ordered a suit of "American Broad Cloths" for himself and a riding habit for Martha. Unfortunately, despite subsidies and tax breaks from the state of Connecticut, the Woolen Manufactory was not very efficient. Although Washington appeared at the inauguration "dressed in deep brown, with metal buttons, with an eagle on them, white stockings, a bag, and sword" (according to most accounts; one observer said he wore a "suit of black velvet"), the ensemble apparently did not originate from Hartford. Washington would visit the manufactory on his trip to New England in October 1789 and concede that its products were "not of the first quality."[5]

The question of what he should say at the inauguration was more complex. Washington agonized over his speech for weeks, working alongside his secretary David Humphreys to prepare a seventy-three-page draft. It was probably just as well that he did not attempt to read it at the risk of trying his listeners' patience. The now-fragmentary document nevertheless revealed his thoughts about America's future as he prepared to take the helm. His mind dwelt primarily on one topic: the economy. Beginning with a history lesson, Washington summarized the struggle for independence by recounting the shortage of "Money, the nerve of War," the creation of a treasury "from nothing," and the "load of debt" it left behind. The war also exemplified the intersection of public enterprise and private morality. "The fluctuations of and speculations in our paper currency," he believed, had "occasioned vague ideas of property, generated licencious appetites & corrupted the morals of men." He would bring up the subject of a moral economy again, more sweepingly, in the final version of his address.[6]

The draft address moved on from the past to lay out his vision for the road ahead. The country's future ultimately was industrial, but the transformation would take generations. "We shall not soon become a manufacturing people," he believed. Although the population would boom (as he accurately predicted), creating an abundance of labor, men would prefer working farms over manufacturing so long as the continent's vast land resources lasted. With that in view he saw no value in a crash course of industrialization. Instead,

Americans should "continue to exchange our Staple commodities for the finer manufactures we may want, [rather] than to undertake to make them ourselves." Nevertheless, he thought that products such as "wool, flax, cotton, & hemp" and "leather, iron, fur and wood may be fabricated at home with great advantage . . . Especially by the introduction of machines for multiplying the effects of labour, in diminishing the number of hands employed upon it." Agriculture, then, must be the primary focus—but always with an eye toward the coming days when America would both serve as the world's breadbasket and stand proud as a manufacturing giant.[7]

Government's role in all this, as he had already written to Jefferson and others, was that of facilitator. By "regulating the coinage & currency of money upon equitable principles as well as by establishing just weights and measures upon an uniform plan," for example, the government could help "make men honest in their dealings with each other." Officials could also "as public or as private men" enlighten the multitudes by working "to improve the education and manners of a people; to accelerate the progress of arts & Sciences; to patronize works of genius; to confer rewards for inventions of utility; and to cherish institutions favourable to humanity." An enlightened electorate would simultaneously buttress the state and, by its industriousness, build the foundations for its prosperity. Most of these lofty goals, though, would remain unspoken on inauguration day.[8]

Washington took the oath of office on April 30 on the balcony of New York City's Federal Hall. He then retired to the Senate chamber to deliver his inaugural address. An attack of nerves made him mumble and fidget. Fortunately he had reduced his address to a fraction of its original length. The details he loved so well were gone, replaced by generalities. Of money he had little to say, except that he would refuse to accept a salary and asked only for reimbursement of his expenses (he did, however, endorse salaries for senators and congressmen).

But one primary theme remained from the discarded draft. This was morality, and its place in the success of the great American experiment. Nature itself ordained morality, in Washington's worldview, and it fueled the work ethic of enlightened people left free to pursue their interests. They would inevitably be industrious. In turn, their industry promoted private virtue even as it generated wealth. The process was self-sustaining; government need only clear the stage. Such was Washington's meaning when he declared hopefully that "the foundations of our national policy, will be laid in the pure and immutable principles of private morality" and "that there exists in the œconomy and course of nature, an indissoluble union between virtue and happiness." These were the principles that would inspire his conduct as president.[9]

Washington would need inspiration in plenty, for the challenges facing him were great. The Constitution set the framework for the new Federal Government, but many of its definitions were vague. Presidential powers, which Washington carefully underlined and bracketed in his printed copy of the document, remained indistinct. To a degree the new president would define them himself, just as he helped shape the government by setting precedents for its future operation.

As president, Washington knew that he had to set a constant public example. Everything he did would be scrutinized and emulated. His many charitable donations, for example, were regularly published in the newspapers. When he made a small contribution in January 1791 to a charity providing for Philadelphia's poor, he told his secretary Tobias Lear to let it be known that such publicity was "not agreeable to the President," but of course the newspapers ignored him as he knew they would. The example of charity was deliberate, but he avoided ostentation.[10]

Nothing worried Washington more than identifying the right people to staff his Cabinet (not yet called by that name). In the helter-skelter of creating the government, there had been no time to fix upon candidates in advance. For months he had to carry most of the administrative burden on his own back. The biggest burden was in the realm of finance where, lacking a designated secretary of the Treasury, he had to confront the nation's dangerous problems head on.

Congress, still debating whether it alone should set economic policy, or leave that to the executive branch, established a Treasury Department on May 21, 1789. This at least was a positive step, and the president followed it up by writing on June 8 to the three-man Board of Treasury demanding "a full, precise and distinct Idea of the various transactions arising under it," along with an outline of its powers under the new Constitution. The Board replied with multiple lengthy reports that Washington perused line by line.[11]

The Board's massive report of June 15 on domestic and foreign debt stunned Washington. The nation's total domestic debt, he learned, was $27,383,917.67. Its foreign debt, arising from war loans from France, Spain, and Holland, was $10,070,307. These totals were exclusive, however, of substantial interest. On domestic debt alone, the interest arrearage due to be paid to 1789 was $11,519,646. Trivial figures today, they amounted to a crushing burden for a new nation just emerging from years of war and weak government. And they were getting worse. Overall, national debt with interest due rose from $39 million in 1783 to $53 million in 1790, alongside another $25 million in debts owed by the states.

Spending long hours hunched over his desk, Washington compiled lengthy notes summing up the debt problem. It originated, he wrote, in the war and the inherent weakness of the Confederation system. And while the reformed Constitutional government was more efficient, its inherited fiscal difficulties might prove insuperable. "For this large balance of public paper," he observed, "there is no reason to presume that funds in the least adequate have been provided by the several States." As he tabulated it, in 1786 alone no state had provided a penny to service the national debt, and the total due from the states to the government was $7,003,725. "Hence it appears," the president continued, that "there never has been a disposition at any one period, in a majority of the States, to collect Taxes; notwithstanding the easy & advantageous terms on which such payments might have been made." The Continental Congress had attempted to tackle the debt back in 1783 by imposing an impost, but the measure never came into effect and the states had continued to service—or not—their domestic and foreign debt by their own methods.[12]

Taking due account of the president's observations but still uncertain how to proceed, the Board could only recommend that the states be required to pay their debts by installments in specie rather than paper money; it also proposed shell games such as transferring French debt to Holland. There, though, the board members also ran into the problem of what to do about invisible debts arising from secret aid that the French had supplied before their formal intervention in 1778. American and French government accountants even bickered over a "lost million" of secret debt, creating a controversy that would entertain lawyers well into the nineteenth century.

Average Americans knew little about the national debt. Many of them were just struggling to get by. In his first weeks as president, Washington was nearly smothered by applications for office and pensions accompanied by hard-luck stories of personal fortunes destroyed by wartime dislocation or worthless currency. Some came from war widows with destitute children. Washington's own foresight in sinking his wealth into stable assets like land had shielded his estate from disaster, but he knew many others who had not been so prudent or lucky. To them he was generous in his charity, drawing on his own limited resources to assist the needy. Restoring national confidence was both more difficult and more important. Just as he had during the war, though, Washington realized that he could play a potentially decisive role in creating a mood of optimism and trust in the national government that would help steady the currency and foster conditions conducive to growth.

Establishing the public credit was the president's number-one priority. The initial steps toward achieving this were obvious if not easy. The first thing was to dispense current obligations and place the government on a sound fiscal footing. One of Washington's first acts as president was to ask Congress for new excise taxes and tariffs to service interest payments. The Tariff Act of 1789 imposed duties—to be collected by a new customs service—on various imports, especially manufactured goods. This of course benefited domestic manufacture even as it buttressed public faith in the government's ability to fund the debt. The move also reassured foreign creditors already encouraged by news of the establishment of a stable national government under Washington's leadership. In an August 1789 memorandum concerning negotiations for a new loan from Holland, Washington observed how the efficient operation of the "New Government, has given great strength & stability to our Credit" and had "the most certain & solid effects" on Dutch "Gentlemen Bankers." His reputation abroad as a man of prudence and business also had an impact.[13]

However sterling Washington's reputation and however correct his goals, they alone could not suffice to put the nation on the right track. He needed the right people to execute his vision—everyone from Cabinet members to consuls and revenue collectors. He even had to appoint lighthouse keepers. For every position there could be dozens of names to vet. For secretary of the Treasury, the choice seemed obvious: financier Robert Morris, who had worked so heroically to stabilize the currency in the latter days of the Revolutionary War. Morris, though, declined the post, suggesting Alexander Hamilton in his place. Washington liked Hamilton, but knew that selecting him would court controversy. Though undoubtedly brilliant, Hamilton also was a lightning rod. Anyone standing by his side would likely get burned.

Born out of wedlock in the West Indies, probably in 1757, Hamilton was orphaned at an early age and made his living working for a mercantile firm trading between New England and the Caribbean. He came to North America to finish his education in 1772. During the war's first stages, he commanded a company of New York provincial artillery before becoming one of Washington's many rotating aides-de-camp in 1777. The general did not necessarily favor all of his aides and secretaries. Most of them subsequently faded into obscurity. Hamilton, though, stood out for his intelligence, efficiency, and charisma. He could also be fiercely—if not, as it turned out, consistently—loyal. During the Valley Forge winter crisis of 1777–1778, he served as Washington's hatchet man, leading the drive to isolate and defame detractors such as Thomas Conway and Horatio Gates, and helping to cement his master's place at the head of the army. Inevitably, Hamilton and Washington—both headstrong men—fell out. In February 1781, Hamilton resigned from the general's staff in a huff after the two had a heated exchange over minor punctilio. The two eventually made up, however (an unusual instance among Washington's frequently long-lasting feuds). At Yorktown, Hamilton was awarded a leading role in the victorious assault on British Redoubt No. 10.

Just before his tiff with Washington, Hamilton's name had come up in connection with the Minister of Finance post that the Continental Congress eventually awarded to Morris. Since then he had applied himself to the study of economics and finance. Washington was most impressed by Hamilton's authorship, with James Madison and John Jay, of the *Federalist Papers* in 1787–1788. Hamilton regularly sent his installments of the *Papers*—written under the pseudonym *Publius*—to Washington, who promised that they would hold "a most distinguished place in my library" and "merit the notice of Posterity; because in it are candidly discussed the principles of freedom & the topics of government, which will be always interesting to mankind so long as they shall be connected in Civil Society." This work helped to temper

Washington's concerns about Hamilton's prickly personality and proclivity for making enemies.[14]

On March 24, 1789, amidst the hurry of preparing to assume the presidency, Washington opened a letter from an anonymous correspondent warning him to "beware of the artful designs, and machinations of your late Aid de Camp; Alexander Hamilton; who, (like Judas Iscariott) would for the gratification of his boundless Ambition, betray his Lord, and Master." Though making no outward comment, he filed the letter carefully away among his papers. Many others at one time or another maligned Hamilton's character. The important thing for Washington, though, was that Hamilton both was intellectually talented and shared his sense of how to solve the debt problem, ensure fiscal stability, and foster prosperity. As president, he was not looking to turn the ship of state over to a new captain. He wanted a man who would stand at the helm by his side.[15]

No shrinking violet, Hamilton clearly wanted to be secretary of the Treasury. For his part, Washington could not afford to postpone addressing the nation's diverse economic challenges. He wasted no time in nominating Hamilton for the post on September 11, 1789, along with Nicholas Eveleigh of South Carolina as comptroller, Samuel Meredith of Pennsylvania as treasurer, and Oliver Wolcott, Jr., of Connecticut as auditor. Congress confirmed all four within the next couple of days, and the president immediately put them to work. That they had much to do became obvious with the number of employees they had to hire—three dozen, eventually, far more than any other government department.

Washington was not in the habit of allowing anyone who worked for him to operate independently. As a military and civilian leader he often micromanaged his subordinates, and at the very least he set specific goals and conducted thorough reviews. This principle operated independently of personal trust. Friends, family, and colleagues alike bore his watchful gaze. The more important their work, the more likely he was to look over their shoulders.

Hamilton, too, labored under steady oversight during Washington's first presidential term. There were no Cabinet meetings. The president did, however, consult with each of his deputies frequently, sometimes through formal written reports but more often in lengthy personal conferences. Some, like

Jefferson, kept extensive written records of these conversations. Others did not. In any event, even though there is no extensive written record of the president's consultations with Hamilton, there is no reason to believe that Washington—always a stickler at punctilio—treated his secretary of the Treasury any differently during his first term (the second term was different, as we shall see). Had he displayed any such favoritism, it would have caused immediate friction.

Busy as a mole for three months, in early 1790 Hamilton began churning out a series of extremely important reports to Congress on public debt, a national bank, a national mint, and manufactures. The reports were his own, but were inspired by the president's economic vision. The first, submitted to Congress on January 14, was the most important and iconoclastic. Its central idea was that the government should not exert itself to pay off all its domestic and foreign obligations entirely and immediately. Instead, it should finance its debt by regularly paying off the interest on loans but borrowing, at least in the short term, to repay principal. This conceded a more or less permanent or revolving debt, but also helped to establish the government's domestic and international credit by reassuring creditors that it would reliably discharge its obligations. Federal bonds would come to be regarded as secure investments. The proposal also engaged American investors to realize that their prosperity depended on the health of the government, and vice versa—creating one of those communities of interest of which Washington was so fond. To fund debt payments, Hamilton proposed import tariffs and duties on distilled spirits, among other taxes.

Even more controversially, Hamilton argued that the federal government should assume responsibility for all state debts. Virginia had discharged its own debts faithfully, while states such as South Carolina and Massachusetts had not. All, however, would have to bear an equal responsibility for paying them off through the new program. Washington and Hamilton both knew that this idea would be divisive. They could also have predicted the repercussions of the Treasury secretary's further proposal that all government securities should be fully redeemed at face value. No one was more aware than the president that many of the soldiers who originally owned these notes had sold them off for a pittance long before, believing with good reason that they would always be worthless. The speculators who bought them would now reap the reward. However, two vital principles would be established: that government notes held consistent value and that investors had a right to profit from the securities market.

At this critical moment, sickness and overwork threatened to end the president's life. Rushing back and forth between offices to put out bureaucratic fires, wading through masses of paperwork, wrestling with irate congressmen, and shooing away importunate office-seekers in early April, Washington's legendarily robust health began to weaken. Observers noticed a flush to his cheeks and that he had lost weight. Ignoring friends' advice that he consult a doctor, the president adjourned to Long Island later that month and spent a week riding about the countryside with only a small entourage. The exercise helped for a little while, but after returning to the city he contracted an ear infection and temporarily lost most of his hearing. The illness turned out to be influenza. In mid-May he was totally bedridden, wracked with fever. Doctor's treatments, including liberal doses of "James's Powder," were useless, and by May 16 the doctors confessed they had "no hopes of his recovery." Spitting blood, hiccupping, and rattling in the throat, he seemed near death. Unable to bear the sight, Martha fled the sickroom.[16]

Incredibly, Washington recovered. Within a few days he was sitting up in his easy chair, trying his caregivers by fretting constantly about the national debt. By late May he was cleared to return to business, but only gradually; a three-day fishing trip to New Jersey in early June helped to complete his convalescence so that he could again take charge. His first full days back at work must have left him yearning for his sickbed. Foreign debt was looking especially worrisome as the frustrated and cash-strapped French ostentatiously prepared to sell off their American debt to speculators. Fearing the devastating impact that this measure would have on the government's international credit, the president directed American bankers in Amsterdam to negotiate an emergency loan of 3 million florins from the Dutch to begin repaying principal on French debt. They successfully concluded the deal, and Congress approved ex post facto. On other matters, though, the delegates came around only slowly. They approved most of Hamilton's proposals on debt in the summer of 1790, but pushed back on securities and the assumption of state debt.

Hamilton refused to wait for Congress to resolve its divisions before pressing ahead with the next stages of his economic plan. The president also was impatient to establish a coherent policy, however much strain the effort put on his shaky health and the untested political system. On December 13, 1790, Hamilton submitted to Congress his Report on a National Bank. Just six weeks later, on January 28, 1791, he tendered his Report on the Establishment of a Mint. The proposals contained in both reports aimed at stabilizing the currency, establishing public credit, and creating a secure environment for investment.

Capitalized as it eventually would be at $10 million, the National Bank would establish a system of currency and exchange that could respond flexibly to the economic climate rather than to state politics. It would serve as the government's lender of first resort, and as a depositor for federal funds. The Bank also could issue bonds as currency usable for paying taxes and redeemable as specie. This in turn would encourage investment and inject wealth into the economy as capital became available for investment. With the establishment of a mint, the appearance of standardized gold and silver currency, and the circulation of specie in dollars would further stabilize exchange and build national credit. These would encourage further specie circulation, eliminating the cash-scarcity that had long hindered growth. Building mobile capital would invigorate an economy still struggling to overcome a history of colonial dependence and wartime dislocation.

At first, the proposals made progress. A bill incorporating subscribers to the Bank was introduced in Congress on January 3, 1791. The Senate passed it on January 20, and the House debated and then approved it by a vote of 39 to 20 on February 8. The president found it on his desk for signature six days later. Derided though he sometimes has been as Hamilton's cipher, Washington refused to approve the plan immediately. Instead he asked Jefferson, Madison, and Edmund Randolph—no friends of Hamilton's—for their written opinions. They all replied at length that they thought the Bank was unconstitutional.

Concerned, Washington passed their letters on to Hamilton for his response and meanwhile asked Madison to prepare a veto message in case he rejected the bill. The president then conferred extensively with Madison, who argued that the Bank was not only unconstitutional but also benefited a small number of wealthy New England speculators rather than the public. Madison recalled that Washington "listened favorably" to his views "without committing himself in any manner," but that he clearly had doubts. "The constitutionality of the national Bank, was a question on which his mind was greatly perplexed," Madison remembered. He believed in the "utility of the establishment" and was disposed "to favor a liberal construction of the national powers"; but on the other hand he knew that many of the state conventions might not have ratified the Constitution if they thought it would authorize the government to assert such a powerful role in the economy.[17]

As his investigations continued, the president's mood turned increasingly grave. Madison by contrast relaxed as a veto looked increasingly likely. Hamilton, who had sequestered himself for days to work on his report, finally submitted his "Opinion on the Constitutionality of an Act to Establish a Bank" to Washington on February 23. A thirteen-thousand-word blockbuster, it asserted the authority of Congress to enact broad legislation on the basis of Article I, Section 8 of the Constitution—a concept that later generations referred to as the doctrine of implied powers. Hamilton's late submission gave the president little time to spare—two days, in fact, under the terms of the Constitution. After perusing the document for several hours, Washington closeted himself with Hamilton throughout the morning and afternoon of February 24. The morning of February 25—the final day—found the president still undecided. With only hours remaining it was looking like the administration's first political nail-biter. "There was general uneasiness," John Rutledge, Jr., later recalled. "The President stood on the brink of a pre[ci]pice from which had he fallen he would have brought down with him much of that glorious reputation he has so deservedly established." Finally, Washington made up his mind. There would be no veto.[18]

There was considerably less fanfare about the Mint than about the National Bank—which is not to say it came to pass more quickly or easily. Washington had long advocated "Uniformity in the Currency," as he had informed Congress in a speech on January 8, 1790. He also was eager to establish a system of uniform weights and measures to oil the wheels of commerce. The president brought up the topic with Congress repeatedly, beginning with the draft of his first inaugural address and continuing throughout his first term. He even expressed strong hopes that "an uniformity of weights and measures could be established upon a proper foundation throughout the several nations of Europe and in the United States" to encourage international trade. Jefferson, meanwhile, performed important work in planning for a national coinage. The president urged him on, determined not to permit any measure that would involve producing coinage overseas.[19]

Even after Hamilton's report on the Mint, however, Congress seemed reluctant to act to establish a uniform currency, let alone a stable system of weights and measures. Just like during the Revolutionary War—albeit now of course with more civil authority—Washington had to act as a catalyst. Fed up with the delays, he lectured Congress on October 25, 1791, about the vital importance of creating a Mint, not least because of "the scarcity of small change, a scarcity so peculiarly distressing to the poorer classes." That did the trick. Six days later the Senate established a committee to consider the subject, and Robert Morris presented a bill to that effect on December 21. Debate and other delays would prevent Washington from signing it into law until April 2, 1792. His dream of uniform national weights and measures, however, would not be realized during his administration; and his vision of a transatlantic system remains unachieved even today.[20]

---

SETTLING THE DEBATES OVER THE DEBT, the National Bank, and the Mint helped to establish fiscal stability. That in turn fostered national harmony, but unity would prove elusive unless Congress and the president could agree on the permanent location of the national capital. Few projects were dearer to Washington's heart. In June 1790 Hamilton, Jefferson, and Madison met for dinner to strike a deal by which the Treasury secretary would receive approval of assumption of state debts in return for conceding that the nation's capital would not be New York City, as he had hoped, but be constructed along the banks of the Potomac. For the president the deal was a win-win proposition, and it is hard to believe he had not approved it in advance if not actually suggested it.

By the terms of the Residence Act in July 1790, Washington was left free to choose the site of the city to which the government would move ten years later. That autumn he rather ostentatiously poked around the banks of the upper Potomac to explore possible sites, but by November he had already fixed on the area around Georgetown, Maryland. A proclamation made it official two months later.

The conflict of interest was readily apparent. John Adams later griped that placing the Federal City on the Potomac so close to Mount Vernon raised the value of Washington family lands "a thousand percent at an expense to the public of more than his whole fortune." The president's hesitation over Hamilton's proposal to create a National Bank in New York may even have emanated from fears that the measure would suck the life out of the Federal City. Fisher Ames, one of Hamilton's allies, boasted that the National Bank would transform New York City into "the great centre of the revenue and banking operations of the nation. So many interests will be centered here, that it is feared that, ten years hence, Congress will be found fast anchored and immovable." As Ames's observation implied, however, the president's personal interests were not the only ones at stake in the capital's location. Many prominent mid-Atlantic entrepreneurs hoped that the Federal City would serve both as a political center and a commercial hub for western navigation and expansion—a central element of Washington's plan to bind east and west into a united polity.[21]

Washington's efforts to lay out and construct the Federal City reflected his desire that the project generate profit for all involved without becoming a burden on the government's still fragile finances. During the first few months of 1791, he appointed city commissioners, closely supervised a surveyor and an engineer tasked with studying terrain, and negotiated with local proprietors who received city lots in return for ceding their land. Jefferson assisted in developing the project, but the president determined boundaries, buildings, and terms of land acquisition.

Toward the end of March, Washington announced that the city would encompass 6,111 acres, or 9.5 square miles, laid out in designated lots divided by streets. His initial construction plans were economical, although Pierre L'Enfant's later intervention would ensure a more grandiose vision.

Even then, though, the president oversaw the process with his customary care in order to guard against wastage and corruption. He took the lead in enticing entrepreneurs to invest in the city, setting the example by purchasing lots there and building houses. Toward the end of his life he collected rents from them as a landlord.

It would take a decade to make the Federal City habitable, and many more years would pass before it became a fixed symbol of national unity. Until then Washington tangibly united the nation in the symbol of his person. He realized that fact without a hint of vainglory. Profoundly self-aware throughout his life, he also knew what it meant to be a leader. His job was to unify—to be, as many called him, a linchpin. To do so effectively, he needed to be visible. Moreover, through his travels around the country, his footsteps would become tangible links in the chain binding the disparate states into one dissoluble (he hoped) union.

No pomp and circumstance accompanied his rain-soaked departure from New York City on October 15, 1789, for the first stage of a journey to New England. In his mind he was traveling "to acquire knowledge of the face of the Country the growth and Agriculture thereof and the temper and disposition of the Inhabitants towards the new government." In keeping with his habit of studying a project from all angles, Washington noted the state of home and public building construction, transportation, and communications at every stage of his journey. He chatted with farmers about their crops, livestock, and profits. The information was useful, but his interaction with the common people was even more important.[22]

Commercial activities fascinated the president, as did manufacturing establishments. His itinerary included manufactories for sailcloth and cordage, cotton, leather, glass, and clothing, and he met with inventors, too. In Boston he sipped Thomas Fielder's "supposed improvement in the Article of American Rum," gazed at a mechanical boat that worked as it seemed by "Magic," and provided the inventor with a small "loan" of $20 to support his development of a "Machine for improving Agriculture." Much the same learning process accompanied his tour in the spring of 1791 to the southern states, where he discovered to his pleasure that the people practiced "industry and frugality." He also learned that thanks to the more settled economy, "the farmer finds a ready market for his produce, and the merchant calculates with more certainty on his payments." On both these trips, though, the president endured an exhausting series of public festivities and portrait sittings as the American people tried to come to grips with their new leader. He grumbled but submitted to these trials, which he knew served the public.[23]

Despite all of his conspicuous manufactory visits, Washington understood that agriculture would continue to dominate the economy during his lifetime and for decades thereafter. Most of the inventions that he inspected in the course of his travels were designed for farm use. There initially seemed to be little he could do, though, to further agricultural prosperity from his presidential office.

Baron Friedrich von Poellnitz, a quirky Prussian nobleman who owned a small experimental farm on Manhattan, was one of many to belabor the president with sweeping plans for overhauling American agriculture. Washington studied the baron's plans with interest but admitted to him that "in my public capacity, I know not whether I can with propriety do any thing more" than to forward them to Congress. "Whatever wise & prudent plans" the delegates "deemed most feasible & effectual (as being clearly within the functions & abilities of the general Government)," he promised, would "meet with my ready & hearty concurrence."[24]

Washington's wariness was a product of both expediency and principle. Any attempt to extend executive control over the economy, he knew, would be viewed with immediate suspicion. He also firmly believed that government could not command production. Public figures such as he could nevertheless promote innovation and development so long as they did so as individuals acting in a private capacity. As president, he would accomplish some of his most important work when he was not being presidential.

Fortunately, Washington did not have to spend all of his time in public office away from Mount Vernon. He returned there as often as his official duties allowed, and worked to maintain and improve the estate. Never had his personal entrepreneurial activities been more public. Far more than during the Confederation period, Americans observed the examples he set in his farming. Visitors studied and newspapers reported his innovations, while inventors plied him with every imaginable gimmick. The advertising value of even an unofficial presidential endorsement was fantastic. Where Washington became a consumer, the producer reaped immense profit.

The president had to be careful on grounds of propriety just as he was always cautious in adopting new technologies. While every invention caught his interest, only a minority caught his fancy. In November 1791, Irish agriculturalist Charles Vancouver sent the president a "curiously invented plough." Washington declined to accept the gift on ethical grounds. And though he said that he would be happy to pay for it, he confessed that the device seemed too complex for use by unskilled labor—specifically, slaves. "All machines used in husbandry that are of a complicated nature," he told Vancouver, "would be entirely useless to him, and impossible to be introduced into common use where they are to be worked by ignorant and clumsy hands, which must be the case in every part of this country where the ground is tilled by negroes."[25]

Jefferson thought as Washington did on the importance of promoting American agriculture and related innovations in farming practices and manufacturing. Before their falling out during the president's second term, the two men acted in concert through public peregrinations that left no doubt about their shared hopes for agricultural improvement. On the morning of August 22, 1791, Jefferson and the president breakfasted together in Philadelphia and then sallied out across the Market Street Bridge to a farm along the Schuylkill River owned by Samuel Powel, president of the city's agricultural society. Powel had just acquired a new threshing machine created by inventor Alexander Anderson, and Washington and Jefferson spent the rest of the morning there looking over its components and watching it in operation.

Jefferson also exploited the president's notorious sweet tooth in order to sell him on the idea of expanding domestic maple sugar production to Virginia. In the same month that he visited Powel's farm, Washington received a shipment of some New York–produced maple sugar from entrepreneurs Arthur Noble and William Cooper, who boasted that "in a few years" they would manufacture enough of the stuff to "supply the whole United States." Jefferson backed them up by sending the president a packet of sugar maple seeds. Possibly smacking his lips with pleasure, Washington recorded his "great pleasure" at "the progress of that promising manufacture" and planted Jefferson's seeds at Mount Vernon.[26]

Arthur Young continued to communicate regularly with Washington about agriculture. Since he published their letters with the president's full concurrence, their correspondence became a public dialogue on the state of American farming and the means for its improvement. Both men used the correspondence to instruct, praise, and sometimes berate their countrymen and their governments. In a letter to the president of January 25, 1791, Young complained bitterly of the heavy taxation that Parliament imposed on English farmers. In his response, Washington exploited the opening thus provided to express his "astonishment hardly to be conceived" at "the account of the taxes with which you are burthened." In America, he boasted, "our taxes are light."[27]

Young's letter also included a request for a broad survey of the state of American agriculture, giving Washington an opportunity to conduct private investigations that he would have found difficult to justify in his capacity as president. On August 25, 1791, Washington dispatched a circular letter to gentlemen farmers in Virginia, Maryland, Pennsylvania, New Jersey, and New York asking for detailed information on matters such as land quality and values; rents; crop production and prices; populations of working livestock; prices of meat, butter, and cheese at different market towns; and iron tool manufactories. At Young's behest as well as for his own purposes, the president inquired about "the Taxes in the different States, which may in any way affect the Farmer." Washington dispatched the responses to Young, who published them to enlighten farmers on both sides of the Atlantic about the state and potential of American agriculture.[28]

Washington's correspondence with Young and other British agriculturalists and inventors helped to meld a new community of interest between both nations—this time, founded on mutual enrichment and respect. The results were far more positive than anything the president could have accomplished by attempting to dictate American agricultural reform. Through Scottish lord David Erskine, the Eleventh Earl of Buchan, Washington and American farmers learned of the work of Scottish economist and commercial and agricultural reformer James Anderson. After being introduced by Erskine in the autumn of 1791, Anderson sent the president a packet of rutabaga seeds and a copy of his journal the *Bee, or Universal Literary Intelligencer.* Washington accepted both with pleasure, and went on to purchase all eighteen volumes of the *Bee* along with Anderson's many other important works on agriculture, science, and silk manufacture.

The volumes were destined not just for the president's shelf. Determined that Anderson's work should benefit all Americans, Washington interceded to get Anderson elected to the American Philosophical Society—an organization that the president heartily promoted for its support of invention and innovation. Washington also made certain that the *Bee* and the Scotsman's other works were widely advertised in American gazettes. Through Anderson he acquired and disseminated knowledge about exciting recent discoveries by merchants, economists, scientists, and explorers in places as far afield as India and Russia, and received samples of foreign products such as scientifically engineered hemp seed from Germany.

Contacts with other Scotsmen were equally salutary. Agricultural reformer Sir John Sinclair, who in addition to being a member of Parliament founded and presided over the British Board of Agriculture, became one of Washington's most important correspondents. Sinclair owned a large estate in Caithness that served as a model for advanced methods of agriculture and livestock (especially sheep) breeding. He regularly supplied Washington with updates on his own endeavors as well as official, board-sponsored agricultural statistics, reports, pamphlets, and surveys. Under Sinclair's auspices in 1795, Washington became an honorary member of the British Board of Agriculture—a remarkable distinction for a sitting president who just over a decade earlier had led a violent rebellion against King George III—thereby forging another bond to unite the two countries in peaceful intercourse.

Washington also corresponded with John Anderson, professor of Natural Philosophy at the University of Glasgow and author of such important works as the *Institutes of Physics* (which greatly impressed Benjamin Franklin) and *Essays on Field Artillery Since the Use of Gunpowder in War*. Frustrated by the lukewarm reception that British officials gave to his military inventions, Professor Anderson asked for the president's good offices in laying them before Congress. Washington was so excited by the proposal that he wrote his secretary Tobias Lear (then in London) on May 6, 1794, that "I wish most sincerely that some inducement could be offered Professor Anderson which would bring him to this Country. His labours are certainly ingenious, & worthy of encouragement." Unfortunately, Congress did not take up the proposal.[29]

The American president's interest in promoting innovation in agriculture and manufacturing—which he shared with Jefferson and many others, but in a far more public role—quickly became common knowledge throughout the western world. This in turn inspired further innovation, as well as the flow of information. Hearing that Washington was intrigued by improvements in threshing machines, German-American merchants Frederick and Henry König of Baltimore contacted famed German agricultural economist Georg Friedrich Wehrs. He "without losing a moment endeavoured by every Exertion in my Power to procure" for the president "Draughts, Models and explanatory Information of the best Threshing Machines hitherto known." In January 1793, Wehrs sent these documents to Washington along with information on paper and silk manufacturing, economics, and "a Small Treatise on the Preparation of Superfine wool for manufacturing fine cloth and other sorts of stuffs."[30]

Given his druthers Washington probably would have loved nothing better than to tour Great Britain—his lack of language skills made him feel insecure about visiting the Continent—to meet his new friends and witness firsthand their accomplishments in agriculture and industry. His youthful yearning to see London likely never left him, although he might have contemplated the prospect of an awkward meeting with King George III with considerable unease. Unfortunately, no sitting president could sail for Europe in an era when overseas travel involved a time commitment of months.

Washington's secretary and confidant Tobias Lear, however, could and did. In August 1793, Lear amicably resigned his secretarial post to invest his time in a new mercantile firm he had founded, T. Lear & Company, with its headquarters in the Federal City. Learning that Lear would soon set sail to establish mercantile contacts in Holland, England, and Scotland, Washington enjoined him to investigate and report minutely about European agriculture, manufactures, and commerce. He also asked Lear to visit his luminary friends. After a stormy twenty-eight-day winter passage that ended in Glasgow, Lear spent two weeks "viewing the several large manufactories in the City and its neighbourhood," including textile and glass establishments. He took copious notes, especially regarding their use of steam power, and sent these along with samples of their products to Washington. After celebrating Christmas Lear set out for Edinburg, and then conducted a tour to visit factories in towns like Leeds, Manchester, and Sheffield on his way to London—becoming an eyewitness to the dawn of the Industrial Revolution.[31]

In the course of his meanderings, Lear studied British agricultural and gardening practices. He dispatched some five thousand white thorn plants to Washington for planting at Mount Vernon. Lear also visited the president's friends, such as the Earl of Buchan, John Sinclair, Professor John Anderson, and of course Arthur Young. Washington spoke fondly and often of Young, so much so that Lear probably expected to tremble before his personal and intellectual presence. Reality was a little disappointing. Young was thin, moderately tall, and with "an interesting countenance, aquiline nose & good eye." He spoke energetically and intelligently. Lear was shocked to discover, however, that far from adulating Young, some of his countrymen considered him a bit of a windbag. A number of Young's closest acquaintances, Lear told Washington, looked on him "rather as a theorist on the subject of farming—and even say that he never made half the experiments of which he has published the result—and his own farm is said to be one of the most slovenly in the part of the Country where he lives." Everyone, however, admitted that he had "done very great good to the cause of agriculture, by his writings and perseverance." Lear also learned that while British aristocrats and merchants still were a little touchy on the subject of America, entrepreneurs and manufacturers almost uniformly viewed Americans and Washington in a positive light.[32]

———————

COULD AMERICA FOLLOW GREAT BRITAIN'S EXAMPLE in building a profitable manufacturing sector that was independent of rather than subsidiary to agriculture? This—although it was not immediately obvious—would be one of the first areas in which Washington and Jefferson parted ways. The president was no rampant industrialist. While Jefferson envisaged a largely agricultural future for the United States, however, Washington cautiously endorsed a gradual expansion of the manufacturing sector. So long as the demand for agricultural labor remained high, so-called cottage industries—dominated by women—could carry much of the workload. "I would not force the introduction of manufactures, by extravagant encouragements, and to the prejudice of agriculture," Washington explained to Lafayette in January 1789, "yet, I conceive, much might be done in that way by woman, children & others; without taking one really necessary hand from tilling the earth."[33]

The president did not expect the agricultural labor shortage to last forever. He expected a population boom and encouraged it through immigration. Knowing as he did so many prominent Scottish agriculturalists, Washington favored the settlement of large numbers of Scots—especially Highlanders—in the United States, calling them "a hardy industrious people, well calculated to form new settlements—and will in time become valuable citizens."[34]

Just as he had learned at Mount Vernon after switching from tobacco to wheat in the 1760s, more labor meant more hands for manufacturing. Washington became more and more enthusiastic over time about creating the conditions whereby American industry could thrive. Telling Jefferson (then still in France) in February 1789 that promoting "manufactures" was among "the greatest & most important objects of internal concern, which at present occupy the attention of the public mind," Washington argued in favor of promoting the domestic textile industry—especially cotton, which would "be of the most immediate and extensive utility."[35]

Just before writing to Jefferson, Washington had entertained James Milne, the entrepreneurial son of British Lancashire cotton manufacturer John Milne, at Mount Vernon. Over dinner, the younger Milne explained his plans to establish textile manufactories in Georgia and South Carolina. The concept worked Washington up into a lather of excitement. "The increase of that new material and the introduction of the late-improved Machines to abridge labour," he enthused to Jefferson, "must be of almost infinite consequence to America."[36]

In his eagerness the president almost forgot—or tried not to remember—the difficulties that British laws placed in the way of acquiring new technologies. In November 1789, after returning from New England where he had witnessed both the potential and the limitations of American manufacturing, Washington read a letter from Welsh woolen manufacturer Thomas Howells. In it Howells expressed to the president his desire to export skilled workers and advanced technologies to America, where they would establish a chain of wool manufactories. This would of course violate British law, which prohibited the export of either; but Washington brushed aside the legal difficulty. Admitted self-interest jacked his enthusiasm. If such manufactories cropped up in northern Virginia, he imagined, they would provide immediate outlets for his own wool, and lead planters across Virginia to raise more sheep—that portion of his stock in which Washington confessed he took "most delight."[37]

Jefferson was less enthusiastic. After Washington promoted Howells's scheme to the Virginia legislature—sparking some interest—Jefferson and Attorney General Edmund Randolph intervened. The president of the United States, they warned with reason, should steer clear of involving himself in what would be regarded as a "felony" in Great Britain. Not until 1808 would Thomas Howells's son Joseph (ancestor of author William Dean Howells) come to America and settle in Ohio to pursue his father's and the president's dream of establishing American wool manufacturing.[38]

Washington, though, did not give up. In December 1789 he met with Thomas McCabe, Jr., son of a prominent Belfast manufacturer, to discuss the plausibility of transferring British cotton manufacturing technology to the United States; and in July 1791 he met with McCabe's friend William Pearce, a Manchester artisan seeking to promote his British-designed loom. Financially backed by Hamilton, among others, Pearce succeeded in establishing a cotton manufactory in Philadelphia. He took George and Martha Washington and many members of the Cabinet on a tour of the facility in June 1792, prompting the president to urge his deputies to brainstorm ways they might encourage it and similar enterprises.

Therein lay a thorny problem. When it came to agriculture, Washington was hands-off: though inefficient, the sector already dominated the national economy and could best be aided by the dissemination of knowledge of improved technologies and better farming practices. Manufacturing, though, did not exist on any scale because of the colonial system's toxic legacy and the British laws against the export of skilled workers and technologies to America. Although Washington had initially hoped for an influx of French and other Continental European know-how, time revealed just how little these countries had to offer in comparison with Great Britain.

How, then, could the government encourage manufacturing? The question baffled Washington. The passage of the Patent Act for the "Encouragement of Arts and Sciences" in 1790 offered protection to American inventors but gave no substantive support to domestic manufacturing. Washington pondered working to build manufacturing through the agricultural sector—for example, "encouraging the growth of Cotton, & Hemp" because of "the advantages which would result to this Country from the produce of articles which ought to be manufactured at home." Likewise with sheep: encouraging farmers to raise them more extensively, he thought, "might be made not only a most profitable subject to the farmer, but rendered highly important in a public view, by encouraging extensive establishments of woollen manufactories from the abundance of wool which they could furnish." Simply "encouraging" or leading by example, though, could foster manufacturing only over the long term. The British government provided bounties or subsidies to promote certain industries it deemed important for the national welfare, and Washington had to admit that such were the only means he could think of to "*effectually*" encourage manufacturing. But were bounties appropriate or even constitutional?[39]

Hamilton thought so. He was already at work in developing a Society for Establishing Useful Manufactures that would create a model industrial town in Paterson, New Jersey. And in his "Report on the Subject of Manufactures" of December 5, 1791, he bluntly proposed that the government follow the British example of subsidizing certain manufactures. Jefferson, though, bitterly opposed the idea as conducive to "unlimited" government. Conversing with the president on February 29, 1792, the secretary of state argued forcefully that "the Report on manufactures which, under colour of giving *bounties* for the encouragement of particular manufactures, meant to establish the doctrine that the power given by the Constitution to collect taxes to provide for the *general welfare* of the U.S. permitted Congress to take every thing under their management which *they* should deem for the *public welfare*, & which is susceptible of the application of money."[40]

This was one time Hamilton did not get his way. Either because he did not wish to alienate Jefferson and Madison—for whom the report on manufacturing was the proverbial last straw—or, more likely, because he could not make up his own mind on the question of subsidies, Washington refused to promote the report and Congress never took it up. Thus, when on May 25, 1792, a certain "B. Francis" wrote to the president expounding on America's limitless mineral resources, which he said would "promote Industry, the study of chymistry, and the prosecution of Manufactures" if the government subsidized their exploitation, Washington deferred to Jefferson. He replied on the president's behalf a month later that "the subterranean riches of this country not yet explored are very great, but the exploring [of] the mineral kingdom, as that of the vegetable & animal, is left by our laws to individual enterprize, the government not being authorised by them to interfere at all: consequently it is not in the power of the President to avail the public of the services you are pleased to tender in this line."[41]

DEBT, CREDIT, AGRICULTURE, AND MANUFACTURING were all important, but to Washington's mind nothing was more vital to the future survival of the United States than the development of free, safe, and thriving systems of internal and external commerce. Domestic commerce took precedence for its role in fostering national unity. In his draft inaugural address, Washington had promoted international commerce out of a belief that "a sense of reciprocal benefits will serve to connect us with the rest of mankind in stricter ties of amity." However, he thought that "an internal commerce is more in our power; and may be of more importance." It would in time "exterminate prejudices, diffuse blessings, and encrease the friendship of the inhabitants of one State for those of another."[42]

The government's role in this process was easier to delineate than its place in, for example, manufacturing. Its business was—along with private investors— to help create the structure and conditions by which such commerce could take place. Communications were essential. Writing to Congress on October 25, 1791, to urge the creation of a post office and post roads "on a plan sufficiently liberal and comprehensive," the president pointed out that "safety and facility of communication" would both bind together the far-flung "Western and Northern parts of the Union" and diffuse "a knowledge of the laws and proceedings of the Government; which, while it contributes to the security of the people, serves also to guard them against the effects of mis-representation and misconception."[43]

Ultimately, though, the government's purpose in promoting the development of internal infrastructure was not to expand its ability to exert political control but to foster prosperity. Washington believed in a strong and stable federal government. He did not, however, believe that it was the government's role to enforce national unity. That, he thought, depended on commerce. It was for this reason that the government had a duty to help build nodes of transport and communication—so that the people could, through free exchange, forge their own national community of commerce. Although Washington promoted the development of post roads and where possible improved land transportation routes, mass road paving was out of the question.

Water-borne commerce held vast potential. Though he had a personal interest in the Potomac, Washington imagined a national network of many waterways linked by canals. Within a decade, he predicted to the Earl of Buchan on April 22, 1793, that "if left undisturbed we shall open a communication by water with all the Lakes Northward & Westward of us with which we have territorial connections; and an inland navigation in a few years more from Rhode Island to Georgia inclusively. . . . To these, may also be added, the erection of bridges over considerable Rivers, & the commencement of Turn-Pike Roads as further indications of the improvements in hand."[44]

Still, the Potomac remained for Washington the prince of American waterways. The "Potowmac River then, is the centre of the Union," he wrote to Arthur Young on December 5, 1791. "It is the River, more than any other, in my opinion, which must, in the natural progress of things, connect by its inland navigation . . . the Atlantic States with the vast region which is populating (beyond all conception) to the Westward of it. It is designated by law for the seat of the Empire; and must, from its extensive course through a rich & populous country become, in time, the grand Emporium of North America." With the letter the president enclosed a "general Map of North America," upon which he fussily traced the outlines of the Federal City along with the Potomac and all its tributaries. Poring over the map during long hours in his study and drawing upon his personal observations during his rambles across the mid-Atlantic, Washington had assessed each of these tributaries and the costs of making them navigable.[45]

Unfortunately, the Potomac Company that Washington had labored so diligently to found, and in which he still held stock, had not so far lived up to expectations thanks in part to the incompetence of its engineer, the inventor James Rumsey. By the time he became president, Washington was no longer closely involved in the company's operations, and after Rumsey died in 1792 the venture went adrift, not to revive until after the turn of the century. His dream still survived as he held out hope that the construction of the Federal City would renew interest in the project.

Private investment would take the primary role in realizing the vision of western navigation and expansion. Government had a limited role to play in maintaining if not developing commercial infrastructure. When melting Delaware River ice broke up an important commercial pier below Philadelphia in the spring of 1792, for example, Washington approved an appropriation of $2,000 for its restoration. By principle, though, he never considered pushing westward navigation or national transport and communications as massive public works projects. The American people, he could only hope, would catch on to his enthusiasm and invest heavily in schemes to develop the Potomac and other rivers. It was up to local governments from the county to the state level, meanwhile, to authorize and seek funding for the construction of roads. Until then, he had to think in broader terms about uniting east and west in a truly continental economy.

Native Americans were integral to his vision. Relations were uneasy as white settlers encroached on their land and they retaliated with sporadic raids and killings, especially in the Ohio and Kentucky country. Contrary to myth, though, Washington preferred to avoid military means of dealing with this issue. He never considered any form of genocide or ethnic cleansing. Rather—in keeping with his view of human relations generally—he sought peace as a prerequisite to commerce, and commerce as a means of maintaining peace.

White and Native Americans, the president imagined, could live side by side if they developed a community of interest through trade. But the link had to be direct. While negotiating a treaty with the Creek Nation in the summer of 1790, he discovered that British middlemen dominated commerce with them by importing English goods through Spanish ports. This had to end for many reasons, only one of which was the need to establish direct (and presumably positive) relations between natives and the United States. Up to this time, after all, depredations against the Native Americans had been at the behest of Spain, Great Britain, and France.

Addressing the Senate on August 4, 1790, the president contended that "As the trade of the Indians is a main mean of their political management, it is therefore obvious, that the United States cannot possess any security for the performance of treaties with the Creeks, while their trade is liable to be interrupted or withheld, at the caprice of two foreign powers. Hence it becomes an object of real importance to form new channels for the commerce of the Creeks through the United States." In accordance with this principle, enshrined that summer in an act of Congress, a secret article was added to the Creek treaty requiring that after 1792, commerce with them would "be carried on through the ports, and by the citizens of the United States."[46]

Hard facts, unfortunately, progressively battered Washington's vision to pieces. As fighting between settlers and Native Americans in the Ohio Region spiraled out of control, Arthur St. Clair, governor of the Northwest Territory, concluded that only war could break the cycle. The president reluctantly complied with his demand to launch punitive expeditions against the Native Americans. These resulted in two major disasters: General Josiah Harmar's defeat in October 1790 and St. Clair's defeat in November 1791.

On October 25, 1791, just before news arrived of the St. Clair disaster, Washington had hopefully suggested that commerce with the Native Americans "should be promoted under regulations tending to secure an equitable deportment towards them, and that such rational experiments should be made, for imparting to them the blessings of civilization, as may, from time to time suit their condition." The twin military catastrophes of 1790–1791, though, left the Northwest Territory essentially ungovernable, forcing the president to choose between abandoning the region to British influence and imposing control by force. There was no real choice. In August 1794, General Anthony Wayne decisively defeated the Northwestern tribes at the Battle of Fallen Timbers. In the aftermath of this battle, Native Americans were forced to cede much of their land in the Ohio region. And following the Jay Treaty of 1795, the British finally pulled out of forts they had continued to occupy in violation of the 1783 Treaty of Paris. The United States had won a "victory," but established an ugly precedent that Washington had never wanted to set.[47]

---

A NATIVE AMERICAN CONFLICT WAS SURVIVABLE, but a foreign war might not be. No one knew better than Washington what another war might do to the economy, politics, and society. That was one of the reasons why, as president, he sought to avoid foreign entanglements. Peace was indispensable for national prosperity to develop. To Lafayette he wrote on January 29, 1789: "While you are quarreling among yourselves in Europe—while one King [George III] is running mad—and others acting as if they were already so, by cutting the throats of the subjects of their neighbours: I think you need not doubt, My Dear Marquis we shall continue in tranquility here—And that population will be progressive so long as there shall continue to be so many easy means for obtaining a subsistence, and so ample a field for the exertion of talents and industry." Avoiding foreign entanglements, though, did not entail withholding commerce. Washington was determined to place the United States firmly within the global economy—again creating communities of interest, this time across the seas.[48]

Overseas commerce was already developing before Washington became president. "Commerce to the East Indies is prosecuted with considerable success," he exulted to Jefferson on August 31, 1788. "The Voyages are so much shorter & the Vessels are navigated at so much less expence, that we hope to rival & supply (at least through the West Indies) some part of Europe, with commodities." Thanks in part to the success he achieved early on at establishing American financial credit abroad, this commercial expansion could be expected to continue more or less on its own account provided no obstacles were thrown in its way. It was clearly not government's role to command commerce. Here as elsewhere, though, Washington knew that there was much he could do personally to foster it.[49]

Projecting confidence abroad formed a focal point of Washington's strategy for promoting international commerce. His official and private letters to overseas friends, acquaintances, diplomats, and merchants oozed optimism on the goodwill and economic potential of the United States. He became particularly vociferous at times of internal crisis, counteracting perceptions of American weakness or discord. In early 1792, with the United States in the grip of a financial panic, he contacted all of his European associates to let them know that his country remained a haven of peace and prosperity in a world torn by war. For the most part he repeated a number of stock phrases, as in a letter to Lafayette on June 10, 1792: "The affairs of the United States still go on in a prosperous train," he wrote. "We encrease daily in numbers & riches, and the people are blessed with the enjoyment of those rights which can alone give security and happiness to a nation." The propaganda remained unremitting throughout his presidency.[50]

American merchants embraced Washington as a symbol of trade and prosperity. Closeness to him also lent them legitimacy. In July 1792 the president announced his plans to pass through Baltimore on his way to Philadelphia. Soon thereafter he received a letter from the merchants of Baltimore "who have a sincere love and attachment for you [and] wish very much to give you a public dinner." Just as during his trips to New England and the South, Washington agreed despite his aversion to "formal & ceremonious engagements." Most everywhere he went as president, the story was the same.[51]

Washington also acted symbolically through his purchases of exotic goods from foreign ports, which he did in part as a means of encouraging the American mercantile community. Mount Vernon's gardens and greenhouse became botanical wonderlands of rare plants. In September 1789, the president wrote to Margaret Tilghman Carroll of the Mount Clare estate in Baltimore asking her to send him a small shipload of some of the imported fruit trees, herbs, and ornamental plants that bedecked her magnificent greenhouse. She complied with a profusion of orange and lemon shaddocks (or pomelos), scented shrubs, aloes, and marjoram. Consigning these to a skilled gardener he had just imported from Bremen, Germany, Washington purchased a wide variety of tropical plants over the following years, especially fruit. He loved how the plants looked but also cherished their value, instructing his gardener to "raise large Nurseries of the most valuable sorts; as well for the purpose of sale" as for pleasure. For the Mount Vernon household—often for Martha's pleasure—he ordered Chinese and Indian porcelain, tableware, ornaments, and muslin and jaconet cloth from American merchantmen docked at Alexandria. Here and on his visits to port cities on his travels around the country, the president made it a point to publicly inspect vessels engaged in the Asian trade, and applaud their work.[52]

Visiting these merchantmen exposed the president to some of the most colorful characters he ever encountered. One of them was the eccentric and wealthy Irishman John O'Donnell, who lived in India for sixteen years as an employee of the East India Company before sailing his merchantman *Pallas* from Canton, China, to Baltimore in 1785. His crewmen were all Indian and Chinese, and their cargo—the first to be carried direct from Canton to Baltimore—generated a sensation. Washington drooled at the prospect of catching "great bargains" from a ship carrying exotic goods not subject to the usual duties and tolls coming from British carriers. So he contacted his former aide Tench Tilghman, then living in Baltimore, and asked him to purchase a long list of items such as fabrics, tableware, tea, and handkerchiefs. Through Tilghman, he and O'Donnell exchanged hearty greetings and expressed their desire to meet. Washington was particularly eager to gaze upon the merchantman's crew because "from my reading, or rather from an imperfect recollection of what I had read I had conceived an idea that the Chinese though droll in shape & appearance, were yet white." Unfortunately, O'Donnell priced his goods "extravagantly high" out of the knowledge that he had temporarily cornered the market on Asian goods. As a result, Tilghman refused to purchase any of them at the public sale.[53]

Though American buyers did not prove as gullible as he had hoped, O'Donnell enjoyed being the center of attention so much that he decided not to leave. Instead he purchased 2,000 acres of Baltimore waterfront land, where he constructed an elegant oriental mansion called Canton and entertained legions of awestruck guests. He hoped more than anything to include Washington among them. The master of Mount Vernon always seemed too busy, though, so after the inauguration O'Donnell rushed off to New York City to meet Washington in his official abode. There the Irishman put his storytelling gifts to full use, beguiling the president with tales of oriental mysteries, including the Indian hookah. Washington must have cocked an eyebrow at this. Later, on passing through Baltimore on September 9, 1790, the president was startled to encounter one of O'Donnell's Asian servants proffering the "Indian Apparatus for Smoking" and proposing to "shew the President's Servant it's use, and the Manner of preparing the Tobacco for Smoking." Whether the hookah ever occupied the president's leisure moments is unknown, but he and O'Donnell stayed in touch for many years.[54]

An old nemesis helped foster the growth of American commerce in Asia. In the mid-1780s Lord Cornwallis, then governor general of India, opened up ports in the subcontinent to American vessels. By the early 1790s the Indian trade had become prolific enough to merit the appointment of an American consul, who Washington nominated to the Senate in November 1792. Further consular appointments to places like the Dutch East Indies and China followed in due course.

There were nevertheless significant limits to what the president could accomplish. On December 13, 1791, the Providence merchants Brown & Francis wrote to him requesting that he draft them a letter of endorsement for a $100,000 loan they sought from bankers in Amsterdam. They promised to use the money to build a large American merchant vessel for the Asian trade with the purpose not just of profit but encouraging the growth of a large American merchant fleet. Washington took their proposal into "serious consideration." He was on record as favoring the construction of American merchant ships, having exhorted Congress on December 8, 1790, to offer "such encouragements to our own navigation as will render our commerce and agriculture less dependent" on foreign shipping. Regretfully, though, he informed Brown & Francis on January 7, 1792, that despite "every disposition and wish to promote the commercial interests of our Country, and to countenance the laudable undertakings of its enterprising citizens," he could not endorse their loan request because in doing so "it would be almost impossible to separate my private from my official character." Far from being offended, the merchants built their vessel anyway, naming it the *President Washington*, and dispatched it to the East Indies. There, like good capitalists they sold the ship for a superior foreign-built vessel. Named the *Illustrious President*, it took up a symbolically significant trade between Asia and Ostend.[55]

In other parts of the globe, too, Washington's name symbolized the projection of American commerce—if not power—abroad. In April 1792 the

American merchant and explorer Joseph Ingraham, sailing the Brigantine *Hope* on a course from Boston to northwest North America, and to China and back, sighted a group of seven new islands in the Marquesas chain in the South Pacific. He named the first of them Washington's Island. Elsewhere, the sloop *Lady Washington* was among a number of vessels owned by a group of Boston merchants trading sea otter furs from northwestern America to China. One of the merchants, Joseph Barrell, sent Washington an otter fur in November 1793, pointing out that it had been carried from America to China and on around the world to Boston. The president proudly adorned his saddle with it.

Although he was no sailor, Washington would always fondly remember his youthful journey to Barbados, and his admiration for seagoing men was profound. When his friend Alexander Spotswood announced in February 1792 that his young son sought a berth on a vessel bound for the East Indies and asked for a letter of recommendation, the president happily obliged. "I am pleased," he told the elder Spotswood, "to find that there are some young Gentlemen of respectability, stepping forward with ardor in a profession, where they may render service to their Country at a future period."[56]

In a world that had already seen no fewer than four major wars in less than a century and was already sliding into a fifth, commercial conflict was inevitable. Washington encouraged the quick negotiation of commercial treaties with all the European powers, although Jefferson, ambassadors, and consuls handled the details. Throughout the president's first term, however, Congress seemed prepared to carry over resentment against European commercial restrictions and raids into tariff contests if not wars.

Washington and Jefferson both walked a fine line between failing to uphold American rights on the one hand and imposing excessively provocative retaliatory measures on the other. Both men understood that American commerce needed peace if it was to grow. Congress, however, sparred with the British—imposing, for example, heavy duties on imports of tin from Cornwall in 1792—and with the French, whose merchants decried the slow repayment of American war debts and whose increasingly radical series of administrations imposed severe duties on American imports.

The president did not waste his time railing against these contests. Instead, he focused his energy on securing measures for the protection of American commerce overseas. In his draft for the inaugural address he had written: "As our people have a natural genius for Naval affairs & as our materials for navigation are ample; if we give due encouragement to the fisheries and the carrying trade, we shall possess such a nursery of Seamen & such skill in maratime operations as to enable us to create a navy almost in a moment." Though he had been sounding the same clarion call since the end of the Revolutionary War, however, a breathtakingly naïve Congress would continue to ignore him until 1794. The results of this neglect would come close to plunging the nation into the very type of war that demilitarization was intended to prevent.[57]

CHAPTER EIGHT

# KEEPING THE PEACE: WASHINGTON'S SECOND TERM

AS WASHINGTON BEGAN WHAT HE ANTICIPATED TO BE THE final full year of his presidency in 1792, he could look back with satisfaction on his accomplishments. The government functioned with suitable efficiency. The site of its future seat had been determined. Debt was under control. The currency—despite some scary moments—was stable. Public credit had been established at home and abroad. The Bank of the United States, which had been subscribed with "astonishing rapidity," seemed to be working well in discharging public debt and sustaining financial liquidity. The United States was at peace, free of domestic rebellion or foreign war, allowing agriculture, industry, and commerce to develop.[1]

Reflecting his belief that he had fulfilled his task of putting the national machinery in motion and nudging the American people toward prosperity, the president's messages to Congress expressed unbridled optimism about the future. In some parts of the country there were murmurings about various facets of his policies, but Washington sincerely hoped and expected to retire at the end of his first term. He had already lived well beyond the life span of most male members of his family going back three generations, and he sensed that his physical and mental faculties were beginning to fade.

The country, however, was not yet ready to do without him. If anything, Americans were feeling increasingly insecure. Many of their worries originated with the financial panic that hit New York City early in 1792. The cause was speculation. William Duer, who had served as a New York congressman during the war and as secretary to the Board of Treasury during the Confederation, briefly held the office of assistant secretary of the Treasury under Hamilton in 1789–1790. During this time he and some associates amassed a small financial empire through speculation in western lands and other schemes. Duer also fell into $200,000 of debt. Rather than mend his ways, in 1791–1792 he speculated heavily in government bonds, stretching his personal credit well beyond its limits.

Securities prices peaked in January 1792, but Duer's edifice began to crumble as his debt payments fell due. On March 9, the day after the Bank of the United States stopped extending him credit—with the US comptroller seeking desperately to recover Duer's debt in anticipation of his coming bankruptcy—he suspended payments altogether. His downfall not only ruined those who had invested in his schemes but also caused a collapse in government securities. Duer and his primary associate were thrown into prison, partly to protect them from angry mobs, but outside their cell bars the crisis continued, hitting its peak in May. For a time financier Samuel Blodget—who had built his fortune in the East India trade—suspended a vital loan he had prepared for construction of the Federal City. Hamilton finally ended the crisis by shoring up government securities and restoring public confidence, but his efforts won him scant applause. For men like Jefferson, the Panic of 1792 served as a dire warning. So long as Hamilton and his friends oversaw the economy, he believed, the speculators would be in control.

Washington watched the approaching political storm with dread. With each passing day it engulfed him further, dissipating his dreams of a peaceful retirement. Conversations with the secretary of state worsened the president's anxiety. Jefferson hated Hamilton. Toward Washington, he paradoxically adopted an attitude that combined contempt and hopefulness—contempt for the president's inability to discern Hamilton's nefarious schemes, suggesting feeble-mindedness; and hope that Washington would wake up and side with the angels. Jefferson recorded his private conversations with the president with an eye toward self-vindication, while possibly twisting or exaggerating Washington's words so that, if he failed to come around, readers could assume it was because of weakness of mind.

In a private exchange on February 29, Jefferson recorded Washington as whining that "he really felt himself growing old, his bodily health less firm, his memory, always bad, becoming worse, and perhaps other faculties of his mind shewing a decay to others of which he was insensible himself." Jefferson by contrast posed as a trusty public servant, warning eloquently that the Hamiltonians were erecting a corrupt edifice "contrived, for deluging the states with papermoney instead of gold & silver, for withdrawing our citizens from the pursuits of commerce, manufactures, buildings, & other branches of useful industry, to occupy themselves & their capitals in a species of gambling, destructive of morality, & which had introduced it's poison into the government itself." Washington might well have recorded these conversations differently; but his worry was real.[2]

The storm's first lightning strike came in the form of a long letter from Jefferson to the president on May 23, 1792. The secretary of state began by acknowledging Washington's desire to retire. Under less worrisome national circumstances, he said, he would encourage him to step down for his own benefit. But now, Jefferson warned, "the public mind is no longer so confident and serene." Danger was afoot—Hamilton's policies pointed toward national bankruptcy and the return of monarchical government. The jeopardy originated, Jefferson contended, in a public debt that had been "artificially created" and then not only sustained but also increased to a level "greater than we can possibly pay." The "accumulation of debt has taken forever out of our power those easy sources of revenue," he continued, that would otherwise enrich the country. Washington, also averse to debt, might well have seen merit in the argument, although it explicitly condemned Hamilton's rotating debt system.[3]

The secretary of state then turned to taxes. Instead of reserving taxation—particularly the "odious" excise—only for "extraordinary calls" such as war, the government placed the people under a constant strain which "produces clamour, and will produce evasion." Their unrest would eventually force the government to react by exerting coercive control over the whole country—all because of the need to service the ongoing debt through taxation. And now,

Jefferson raged, the government was beginning to transfer its debt overseas. The inevitable result would be for hard currency to flow outward while the United States printed paper money to cover up a massive loss of real wealth. Rascals like Duer would speculate in paper money that was "barren & useless," drawing money away from "commerce & agriculture" where it would have had a fruitful impact. Using Washington's own language of a moral economy, Jefferson warned that the result would be to encourage "vice & idleness instead of industry & morality."[4]

Jefferson was only getting started. "That the ultimate object of all this," he thundered, "is to prepare the way for a change, from the present republican form of government, to that of a monarchy of which the English constitution is to be the model." Already he observed the growing "corruption of the legislature" by "Monarchical federalists" who used monetary policy to carry out their insidious plots. Though Jefferson did not mention Hamilton by name, his target was obvious.[5]

The conclusion was particularly jarring. "I am perfectly aware of the oppression under which your present office lays your mind," Jefferson told Washington, "& of the ardor with which you pant for retirement to domestic life. but there is sometimes an eminence of character on which society have such peculiar claims as to controul the predilection of the individual for a particular walk of happiness, & restrain him to that alone arising from the present & future benedictions of mankind. this seems to be your condition, & the law imposed on you by providence in forming your character, & fashioning the events on which it was to operate: and it is to motives like these, & not to personal anxieties of mine or others who have no right to call on you for sacrifices, that I appeal from your former determination [to retire] & urge a revisal of it." If Washington could just see the nation through the current "crisis," he could retire in "one or two" years.[6]

Fortunately for the president's peace of mind, he did not receive this letter for over two months. Jefferson directed it to Mount Vernon, which Washington had just left, and it only reached him in Philadelphia in July. Then there was no avoiding it. On July 10, openly distraught, he engaged Jefferson in a grueling conversation. In Jefferson's account, the president complained that "the subject was painful, to wit his remaining in office which that letter solicited." His wish to retire, he said, was "sincere," and he well knew that if he returned for another term, quitting before its end would be out of the question. Washington feared that other men would say that his stated longing to retire was "mere affectation, & that he was like other men, when once in office he could not quit it."[7]

Making an unusual admission even in private conversation—if Jefferson transcribed it accurately—the president confessed that "he was sensible too of a decay of his hearing [and] perhaps his other faculties might fall off & he not be sensible of it." Shifting apparently from sorrow to anger, Washington fretted that attacks on federalism by Jefferson and his friends "had been carried a great deal too far," and that there was no monarchist plot. Indeed, if anyone was fomenting monarchism it was Jefferson's own allies like shock journalist Philip Freneau, whose fulminations against the excise would generate unrest leading to "a separation of the union, the most dreadful of all calamities," and provoke an authoritarian reaction. Freneau's implications in his paper that Washington was "too careless to attend to" or "too stupid to understand" the Hamiltonian economic measures he had signed were particularly infuriating. Washington had never, he insisted, put his name to any legislation that he did not regard on the whole as beneficial. That included, he said pointedly, the Bank of the United States. He had never seen a logical argument against it. The American people, he contended, were "contented & happy"—if only Jefferson and his friends would stop trying to stir them up.[8]

The exchange became testy. "A considerable squadron" of Hamilton supporters in Congress, Jefferson insisted, was composed of northerners "devoted to the paper & stockjobbing interest." It was from them that the cancer of corruption spread in the form of a "legislature legislating for their own interests in opposition to those of the people." Washington's rejoinder failed to impress the secretary of state, whose pen dripped sarcasm as he later recorded the conversation. The government "had not increased the debt, for that all of it was honest debt," and the excise was "one of the best laws" imaginable, he put down the president as exclaiming. Jefferson then bemoaned having agreed to the federal assumption of state debts, which prevented them from being paid in a way "acceptable to the people, by a direct tax in the South, & an excise in the North." Still then, Washington fired back, the debts "would be paid by the people." At which point, "finding him really approving the treasury system[,] I avoided entering into argument with him on those points," Jefferson gave up in disgust and left the room.[9]

A shaken Washington returned to Mount Vernon, seeking the soothing embrace of his farms as he mulled the country's predicament. For about a week he stayed entirely away from his desk, if the absence of letters from this period is any indication. Instead he probably rode about the estate, consulting with overseers and studying his growing crops as harvest-time approached. Unfortunately the rest period failed to clear his mind adequately, for when he finally returned to his study and took up his pen he committed a regrettable blunder. Writing a "private & confidential" letter to Hamilton on July 29, Washington presented Jefferson's objections as laid out point by point in his May 23 letter. Without actually naming the secretary of state, the president disingenuously claimed to have gathered his material from various individuals "as well as my memory serves me." Continuing in the same indirect vein, he affected to seek Hamilton's feedback only as an information-gathering exercise, "wishing to have before me *explanations* of as well as the *complaints* on public measures in which the public interest, harmony and peace is so deeply concerned."[10]

The letter was astonishingly naïve, especially for a politician as experienced as the president. In earlier debates over Hamilton's policies, Washington had passed his subordinates' letters back and forth with their full knowledge and consent, as a matter of course. The situation now, with the secretaries of state and the Treasury literally at each other's throats and his own intellectual prowess under attack, was quite different. Although Washington attempted to maintain secrecy, his appeal to Hamilton only reinforced—to contemporaries and posterity—the perception that he did not in fact understand his own administration's economic policies, and needed an expert to explain them. Perhaps he really did believe that his mental faculties were declining. More charitably, Washington's letter constituted an acknowledgment that a major political blow-up was approaching, and that he would probably have to remain in office to face it down. From that angle his continued service would appear as an act of noble self-sacrifice, if not of wisdom.

Washington also succeeded in completely infuriating Hamilton. In a long response recapitulating his policies and denouncing his critics, the secretary of the Treasury growled that "I cannot be entirely patient under charges, which impeach the integrity of my public motives or conduct." Washington tried to calm his deputy even as his own fears grew that a spirit of faction was bent on tearing the country apart. What this spirit threatened most was prosperity.[11]

Turning to Jefferson in anguished appeal, he wrote on August 23: "How unfortunate, and how much is it to be regretted then, that whilst we are encompassed on all sides with avowed enemies & insidious friends, that internal dissentions should be harrowing & tearing our vitals." Paranoid convictions that political opponents were enemies of mankind rather than comrades with different points of view made compromise impossible. Without that, government could not function. "Without more charity for the opinions & acts of one another in Governmental matters," he chided, "I believe it will be difficult, if not impracticable, to manage the Reins of Government or to keep the parts of it together." As a result, "the fairest prospect of happiness & prosperity that ever was presented to man, will be lost—perhaps for ever! My earnest wish, and my fondest hope therefore is, that instead of wounding suspicions, & irritable charges, there may be liberal allowances—mutual forbearances— and temporising yieldings on *all sides.*" In a similar letter to Jefferson's ally Edmund Randolph three days later, Washington warned that political dissention would "Mar that prospect of happiness which perhaps never beamed with more effulgence upon any people under the Sun—and this too at a time when all Europe are gazing with admiration at the brightness of our prospects."[12]

He might as well have appealed to the reason and good feelings of a brawling pair of rabid dogs. Hamilton frothed that the friends of anarchy were "as inveterate as ever" and organized in a "formed party" that sought to "subvert the Government." Jefferson raged at Hamiltonian "schemes" to "demolish the republic." Refusing to continue serving as secretary of state for much longer, let alone seek the presidency, Jefferson warned ominously that "I will not suffer my retirement to be clouded by the slanders of a man [Hamilton] whose history, from the moment at which history can stoop to notice him, is a tissue of machinations against the liberty of the country which has not only recieved and given him bread, but heaped it's honors on his head."[13]

Washington knew what that meant—ostensibly retired at Monticello, Jefferson and his friends would continue to wage destructive war through the press. From then on Jefferson—transfixed by nightmare visions of monarchists slithering out of the woodwork even though Washington insisted that there were not "ten men" in the country of that cast of mind—firmly resisted all further appeals. His inveteracy left Washington with no choice but to listen when Hamilton beseeched him not to "leave the business unfinished and in danger of being undone" and, instead, remain in office a "year or two more" in order to permanently establish "public Credit and public Order." Even Madison suggested that another term in office would "give such a tone & firmness to the Government as would secure it against danger" from faction.[14]

Surrounded by angry men, Washington turned to a woman in his moment of crisis. Elizabeth Willing Powel and her husband, Samuel, the latter a former mayor of Philadelphia and a founder of the University of Pennsylvania, were close family friends. Over the years Washington increasingly turned to Willing Powel as a sort of confessor. On November 15 the couple visited the president in Philadelphia, where he engaged her in an emotional conversation, pouring out his worries for the country and himself. Neither recorded their words, but clearly the topic uppermost on Washington's mind was whether he should return for a second term.

Two days after they parted, she penned a deeply thought letter that may finally have made up his mind. Her arguments appealed not to his own prestige but to the welfare of the American people, and the essential task of preserving the economic system he had erected for their future prosperity. The "Repose of Millions" depended on his return, she declared. If he departed, antifederalists would use his resignation "as an Argument for dissolving the Union, and would urge that You, from Experience, had found the present System a bad one, and had, artfully, withdrawn from it that you might not be crushed under its Ruins." "For Gods sake," she concluded, do not abandon the people's "Welfare" for ease in retirement.[15]

A confluence of people and forces convinced Washington to return to public service. Jefferson and Hamilton—bitter enemies ironically working in concert to keep the president in office—succeeded in winning him over not so much from the content of their arguments as from the threat their feud posed to the nation. Willing Powel capped it all by pointing out Washington's duty to sacrifice his own welfare for that of the people in order to secure national prosperity.

Washington also could not help wondering how the nations of Europe would react to a scene of deepening political chaos. At worst, they might swoop in to reclaim part or all of their old North American possessions; at the least, their lack of confidence in the durability of the American experiment would wreck the international credit he had worked so hard to establish, imperiling foreign loans and damaging the financial system. With what strength remained to him, he would once again have to serve as the nation's linchpin. This time, though, he acted not just with a sense of reluctance but with a deep bitterness that would mar his second term. Henceforward his efforts would have one primary focus—secure internal and external peace and stability, above all, as the foundation of prosperity.

---

WASHINGTON TOOK THE OATH OF OFFICE for his second term as president of the United States in the Senate chamber on March 4, 1793. A month later he went to the circus with Samuel and Elizabeth Powel, forgetting his worries as he marveled at the equestrian demonstrations. Despite all the drama of the previous months, there was no immediate political explosion. Unlike in his first term, when he had communicated with his secretaries and ministers largely through writing or informal conversation, in his second term Washington brought his Cabinet together in regular meetings similar in format to his wartime councils of war. Jefferson remained committed to resigning his post as secretary of state at the end of 1793, and there was no face-off between him and Hamilton.

Discussions over the economy remained largely muted. The financial panics that Jefferson had predicted in a system allegedly beholden to speculators did not materialize. Washington brooded about debt, telling Congress on December 3, 1793, that "No pecuniary consideration is more urgent, than the regular redemption and discharge of the public debt: on none can delay be more injurious, or an œconomy of time more valuable." However, aside from a brief spat with Hamilton over the president's decision to discharge part of the remaining French debt in kind (through the delivery of American flour and other commodities to France and Hispaniola), this faded as a subject of debate. The final payments would be made in 1795, allowing Washington to proclaim proudly to the House on January 19, 1796, that the national war debt had been liquidated—though enemies would contend it had really only been transferred.[16]

Tax did not fade as a subject of contention. On December 13, 1790, in his first report on the public credit, Hamilton had recommended duties on imported spirits as well as a national tax on domestic spirits. After extended debate Washington signed the measures into law on March 3, 1791. Revenue districts were established in each of the fourteen states, and the president was tasked with appointing supervisors and revenue inspectors within each district. Drudging through the exacting process of choosing candidates in consultation with Hamilton, he produced a list of names and appointed them by executive order on March 15. With this tedious but necessary business over, he turned to other matters.

By early 1792, unfortunately, it became apparent that tax collection had faltered because of local resistance in many districts. It was worst in the South and above all in the isolated mountainous regions of western Pennsylvania, where feisty recent Scots-Irish immigrants complained that the excise discriminated against small-scale distillers. The frequent insinuations by Jefferson and his allies that the excise might constitute a *casus belli* justifying widespread rebellion made Washington particularly sensitive to the unrest. On September 15, 1792, he issued a proclamation—moderately worded so that he could convince a recalcitrant Jefferson to sign it—ordering the unruly Pennsylvanians to "desist."[17]

They did not desist. Through 1793 the resistance continued to increase, until by the beginning of 1794 collection had become all but impossible in many districts. Revenue officials were beaten and humiliated, and no local law enforcement existed to restrain the disaffected. Radical newspapers egged them on, pointing to the French Terror as an example worthy of emulation. By July Washington was convinced that he faced an incipient major insurgency, and determined to quash it instantly. For him tax collection was a basic function of the federal government, and maintaining the public order a fundamental duty. To allow armed civilians to take matters into their own hands was an incitement to mob rule in which the strong preyed upon the weak and beneficent commerce and industry disappeared.

The issue at question, the president proclaimed as he prepared to march on the insurgents on September 25, 1794, was "whether a small portion of the United States shall dictate to the whole union, and at the expence of those, who desire peace." Leading his assembled army to Carlisle, Pennsylvania, before turning it over to his old wartime comrade "Light Horse" Harry Lee (Hamilton remained in the background), Washington demonstrated his personal commitment to the cause of federal authority, public order, and, above all, peace. The brewing rebellion dissipated.[18]

On the frontier, tensions continued to grow in the wake of Harmar's and St. Clair's defeats. Their continuance threatened the fabric of internal commerce, trade, and westward navigation—and endangered national unity. Washington still hoped that the establishment of peaceful commerce would heal all wounds, telling Congress of his conviction that if Native American trade developed "under regulations calculated to protect them from imposition and extortion, it's influence in cementing their interests with our's could not but be considerable." He gladly approved "An Act to regulate Trade and Intercourse with the Indian Tribes" on March 1, 1793. As events would demonstrate, however, the root of the white–Native American contest was far more intractable than Washington would allow himself to realize. General Anthony Wayne's victory at the Battle of Fallen Timbers in August 1794 bought only a temporary peace. Though he dreamed of peaceful relations, Washington's Native American policies never came close to solving the essentially insoluble.[19]

Foreign affairs assumed a far more threatening aspect, so much so that they came close to consuming the president's second administration. The French Revolution of 1789 had initially appeared as a welcome event. Washington thought it the inevitable outcome of the "abuse of the finances" of France by the nation's prerevolutionary government, and hoped that a moderate Constitutional monarchy would inaugurate a term of stability and peace. Instead, France spiraled into an ever-worsening cycle of violence, symbolically culminating in the execution of King Louis XVI on January 21, 1793. This event and the Reign of Terror that followed—a bloodbath in which the guillotine claimed tens of thousands of victims through 1794—impressed Washington as a perversion of the fundamental principles of law and justice even as it delighted his radical countrymen. He worried less about the spread of the Terror to the

United States, however, than that French sympathizers would goad the nation into a war with France's enemy, Great Britain. And war was bad for business.[20]

Hope, not fear, nevertheless inspired Washington's quest for peace. "If we are permitted to improve, without interruption, the great advantages which nature & circumstances have placed within our reach," he told David Humphreys on March 23, 1793, "many years will not revolve before we may be ranked not only among the most respectable, but among the happiest people on this globe." The advances of the past four years had been astonishing, and the president painted an idyllic portrait of a nation at work. Everywhere Americans were engaged "in objects of the greatest public utility," building canals, roads, bridges, and houses. Such "enterprizes of individuals shew at once," he enthused, "what are the happy effects of personal exertions in a Country where equal laws & equal rights prevail."[21]

The "interruption" he sought to avoid was war. And the "equal laws & equal rights" he sought to maintain were in direct contradiction to what he saw happening in France. He stated the same thing somewhat more explicitly to the Earl of Buchan on April 22: "I believe it is the sincere wish of United America to have nothing to do with the Political intrigues, or the squabbles of European Nations; but on the contrary, to exchange Commodities & live in peace & amity with all the inhabitants of the earth. . . . Under such a system if we are allowed to pursue it, the Agriculture and Mechanical Arts; the wealth and population of these States will encrease with that degree of rapidity as to baffle all calculation." This image of American exceptionalism based on peace and industry was central to his vision of future growth.[22]

The British and French governments, indifferent to Washington's dreams of American prosperity, immensely complicated his efforts to stand aloof. The British in particular behaved arrogantly and committed some atrocities against American shipping. They also instigated Native American unrest on the frontier. Both Great Britain and France, however, enacted competing commercial embargoes that hampered American trade, and both dispatched commerce raiders to the high seas. British and French military vessels frequently entered American ports for repairs, or to purchase supplies and recruit volunteers.

The French, moreover, courted American antifederalists and denounced Washington's refusal to repay what they saw as a moral debt for their aid during the American Revolution. Many Americans shared that sense of indebtedness. Most were content to rail against Washington's administration, or to mutter darkly of regime change. Others, though, including the well-intentioned Harry Lee, chose to offer their services to the French as volunteers. Washington was able to talk Lee out of sailing for France. He knew, though, that popular support for France, if left unchecked, could drag the country into a war that he sought to avoid at nearly any cost.

The alternative to Washington's wished-for peaceful future was almost too terrible to contemplate. Joining the French, who at this time were practically isolated, would effectively if not formally entail a declaration of war on most of the nations of Europe. At a single stroke it would not just damage but *eliminate* American overseas commerce, devastating the economy. Debt would explode, and the currency would collapse. Goaded by the British, Native American tribes would ravage the frontier. Political unrest could tear the young Constitution apart. Worst of all, the British could launch punitive expeditions against the American mainland (as they would during the War of 1812). Bereft of a navy—thanks to many of the same men who now clamored wildly for a war with Great Britain—the United States was utterly incapable of defending its shores. Incredibly, none of this seems to have occurred to the antifederalists who demanded an open alliance with France. Washington, though, could foresee the consequences if he failed to act swiftly to defuse pro-war sentiment.

This sense of urgency informed Washington's neutrality proclamation of April 22, 1793. In it, he declared impartiality in the current European conflict and warned American citizens not to provide material aid to any of the warring nations. Any who did so in violation of international law would forfeit the protection of the United States government and render themselves liable to prosecution.

Jefferson—still secretary of state, albeit a lame duck given his intention to resign at year's end—opposed the proclamation as unnecessary and a violation of the rights of Americans to do as they wished. Hamilton, though, strongly supported it, as did most other members of the Cabinet. British and French warships, already anchored in eastern ports and trading with American civilians (as well as fighting with each other), tested the proclamation in practice just as antifederalists did in theory. Hamilton's assistance proved vital in identifying and prosecuting domestic transgressors, and in formulating the legal arguments to defend the proclamation (he leaned heavily on a seminal 1758 book by Swiss philosopher Emmerich de Vattel, titled *The Law of Nations*). Hundreds of American merchants and tradesmen from cities like Baltimore and Philadelphia signaled their support by signing formal addresses endorsing neutrality. Though they conceded that contraband trade with the British and French "might serve the interests of their commerce for a time," it would prove ruinous in the long term.[23]

The Neutrality Proclamation did not of itself ensure peace. Washington hoped to follow it up with a diplomatic offensive aimed at securing new commercial treaties with the major European nations. France preempted him with a treaty proposal borne by new Minister to the United States Edmond Charles Genêt. Unfortunately, the document that he submitted after his arrival in America on April 8, 1793, did not come close to anything the president had in mind. While entering a full commercial embrace, the minister suggested, France and the United States should also "punish those powers [Great Britain and Spain] who still keep up an exclusive colonial and commercial system, by declaring that their vessels shall not be received in the ports of the contracting parties." In exchange for declaring an embargo against Great Britain—tantamount to a formal declaration of war—Genêt offered territories that France did not control: Spanish-held Louisiana and British-ruled Canada.[24]

Genêt's proposal was an imperialist's dream and a fool's bargain. France, he knew, could do nothing to assist the United States in claiming those territories—the Americans would have to conquer them on their own. In reality, all he could offer was privileged trading status with France—trade that would be impossible to conduct since the British Navy dominated the seas—in exchange for an all-out American attack against Great Britain and Spain. Washington never remotely considered the bargain. Genêt nevertheless remained stateside for several more months, threatening to take his case to the American people and insinuating in the press that the presidential office was tainted with British gold. Washington pressed hard for Genêt's recall until another change of French government in 1794 ended his ministerial status. Ironically, since Genêt's return to Paris would almost certainly have meant his execution at the hands of the new, more radical administration, Washington and Attorney General Edmund Randolph allowed him to remain—quietly—in the United States.

In the short term the Genêt affair helped to vindicate America's neutrality policy, which the Cabinet enumerated in a formal set of rules in August 1793. Congress passed a Neutrality Act in June 1794. In the longer term, the affair helped Washington to make up his mind about whether American economic interests lay more with France or with Great Britain. On the surface, France seemed the better partner. He had dreamed of a broad expansion of Franco-American trade after the war. The French seemed to want to be friends, while the British, with their impressment of American sailors and confiscation of cargoes, seemed indifferent. The brutal violence unleashed by the Terror, how-ever, raised the prospect that close association with France might cause the infection of political radicalism to spread to the United States. If a king could end his life on the guillotine, so could a president.

Washington also looked beneath the surface. Current British policies to-ward the United States were infuriating, but a possible change of ministry to the friendlier Whigs under Charles James Fox promised a more enlightened Anglo-American relationship. At the end of January 1794, Tobias Lear ob-served the opening of Parliament and noted approvingly that "very honorable mention was made of" Washington's recent speech to Congress "as well as of America in general." "Mr Fox in particular," Lear informed the president, "dwelt with enthusiastic energy on the—virtues—the talents—and the pe-culiar good fortune of General Washington. He drew, with much warmth, a lively comparison between the conduct of the American Governmt and that of this Country—much to the disadvantage of the latter. In an animated voice he cried—'All the Kings of Europe when compared with the great & the good Washington appear—small—and I had almost said contemptable'; but says he, in a lower voice, 'I *must* except our own King.'" Lear felt that Fox's "words strike my very soul—I wished to have embraced him for them." Spectacles such as this convinced Washington that British official policies did not reflect the views of their people—and that change was possible if not imminent.[25]

Washington's relationship with Arthur Young and his friends, as well as Lear's reports, had awakened him to Great Britain's economic potential. Since opening his correspondence with Young and other British agriculturalists and entrepreneurs, he had begun to sense a growing community of interest between the United States and Great Britain. The British, already decades ahead of the rest of the world in their agricultural practices and productivity, were also in the first stages of revolutionizing their industry. They had much to offer, both now and in the future.

Lear also had communicated the strongly pro-American sympathies of British manufacturers. The French, by contrast, could offer very little. Since 1783 Washington had grown aware of the backwardness of French agriculture and industry. He had also come to recognize the poverty of France's circumscribed colonial possessions relative to Great Britain's far-flung empire in Asia and the Caribbean. Finally, Great Britain possessed a magnificent navy with a global reach, while the French Navy projected little beyond the mid-Atlantic and the Mediterranean. The British were fearsome enemies—but also valuable friends.

Washington's growing sense that America's interests lay with Great Britain unfortunately coincided in the spring of 1794 with a nasty uptick in British assaults on American commerce. Though he tried to resist popular anti-British sentiment, it demanded an outlet. Prodded by Madison and Randolph—now secretary of state—the president agreed to a series of thirty-day embargoes against the British.

The effects were immediate—not on the British, but on the Americans. The first embargo in April 1794 forced hundreds of Yankee seamen out of work, as Washington learned when he watched them parade angrily through the streets of Philadelphia. The embargo also hit Mount Vernon, forcing him to temporarily shut down his gristmill. Merchants came close to panic. The president's sister Betty Washington Lewis wrote that "we are Extreamly alarm'd here for fear of a War the Merchants here say that it is Inevitable I Expect it is to raise the Price of Goods which has allredy taken Place in regard to Westindia goods, I wish to here from you as I then shall be satisfied of the truth of it, I was in hopes I should never live to see any more of those troublesome times."[26]

Worried that war was imminent despite all his efforts to avoid it, Washington argued for military preparedness. Unfortunately, he was still opposed by men who clamored for war with Great Britain but denounced the creation of a standing army or navy as an assault on their liberties. The president attempted to point out the obvious to Congress, lecturing that body on December 3, 1793: "There is a rank due to the United States among Nations, which will be withheld, if not absolutely lost, by the reputation of weakness. If we desire to avoid insult, we must be able to repel it; if we desire to secure peace, one of the most powerful instruments of our rising prosperity, it must be known, that we are at all times ready for War." Finally, on March 27, 1794, Congress passed "An Act to provide a Naval Armament" that created a United States Navy. It authorized only six ships, however, and on land the president could only build arsenals, improve coastal fortifications, and tinker with the militia system. As before, the United States remained helpless against foreign enemies.[27]

With relations with Great Britain unraveling rapidly, Hamilton dispatched to the president on April 14 a dire warning of future calamity. Pro-war partisans, he said, subverted reason to their emotional vindictiveness against the British. The acts of economic reprisal that they proposed in Congress and the state assemblies—now including sequestration of British debts—would likely lead to war. In that, there would be less to fear from an actual British invasion of the United States than from their all-out assault on America's now-burgeoning international commerce. They would seize American vessels worldwide and hold them hostage until the United States surrendered to prevent economic catastrophe. Even if a full embargo on British commerce did not lead to war, it would wreck "our public and mercantile credit," depriving the United States of critical supplies not available elsewhere. "It gives a sudden and violent blow to our revenue," Hamilton concluded, "which cannot easily if at all be repaired from other resources." The destruction of commerce would undermine the tax base, perhaps bringing "the Treasury to an absolute stoppage of payment—an event which would cut up credit by the roots." With imports and exports alike halted and credit destroyed, the currency would collapse as it had during wartime. Altogether, "these circumstances united may occasion the most dangerous dissatisfaction & disorders in the community and may drive the government to a disgraceful retreat."[28]

Washington acted boldly to head off the disaster. On April 16, 1794, he informed Congress that he had decided to nominate John Jay as an extraordinary envoy to Great Britain, "as peace ought to be pursued with unremitted zeal, before the last resource, which has so often been the scourge of Nations, and cannot fail to check the advanced prosperity of the United States, is contemplated." A suspicious Senate approved Jay's nomination on April 19 by a vote of 18 to 8.[29]

A forty-nine-year-old New Yorker, Jay was one of Washington's oldest and most trusted political associates. During the war he had served as president of the Continental Congress and minister to Spain, and had negotiated the 1783 Treaty of Paris that ended the war. After the war he had helped author the *Federalist Papers,* and since 1789 he had served as first chief justice of the US Supreme Court. No man was better qualified to negotiate a treaty. Armed with instructions composed by Hamilton under Washington's guidance, Jay sailed for Great Britain and after extended negotiation signed a treaty on November 19, 1794.

It was remarkable that Jay secured any concessions at all, for he had little leverage to bargain with. The British agreed—as they were already treaty-bound to do—to withdraw from their posts on American soil, and granted limited additional rights for American merchants to do business in British Asian and Caribbean colonies. All other points of contention would be submitted to arbitration. For Washington, the treaty's details were almost beside the point. The important thing was that it secured a desperately needed term of peace, and took steps toward establishing a community of commerce between the United States and the most powerful—and economically advanced—nation on earth.

The Jay Treaty was only the first of three important treaties that the Washington administration negotiated, all to the same purpose. A Treaty of Peace and Commerce with the dey of Algiers signed on September 5, 1795, provided additional security to American merchantmen in the Mediterranean and Atlantic. More significantly, Washington dispatched Thomas Pinckney—a South Carolinian then acting as the American minister to Great Britain—to Madrid to negotiate a treaty with Spain. In December 1793 a collection of citizens living west of Appalachia had petitioned the president that they were "Entitled by Nature and by stipulation to the undisturbed Navigation of the river Mississippi and consider it a right Inseparable from their prosperity." Earlier attempts to secure this right by coming to terms with the Spaniards in 1785–1786 and 1792 had failed. This one succeeded. The Treaty of San Lorenzo, signed on October 27, 1795, allowed free American navigation through New Orleans and all the way up the mighty Mississippi. The treaty's terms fostered the creation of a Continental market that could grow and develop despite turmoil abroad, and established the first—admittedly tenuous—strands of global trade and commerce between the United States and the vast Spanish empire.[30]

The conclusion of these three important treaties, which collectively secured American commerce in a time of worsening global conflict, was an outstanding accomplishment. But not all Americans saw them in a positive light. The Jay Treaty, which barely passed through the Senate on June 24, outraged antifederalists who thought it a devil's bargain that bought peace at the price of opening the door for a return of British rule. Jefferson and his supporters, now including Madison, savagely attacked the administration in the press. Again there was talk of betrayal, and of monarchist plots. This time, though, antifederalists did more than just talk.

Opposition to the government emerged by the grass roots and spread like a prairie blaze. Community assemblies passed resolutions denouncing the government. Mobs burnt effigies of Jay, and stoned Hamilton when he dared to appear at a public event in New York City. There was talk of the guillotine. Washington enjoyed no immunity from the frenzy. Jefferson's friends in the press mercilessly attacked him as (at best) a fool and (at worst) a closet royalist. With full knowledge of what they were doing, radical journalists republished as genuine letters a series of wartime forgeries that made Washington appear to despise Congress and yearn for the return of King George III. Slanderous accusations appeared in the antifederalist *Aurora* on October 23, 1795, falsely accusing Washington of overdrawing $1,037 from his expense account during his first term in office with Hamilton's connivance. The paper denounced the president's "abuse of power" and "political hypocrisy," and compared him to Caesar and Oliver Cromwell.[31]

The turmoil deeply troubled Washington, but not out of concern for his own grip on power or his safety. Rather, he worried that political factionalism would weaken the government, destroy public order, wreck the national credit, and derail the economy. To Patrick Henry he wrote on October 9, 1795, that "a crisis is approaching, that must, if it cannot be arrested, Soon decide whether order and good Government Shall be preserved, or anarchy and confusion ensue." Though popular clamor continued to rage for many months, to his everlasting credit Washington stayed the course. None of his presidential acts did more to secure the nation's future prosperity than his successful efforts to keep the United States—a mere nestling in a world plagued by fearsome raptors—at peace. He expressed astonishment in a letter to his Scottish friend James Anderson on Christmas Eve, 1795, "that the earth should be moistened with human gore, instead of the refreshing streams which the shedders of it might become instruments to lead over its plains, to delight & render profitable our labours." In America, thanks to Washington, the streams continued to flow fresh and clear.[32]

In 1796, the usual cast of characters began wheedling Washington about a third term in office. If he would just stay on a few more years, they begged, the nation's fortunes could rest secure. Only he could keep political factions under control, and steer the nation safely through the shoals of global uncertainty. Washington did not even begin to consider their pleas. He was tired, and though still mentally vital he was certainly beyond his prime. One of the effects of the constant political attacks on the government during his second term had been to scare away qualified candidates for office. By 1796, his Cabinet aside from Hamilton was mostly staffed by well-intentioned political mediocrities. In these later years there is no question that the president leaned heavily on Hamilton—partly because he lacked other talented, energetic men whom he could consult. Washington knew both that he had reached his physical limits and that fresh faces were necessary.

Hope filled Washington's mind as he prepared his farewell address. Published on September 19 as a message "To the People of the United States," it expressed both gratitude for their trust and optimism for their future. He warned against the perils of disunion, but exhorted that "The name of American, which belongs to you, in your national capacity, must always exalt the just pride of Patriotism, more than any appellation derived from local discriminations." The source of that union—as he had long believed and repeatedly proclaimed—was commerce, which created the great community of interest that would bind the nation together.[33]

Not content to leave it at that, Washington laid out point by point the "commanding motives" for union, in an "unrestrained intercourse" of commerce that would benefit north and south, east and west. Together, they would create "an indissoluble community of Interest as *one Nation*." While "every part of our country thus feels an immediate and particular Interest in Union, all the parts combined cannot fail to find in the united mass of means and efforts greater strength, greater resource, proportionably greater security from external danger." A strong central government helped protect the union, and as such it should be supported and obeyed. But it was not the *source* of union. That depended, alone and entirely, on the people—and not on their words, but on the bonds of mutual interest. The antidote to faction was commerce. And commerce both rested upon and fostered "virtue" and "morality."[34]

Washington could not resist one more exhortation to "cherish public credit" as the "source of strength and security." He warned against the "accumulation of debt," and reminded that all obligations must be discharged faithfully. To that end, he pointed out, "it is essential that you should practically bear in mind, that towards the payment of debts there must be Revenue; that to have Revenue there must be taxes; and that no taxes can be devised which are not more or less inconvenient and unpleasant."[35]

Nowhere, though, did the president suggest that the government's purview extended further than to establish the conditions best suited for natural industry to thrive. The people paid taxes so that they might build their prosperity in freedom. As part of its task, the government must foster "commercial relations" with the world and "Observe good faith and justice towards all Nations," but remain scrupulously clear of entanglements abroad. A wise foreign policy furthered the national defense and protected international commerce, but did not make the mistake of attempting to dictate terms to a process that worked most effectively on its own. "Commercial policy" should not go beyond "consulting the natural course of things; diffusing and diversifying by gentle means the streams of Commerce, but forcing nothing." Abroad as at home, government should let the people do the real work.[36]

There was indeed much work remaining to be done. Washington never claimed to have accomplished more than to help set the nation steadily on its feet and point the way forward. What happened next depended on the American people. Had he not believed in their capacity to create prosperity he would never have assumed public office, let alone relinquished it. Now, though, he had his personal interests to tend to. In retirement, he would speak metaphorically of resting under his own vine and fig tree. But he could never resist looking forward. Far from shutting down and relaxing, he strove to leave one final legacy behind—a prosperous estate that could provide security for his family and offer a lasting example for the future. Looking toward Mount Vernon, Washington rolled up his sleeves.

# CHAPTER NINE

# THE ROAD HOME

NO TRUMPETED FANFARES HERALDED GEORGE WASHINGTON'S retirement from the presidency on March 4, 1797. "Much such a day as yesterday in all respects," he wrote in his diary, referring to the weather, which was crisp and clear. He spent much of his remaining time in Philadelphia packing furniture and cleaning out his desk, or receiving small parting gifts such as a brace of antique Turkish pistols from a local wine merchant. To his old friend Elizabeth Willing Powel he sent his coach horses, in symbol of his return to the life of a humble farmer who no longer needed to parade ostentatiously. Washington's avowed purpose of spending the remainder of his life "seated under my own Vine and fig tree . . . in peaceful retirement, making political pursuits yield to the more rational amusement of cultivating the Earth" nevertheless belied his intention to get back to work—and hard. At his request, the experimental farmer William Hamilton dispatched a shipment of plants timed to meet the former president upon his arrival at Mount Vernon. Washington also sent Scottish agriculturalist Sir John Sinclair some pamphlets on the use of manure accompanied by a letter musing hopefully on the establishment of a board of agriculture in the United States. True to form, he was looking ahead, not behind.[1]

George and Martha left Philadelphia on March 9 for their journey home. They were buffeted by a blustery winter wind, and Martha suffered from a cold she had caught before they left. While she coughed and sneezed by his side, George worried about a bundle of her correspondence that he had accidentally left behind in his presidential desk (Willing Powel saved the letters for him). Still, the couple's mood was relaxed as Mount Vernon came into view. They both liked to be busy, and there was plenty to do. "We are like the beginners of a new establishment," George wrote to Willing Powel on March 26, "having every thing in a manner to do. Houses and every thing else to repair. Rooms to Paint—Paper—Whitewash &ca &ca—But although these things are troublesome, & disagreeable as they will involve us in a good deal of litter & dirt, yet they will serve to give exercise to the mind & body." Within a few days of stepping out of his carriage, he was probably feeling better than he had for years.[2]

The estate had not been totally neglected, since he had visited it regularly during his presidency. The farm managers and overseers who had managed it in his absence, however, were an uneven lot. He had been forced to fire some of them for incompetence. In 1793, he had let Anthony Whitting go after three years because he "drank freely—kept bad company at my house and in Alexandria—& was a very debauched person. . . . [T]his I take to be the true cause why Mr Whiting did not look more scrupulously into the conduct of the Overseers, & more minutely into the smaller matters belonging to the Farms." Other managers were well-intentioned but could barely understand the detailed instructions he plied them with.[3]

In desperation, Washington resorted to platitudes—some derived from the Scottish Highlanders whose legendary thrift he so admired. "There is one rule—& a golden one it is—that nothing should be bought that can be made, or done without," he had lectured Whitting before firing him. "People are often ruined before they are aware of the danger, by buying every thing they think they want; conceiving them to be trifles—without adverting to a scotch addage—than which nothing in nature is more true—'that many mickles make a muckle.'" "Frugality & oeconomy are undoubtedly commendable and all that is required," he told another. Washington often summed up by brandishing one of his favorite adages: "A penny saved, is a penny got." He might as well have quoted Chaucer for all the good it did.[4]

Washington had acquired a competent new farm manager shortly before he retired, hiring Scottish farmer James Anderson (no relation to the agricultural reformer) in October 1796. The two had their disagreements, but Anderson was a hard worker and a creative entrepreneur in his own right. Shortly after Washington returned to Mount Vernon, Anderson suggested erecting a distillery not far from the gristmill in order to produce and sell whiskey. Washington considered the proposal carefully before responding that although distilling was "a business I am entirely unacquainted with . . . from your knowledge of it and from the confidence you have in the profit to be derived from the establishment, I am disposed to enter upon one"—that is, provided "the Distillery shall not appear upon a fair estimate, to be too expensive."[5]

Anderson took to the business of planning the distillery with an enthusiasm that might have made Washington—who abhorred alcoholism—a tad suspicious. Laying out the steps toward getting production under way, the Scotsman pointed out that he would have to transfer his own abode adjacent to the distillery: "the place of Action, as most of the business will be done at that particular Spot." Fortunately, he was reliable. Construction began in the fall of 1797, with slaves and workers erecting a still house and malting house and digging a cellar for storage. Anderson oversaw the construction or purchase of the needed equipment, including troughs, boilers, and copper stills. Knowing that Washington would insist upon it, he also kept a detailed and strictly accurate account of his expenditures. There were no significant cost overruns.[6]

Washington's micromanaging oversight and continuing addiction to platitudes on thrift and economy might nevertheless have tempted Anderson at times to abandon the whole business and return to Scotland. By December construction was well advanced, but His Excellency could not refrain from chiding his farm manager for underestimating the time it took to lug tools and lumber to the construction site. "The man who does not estimate time as money will forever miscalculate," he lectured. Worse, it seemed to Washington that Anderson was trying to accomplish too many things at once, without adequate planning, and talking too much about his intentions before he got down to work. "System in all things is the soul of business," he wrote. "To deliberate maturely, & execute promptly is the way to conduct it to advantage. With me, it has always been a maxim, rather to let my designs appear from my works, than by my expressions." Anderson griped freely, and eventually told Washington directly that his constant interference had "thwarted" his plans for finishing the distillery. However tiresome his lectures may have become, however, Washington was always fair. He reassured the prickly Scotsman—and overlooked his impertinence—and the work reached a successful conclusion by the spring of 1798.[7]

The venture paid off. Anderson's care in constructing the distillery—reinforced by Washington's annoying oversight—ensured that the operation was constructed and operated economically. The general could also thank his own foresight in checking to ensure that there was a market for the distillery's product. Before granting approval for construction to commence, he had consulted his former wartime aide-de-camp John Fitzgerald—who ran his own successful molasses-distilling venture—to ascertain whether whiskey could be sold locally at a significant profit. Fitzgerald correctly assured him that it could. In 1799, the distillery produced an impressive eleven thousand gallons of whiskey that profited Washington $7,500. He passed on the distillery to his family as a going concern, renting it to his nephew Lawrence Lewis in the fall of 1799.

While Mount Vernon echoed to hammers and saws, Washington pondered his western lands and his slaves. In time he came up with a possible solution to the problems posed by both. Not many years earlier he had seized upon every opportunity to snatch up territory from Kentucky to western Pennsylvania and Ohio. The prospect of a rapid development of Potomac navigation added urgency to his campaign, and he hoped to see the fruits in his lifetime. To George Mason's son John, now director of the Potomac River Company, Washington wrote on January 2, 1798, reiterating his passionate belief in expanding western navigation: "To the United States, it holds out the desirable advantage of perhaps the most direct & easiest communication between the Waters of the Atlantic States and the Western country," while "To the Stockholders, the completion of the work promises an ample increasing, and secure interest."[8]

By the mid-1790s, though, it had become clear that the golden dream of westward expansion and commerce would not be realized for years, perhaps decades—eventually coming to fruition with the Erie Canal and other schemes. In the meantime, many clung heedlessly to the golden dream, continuing to pour money into obviously mismanaged ventures that unfortunately included the Potomac Company. When it came to business, though, Washington was no idle dreamer but a hard-headed realist. In 1796, he hatched plans to sell off his western lands and rent his outlying Mount Vernon farms. With the proceeds he hoped "to liberate a certain species of property which I possess, very repugnantly to my own feelings." He meant his slaves.[9]

Despite all of Washington's talents as an entrepreneur, enslaved men, women, and children had by their labor played a vital role in creating his wealth. Time had taught him to view their continued bondage as a grave moral injustice. It was his conception of a moral economy, though, that led him to decide that slavery as a system was not only bound to fail but would, so long as it existed, hinder the growth of national prosperity. In his farewell address, Washington had spoken of a "community of interest" that bound the country together. Echoing John Locke, he believed that men created their own wealth. Their industry enhanced their morality, and vice versa. Fundamentally, though, they produced because it was in their interest to do so. They could enjoy the fruits of their labor, invest their earnings, become more prosperous, and enrich themselves, their families, and their communities.

What incentive did the enslaved have to produce, except their masters' cruelty? As he had told Arthur Young in June 1792: "Blacks are capable of much labour, but having (I am speaking generally) no ambition to establish a *good* name, they are too regardless of a *bad* one; and of course require more of the masters eye than" did free workers. He saw the principle in action himself as, year after year, he struggled to motivate enslaved farm workers who "feel no interest in the Crop." The conclusion was inescapable: enslaved labor was not really free labor. Moreover, by undermining the basic principles of industry, such labor morally degraded not just the slaves themselves but those who owned them. That had certainly seemed true in the case of Whitting, who "finding it a little troublesome to instruct the Negros, and to compel them to the practice of *his* modes, he slided into theirs." It was for this reason above all that Washington came to believe that he needed to free them—albeit, true to the principle of interest, in a way that did the least harm either to the enslaved or to his estate.[10]

Advertisements for these land sales and rentals first appeared on February 1, 1796. Washington was not terribly particular about buyers so long as they seemed trustworthy for payments. But he was unwilling to rent out his Mount Vernon farms to just anyone. He wanted the farms not just maintained but improved. The object was not just to "make the remainder of my days . . . as free from care and trouble as possible," and "to reduce my income (be it little or much) to a certainty," but "to see my farms in the hands of a number of tenants . . . who are professed farmers, who understand and will cultivate them in the manner most approved in England." Ideally, he hoped "to get associations of farmers from the old countries, who know how (from experience & necessity) to keep the land in an improving state rather than the slovenly ones of this, who think (generally) of nothing else, but to work a field as long as it will bear any thing, and until it is run into gullies & ruined."[11]

The best farmers came from Great Britain, especially Scotland, and to them he initially directed his appeals. Washington nevertheless realized that the prospect of dozens of tidy Scottish farmers settling around Mount Vernon was far-fetched, and imagined that in their absence freed slaves could till the fields at modest rents. This would particularly have to be the case if, as he anticipated, he ran into legal obstacles that prevented him from freeing the Custis dower slaves who had in many cases intermarried with his own and produced families.

The dream remained a dream. Though Washington found purchasers for some of his western lands, they turned out without exception to be ne'er-do-wells who signed contracts but never sent a penny in payment. And although he received a few inquiries about rentals, there were no firm commitments. In 1798 English farmer Richard Parkinson inspected some of the land, only to conclude that the soil quality was too poor for his requirements. Reluctantly, then, Washington approached the end of the century with no firm plan for his estate's future.

He did not, however, sit inactive, twiddling his thumbs and waiting for rent payments. The years 1797–1799 were in fact among the most active of his life, if not necessarily the happiest. He hoped to spend the vast bulk of his time working the central Mount Vernon farms and ensuring that his remaining enterprises were passed down, profitable and unencumbered, to his heirs. However, a series of troublesome distractions—personal, local, and national—hindered his efforts to achieve these goals and sometimes even entirely prevented him from tending to business.

Though renovated, the Mount Vernon gristmill required a competent miller to run it efficiently. Unfortunately, Washington's longtime miller Joseph Davenport, who had run the operation since 1785, died suddenly in 1796. His replacement, Patrick Callahan, the general complained, was "far from being an industrious man" and demanded an increase in wages that Washington refused to grant. He *was* willing to offer a good miller annual wages of just over $166 plus "ample" food and wood, a milk cow, a cooper's shop, and a modest house near the mill. Plenty of men would have accepted such terms, but evidently no one of any ability, forcing Washington in 1799 to turn to Davenport's predecessor, William Roberts, whom he had fired back in 1785 for being "an intolerable sot." Inventor William Booker, who knew both Roberts and the general, warned Washington that the miller was still "very fond of strong drink, and when Intoxicated, is very troublesome." He had lost two wives and been thrown repeatedly into prison, all because of his alcoholism. Washington nevertheless gave Roberts a second chance after extracting from him a promise to renounce "Speretus Licquers . . . to the Day of My Death." Alas the poor man showed up at Mount Vernon in the fall of 1799 half-dead from drink and unable to work, leaving the gristmill under temporary management.[12]

Such were among the hazards of running an estate. Nothing, however, could stifle Washington's ambition to maximize his production. In addition to pestering Anderson endlessly about the distillery, the general sent him extraordinarily detailed plans for crop management, labor allocation, building, sales, and so on, enjoining him to "pursue *strictly* the means that are to carry them into effect." Every day, so far as he was able, the aging general rode the bounds of his estate, retiring in the evenings to dine, read the newspaper, and prepare accounts, reports, and other documents regarding the workings of his farms.[13]

Washington also continued to experiment vociferously with new tools and technologies. Booker had received a patent for an innovative threshing machine, and built one for Mount Vernon in the summer of 1797. It failed to work to the general's satisfaction, forcing Booker to return the following summer to repair the device. In the spring of 1798, the general learned about a new wheat scythe, or cradle, being used on the eastern shore that allowed harvesters to catch and lay the grain by hand. Intrigued, he purchased copies of the machine and paid for an expert to train his agricultural workers in its use. He also recalled a new device that he had seen at a "Manufactory of Machines for raking Meadows" in Philadelphia, and ordered a copy for Mount Vernon. Just as in the late 1760s, the estate echoed to the sounds of construction and the clack and rattle of a variety of oddly shaped machines.[14]

The ongoing construction of the Federal City continued to occupy Washington even after his retirement from the presidency. The excruciatingly slow pace of building conspired with instances of inefficiency and even corruption to infuriate him. At least, though, he could step back and leave the worst problems for President John Adams and his administration to solve. This gave Washington time to concentrate on his own investments in two lots north of the Capitol that he purchased for just over $600 in September 1798. He bought the lots purely for profit. Over the next year his contractors constructed two three-story brick houses on the lots. They performed their work so well—of course under the general's strict oversight—that he assessed the lots' total value in 1799 at "$15,000 at least."[15]

Just as the appearance of political factions marred Washington's second term, the slow but inexorable descent of the United States into involvement in international conflict marked the years that followed his retirement. This was for Washington both cause for bitter regret and bad for business. The ill-fated XYZ Affair of 1797–1798, in which French foreign minister Talleyrand demanded bribes from an American diplomatic delegation to Paris, ignited a fury of anti-French feeling in the United States. Washington joined in condemning the French government but was no war hawk; and when the Adams administration called upon him in July 1798 to take the helm of an army formed to repel an expected French invasion, he could barely conceal his disgust. Washington agreed to command the army, but only on condition that he remained at Mount Vernon until such time as an enemy force actually landed. This military absurdity—which would have left Washington entirely unprepared to command the army if an actual war (as opposed to a quasi-war) transpired—is a reflection of the desperation with which he wished to avoid conflict, both for his own and the country's sake. No invasion occurred, but at the time the general bitterly begrudged the many hours he had to waste on routine army administration in the waning years of his life.

Business and politics did not distract Washington from his responsibilities as a family man and, more specifically, a step-grandfather. His step-grandson George Washington Parke Custis, not wholly affectionately nicknamed "Washtub," was a source of endless frustration. In 1797, the seventeen-year-old boy abandoned a place at Princeton that his family had painstakingly secured for him in preference for loafing at Mount Vernon, riding, and hunting. Washington's mind revolted at the idea of his heirs squandering his inheritance in idle pleasures, and labored diligently to whip Washtub into shape. "Rise early," he lectured the boy, "that by habit it may become familiar—agreeable—healthy—and profitable." Punctual, well-dressed appearance at all meals was essential. For the rest of his days at Mount Vernon, the general expected young Custis to devote himself to study, with breaks for light exercise in the afternoons. Only on Saturdays could the boy take time for riding, shooting, or "proper amusements" as opposed to time spent "running up & down stairs, & wasted in conversation with any one who will talk with you."[16]

Washington's words no doubt echoed his mother's practical advice, as well as his continuing regrets for his neglected education. They also reflected his studied opinions about the importance of learning to individuals and society. A "well grounded knowledge," he told Custis, would ensure "your respectability in maturer age; your usefulness to your country; and indeed your own private gratifications." Moreover, although he of necessity had been largely self-taught, Washington was no fan of self-guided learning. "It is from the experience and knowledge of preceptors," he wrote, "that youth is to be advantageously instructed." Unfortunately young Custis remained stubbornly intractable, and fled the general's discipline just as he, as a boy, had fled his mother's firm oversight. Washington's determination that no one of his heirs would be permitted to look on inherited wealth with a sense of entitlement, however, would inform the writing of his will.[17]

———

BY THE BEGINNING OF 1799, Washington sensed that he was approaching the end of his life's term. After dreaming that Martha had died, he conjectured that it might actually portend his own passing. "I may soon leave you," he told her. With the war scare finally fading, he turned the army over to Alexander Hamilton—still young, and a sucker for hard work—and turned his sights wholly back to Mount Vernon. Much work remained to be done. Early that summer, though—watching his crops sprout for what he thought might be the last time—Washington sat in his study to compose two documents: a complete list of his slaves, and a Last Will and Testament.[18]

The connection between the two documents became apparent in the will's fourth paragraph. After mandating that all of his few debts be "punctually and speedily paid" and that Martha have full use of the estate, Washington decreed that "Upon the decease of my wife, it is my Will & desire that all the Slaves which I hold in my *own right*, shall receive their freedom." The very young and the old and infirm, he specified, must be "comfortably cloathed & fed by my heirs while they live," whereas orphan children would be "bound by the Court." While under the court's care, he carefully prescribed, they ought "to be taught to read & write; and to be brought up to some useful occupation." Every particle of his instructions regarding his slaves, he enjoined, should be "religiously fulfilled" by his heirs. For his longtime body servant Billy Lee, Washington granted immediate freedom plus an "annuity of thirty dollars during his natural life."[19]

The bulk of the will dealt with the disposal of Washington's landed property. It was immense. At Mount Vernon his estate sprawled over 7,600 acres. Elsewhere, in Virginia, Ohio, Maryland, Pennsylvania, New York, Kentucky, and the Northwest Territory, he held a staggering 50,975 acres worth, by his estimate, $444,803. In addition, he held interest in 4,000 acres of the Dismal Swamp worth $20,000; lots in the Federal City, Alexandria, Winchester, and Bath, Virginia, worth $24,332; stocks and bonds worth $25,212; and livestock worth $15,653. This brought him to a round total of $530,000. But that was really just a start. In addition to his many possessions—from which he bequeathed the best keepsakes to his many friends—and various small debts owed to him, there were his many active enterprises: his mills, his fishery, and his distillery, among other endeavors. Recent estimates have put their value at about $250,000, putting his total worth at around $780,000. In 1799 there was no Forbes list of the richest men in America—but it is safe to guess that Washington likely would have come in among the top one hundred. The potential of his estate, though, was even greater. Managed carefully, it could be built into not just one but several substantial fortunes.

Remarkably, Washington chose not to pass on the bulk of his estate intact to a few primary heirs. Instead, while leaving Martha in control of his estate during her lifetime and after bequests to charitable educational institutions, he equally divided the residue of the estate among her grandchildren and the surviving descendants of his brothers and sisters—twenty-three people in all. He left no explanation for doing so, but his motives are not difficult to fathom. Caring equally about every member of his family, he wished to give each of them the financial resources to make their way in the world. At the same time, he did not wish to doom any of them to complacency. Believing as he did that industry was inextricable from morality, Washington sought to provide his relations with opportunities to produce their own wealth. It was the richest gift he could imagine.

Composing the will's final lines and signing his name, Washington set his sights on the future. Although he had experienced forebodings of his death earlier that year, with his will complete he looked on that eventuality with equanimity. The date of his demise was beyond his control. What he *could* still control was the land on which he stood and lived—the core of his Mount Vernon estate. In early December 1799, looking forward to the new century due to arrive in a few weeks, he prepared a detailed plan for the work to be performed over the next three years at the estate's three major farms: River, Union, and Muddy Hole. He laid out how, where, and what kind of crops were to be planted, how they were to be fertilized, and how livestock were to be fed and penned. He designated repairs to be made to outbuildings, and fences to be laid. Finally, he pointed out the principles upon which his overseers and laborers should work. "Every attentive, and discerning person, who has the whole business of the year laid before him, can be at no loss to lay it out to advantage," he wrote. Men should be guided by "the Wiseman's saying 'that there is a time, and a season for all things' and that, unless they are embraced, nothing will thrive; or go on smoothly." With these plans and principles in mind, he was eager to see what the future would bring. In 1800, he planned to take the management of his farms entirely on his own shoulders.[20]

It was not to be. Four days after he completed the plan for his farms, Washington's own season arrived. On December 12, he rode out to inspect the farms. The skies poured rain, snow, and sleet, but his mind was preoccupied with his future plans, and he ignored the chill creeping under his collar and down the back of his neck. That night he attended dinner without changing his clothes. The next day it snowed heavily and so he stayed indoors, working at his desk and reading the newspapers. He had developed a sore throat but elected to "let it go as it came." The following night, however, he woke up with his throat dangerously inflamed. His condition continued to weaken throughout the rest of the morning and into the day despite medical intervention that included, according to the backward standards of the time, controlled bleeding.[21]

By afternoon Washington knew he was dying. His first thought was to make certain that Martha had his most recent will. Then he ordered a distraught Tobias Lear to carry on with the copying of his correspondence, and to "arrange my accounts & settle my books." His last words, uttered after begging that he not be placed in the vault less than two days after his death—to ensure against premature burial—were "Tis well." Martha echoed his words. "Tis well," she said, speaking firmly. "Tis All now over. I have no more trials to pass through. I shall soon follow him!" Two years later, she did follow. But before then, she enacted a crucial provision of her husband's will before it actually came due. She freed his slaves.[22]

Martha, like George, had not died at rest—but doing.

# CONCLUSION

IN A FREE SOCIETY NO MAN CAN DICTATE HOW AN ECONOMY functions. George Washington never had the power or the desire to do so. Neither as general nor as president did he command prosperity. Men of talent working alongside him—some lifelong friends and some, alas, eventual enemies—contributed vitally to winning the Revolutionary War, fashioning a Constitution, creating a government, and setting the nation's course. John Jay, Robert Morris, James Madison, Thomas Jefferson, and of course Alexander Hamilton all performed feats that Washington could never have accomplished on his own. Alongside them labored unsung members of the Cabinet and of Congress, state and local officials, accountants, deputy treasurers, financiers, and commissaries. Even they were only partly responsible for creating the prosperous nation the United States was to become. Washington understood above all that it was the people—men and women, rich and poor, enslaved and free—who created the wealth. His job was to free them to do the real work.

Even a free nation, though, needs leaders. In that role, Washington was ideal. As a child, he had learned principles of thrift and self-discipline at his mother's knee. In his teenage years he came to understand what it meant to work hard to earn a salary, and to save and invest. During the French and Indian War, he developed an appreciation for the indispensable necessities that made up the basic ingredients of everyday life for the mass of his countrymen—things like food, drink, clothing, shelter, and, above all, money. He struggled through adversity, and became an advocate for the men he commanded. He witnessed the west's potential, and traced the routes of commerce that would bind it to the east. At Mount Vernon after the French and Indian War, he acquired the skills to build and manage a successful enterprise. Ditching tobacco, he transformed his estate into a multilayered producer of diverse commodities. Washington's struggles in the colonial credit system inculcated in him a horror of debt, and his self-liberation from credit as he shifted to wheat and began selling abroad awakened him to the promise of overseas commerce. These facts helped convince him to support the drive for independence, while the exhilarating experiences of resistance and revolution impressed him with what Americans working in concert could accomplish.

In wartime Washington served as more than just a battlefield leader, or even a military administrator. His understanding of the economic underpinnings of the war effort informed his strategy. So did his certain knowledge that, to survive, the United States had not just to beat the British militarily but to ensure that America emerged from the war with a functioning government and economy, and an intact civil society. This was why he sought to end the war rapidly—an insight that also lay behind his almost instantaneous decision to take the road to Yorktown. It was also during the war that Washington conceived his concept of communities of interest.

Winning the contest for hearts and minds was not just about propaganda. It was not even about driving off the enemy. Fundamentally, it meant developing a sense of shared interest between the government (along with its military arm) and the people. Interest provided individuals with a clear investment in victory. It also bound them together in the cause, and against a common enemy. Even so, by 1783 Washington believed that the United States had just pulled through by the skin of its teeth. The Confederation government lacked the tools to build the bonds of unity. New ideas were in order.

Washington was no philosopher or political theorist. He never dreamed of himself as an economist. Though he identified the problems that the country faced in the 1780s—debt, poor public credit, insecure currency, inefficient government, and so on—the Constitution was not his baby. It was in these years more than any others, though, that he came to appreciate what he could accomplish as a symbol. Although he was not yet holding public office during this period, his fame left intellectuals like Jefferson and Madison in the shade.

Americans looked to him as an example. He kept this in mind as he labored to rework his estate on scientific principles, hailing experimentation, innovation, and industry as principles to guide American farming. In the process of doing so, he established connections with some of the most visionary entrepreneurs of his age. That they were all British was no coincidence.

Prejudice, Washington believed, must not hinder the quest for prosperity. Emotion bound America to France, but interest bound it to Great Britain. Looking behind the still arrogantly imperious British government, he identified a people who stood on the verge of great things. He did not imagine Americans as cheap imitators, much less as humble supplicants to the throne of British prosperity. Rather, he conceived a developing trans-Atlantic community of interest that would develop into an equal partnership to the enrichment of both.

Transitioning from the role of symbolic leader and mediator at the Constitutional Convention and advocate for ratification to president of the United States, Washington focused his efforts on fostering fiscal stability, national unity, and peace as the harbingers of prosperity. He set the tone, but did not shirk the details. Hamilton was a vital member of his Cabinet. As secretary of the Treasury he was the bricklayer if not the sole architect of economic policy. Washington agreed with him on most principles, but not unthinkingly, and blocked or discarded his suggestions where he thought them wrongheaded.

Nor did Jefferson stand on the outside. Though increasingly disdainful of Hamilton, he found a ready ear with the president on matters such as the national currency and international commerce. He, too, played a central role in charting the nation's course. In navigating the dangerous shoals separating France and Great Britain, however, it was Washington who steadied the helm and saved the nation from a ruinous war. Never were Jefferson and Madison more wrongheaded than in their advocacy of close friendship with France on the one hand and an openly provocative stance toward Great Britain on the other. Right, they seemed to imagine, made might. Washington knew otherwise. Lacking an effective army and above all a navy, he knew the United States had no chance of success in a full-scale war with what remained the most powerful empire on the face of the earth. Even if it avoided outright conquest, America would still face ruin, undermining—perhaps permanently—all the work of the past twenty years. For prosperity, Americans needed peace. Washington gave it to them.

In retirement, Washington knew he still had not left the national stage. The floors of Mount Vernon groaned under the weight of scores of visitors. Newspapers—even those who had spent the past few years scurrilously denouncing him—followed his every move. His private actions were still public. And they still had value. On January 18, 1792, Arthur Young had told Washington that "every man should do what good he can to Society; and the quantum in his power will always be in proportion to his celebrity. . . . [F]or a man on whom the eyes of the universe are fixed it is some thing for the good of agriculture to have it known that he regards, practices and studies it."[1]

Frederick the Great, king of Prussia and one of the finest military leaders the world had ever seen, set one kind of example. Like Frederick, Washington had won his share of battles. Young, though, saw his American friend in a different light. "I wish the Western World to give another example," he wrote, "and send new votaries to the Plough because Washington has attended to it." In his fields—brighter than any youth taking on the wilderness, taller than any general on his horse, prouder than any president elected by unanimous consent—stood George Washington, a man of the people following his plough. In that stance he set an example for the world to emulate.[2]

# APPENDIX
## GEORGE WASHINGTON'S ESTATE TODAY

GEORGE WASHINGTON'S IMMEDIATE HEIRS DID NOT DO AN EFFECTIVE JOB of maintaining the estate, let alone preserving or increasing its productivity. By the mid-1800s it had produced few crops and the mansion house had become run down. The owner, John Augustine Washington, Jr., strove unsuccessfully to convince either Virginia or the federal government to preserve the estate. It took a remarkable woman, Ann Pamela Cunningham, to raise the money necessary to purchase the mansion and the tiny remaining estate of 200 acres. The organization she founded, The Mount Vernon Ladies' Association of the Union, took responsibility for the estate and operated and maintained it thereafter. Thanks to the association's efforts over the following century and a half, the estate has returned to prosperity (though it has not resumed its former size).

A visitor to the estate today may bear personal witness to George Washington's entrepreneurship. Complete and accurate reconstructions of the gristmill and distillery are located adjacent to each other and less than three miles from the mansion house. At the gristmill, historical interpreters take visitors through the grinding process step by step. Likewise, the distillery is fully operational. Lucky guests may observe and sometimes even participate in the grueling distilling process. Proceeds of both the gristmill and distillery are available for sale, if not distributed quite as widely as they were in Washington's own day.

Another remarkable reconstruction is the sixteen-sided barn. Completed in 1996, it closely replicates the original so that it is possible to inspect the remarkably complex and innovative architecture. Demonstrations of its original operation take place from time to time, and here as elsewhere historical interpreters ply their vital trade of bringing the past to life for the modern public's enrichment and enjoyment.

Other original operations, such as the fishery, have not been reconstructed. Representatives of Washington's original livestock still walk the estate, though, and interns tend the animals as well as work modest farm plots and operate the smithy. Once again thanks to the estate's historical interpreters, though, it is possible to attain strong impressions of how Mount Vernon would have operated in Washington's day, including the important role of enslaved African Americans. Even better, the estate's superb website includes a digital encyclopedia describing all aspects of Washington's life and endeavors, as well as videos that show estate operations for those unable to view them in person.

Elsewhere, the physical legacy of Washington's entrepreneurship is harder to detect. While a few remnants of his Potomac Company enterprise near Great Falls, Virginia, still exist and his gristmill at Perryopolis, Pennsylvania, has been reconstructed, the houses he built in Washington, DC, are gone and his far-flung properties have long been sold off and developed. To truly understand the legacy of Washington's entrepreneurship, though, all one needs to do is witness the prosperity (not so robust as it once was, true) of the present-day United States.

# BIBLIOGRAPHY

Abbot, W. W., et al., eds. *The Papers of George Washington,* 5 series, 68 vols. to date. Charlottesville: University of Virginia Press, 1976–.

Achenbach, Joel. *The Grand Idea: George Washington's Potomac and the Race to the West.* New York: Simon & Schuster, 2004. *FCL*

Boyd, Julian P., et al., eds. *The Papers of Thomas Jefferson,* 41 vols. to date. Princeton, NJ: Princeton University Press, 1950–.

Brady, Patricia. *Martha Washington: An American Life.* New York: Viking, 2005.

Breen, T. H. *The Marketplace of Revolution: How Consumer Politics Shaped American Independence.* New York: Oxford University Press, 2004.

Brown, Roger H. *Redeeming the Republic: Federalists, Taxation, and the Origins of the Constitution.* Baltimore: Johns Hopkins University Press, 1993.

Chernow, Ron. *Washington: A Life.* New York: Penguin, 2010.

Crowley, John E. *The Privileges of Independence: Neomercantilism and the American Revolution.* Baltimore: Johns Hopkins University Press, 1993.

Dalzell, Jr., Robert F., and Lee Baldwin Dalzell. *George Washington's Mount Vernon: At Home in Revolutionary America.* New York: Oxford University Press, 1998.

Fields, Joseph E., ed. *"Worthy Partner": The Papers of Martha Washington.* Westport, CT: Greenwood Press, 1994.

Fitzpatrick, John C., ed. *The Writings of George Washington,* 39 vols. Washington, DC: US Government Printing Office, 1931–1944.

Freeman, Douglas Southall. *George Washington: A Biography,* 7 vols. New York: Charles Scribner's Sons, 1948–1957.

Grizzard, Jr., Frank E. *George Washington: A Biographical Companion.* Santa Barbara, CA: ABC-CLIO, 2002.

Humphreys, David. *David Humphreys' Life of General Washington: With George Washington's "Remarks,"* ed. Rosemarie Zagarri. Athens: University of Georgia Press, 1991.

Hunt, Elizabeth Pinney, ed. *Arthur Young on Industry and Economics.* Privately printed, Bryn Mawr, PA, 1926.

Klein, Maury. *The Power Makers: Steam, Electricity, and the Men Who Invented Modern America.* New York: Bloomsbury, 2008.

Lengel, Edward G. *General George Washington: A Military Life.* New York: Random House, 2005.

———. *This Glorious Struggle: George Washington's Revolutionary War Letters.* New York: Smithsonian, 2007.

Longmore, Paul K. *The Invention of George Washington.* Charlottesville: University Press of Virginia, 1999.

McCraw, Thomas K. *The Founders of Finance: How Hamilton, Gallatin, and Other Immigrants Forged a New Economy.* Cambridge, MA: Belknap Press of Harvard University Press, 2012.

McCusker, John J., and Russell R. Menard. *The Economy of British America, 1607–1789.* Chapel Hill: University of North Carolina Press, 1991.

Ragsdale, Bruce A. *A Planter's Republic: The Search for Economic Independence in Revolutionary Virginia.* Madison, WI: Madison House, 1996.

Ritter, Halsted L. *Washington as a Business Man.* New York: Sears Publishing, 1931.

Royster, Charles. *The Fabulous History of the Dismal Swamp Company: A Story of George Washington's Times.* New York: Knopf, 1999.

Sydnor, Charles S. *Gentlemen Freeholders: Political Practices in Washington's Virginia.* Chapel Hill: University of North Carolina Press, 1952.

Syrett, Harold C., et al., eds. *The Papers of Alexander Hamilton,* 27 vols. New York: Columbia University Press, 1961–1987.

Toner, J. M. *George Washington as an Inventor and Promoter of the Useful Arts.* Washington, DC: Gedney and Roberts, 1892.

Wood, Gordon S. *The Radicalism of the American Revolution.* New York: Knopf, 1992.

Wright, Robert E., and David J. Cowen. *Financial Founding Fathers: The Men Who Made America Rich.* Chicago: University of Chicago Press, 2006.

Young, Arthur. *Autobiography,* ed. M. Betham-Edwards. 1898.

# NOTES

## Introduction

1. Pass for Jean-Pierre Blanchard, 9 January 1793 (*Papers, Presidential Series,* 11:602–604).

2. GW to Lafayette, 23 December 1784 (*Papers, Confederation Series,* 2:228); GW to Edward Newenham, 25 November 1785 (*Papers, Confederation Series,* 3:387).

## Chapter One: Family Fortunes

1. Quoted in Douglas Southall Freeman, *George Washington: A Biography,* 7 vols. (New York: Charles Scribner's Sons, 1948–1957), 1:38.

2. David Humphreys, *David Humphreys' "Life of General Washington": With George Washington's "Remarks,"* ed. Rosemarie Zagarri (Athens: University of Georgia Press, 1991), 6.

3. Donald Jackson and Dorothy Twohig, eds., *The Diaries of George Washington* (Charlottesville: University Press of Virginia, 1976–1979), 1:7.

4. GW to Richard, 1749–1750 (*Papers, Colonial Series,* 1:44).

5. J. M. Toner, *The Daily Journal of Major George Washington, in 1751–2, Kept While on a Tour from Virginia to the Island of Barbados, with His Invalid Brother, Maj. Lawrence Washington, Proprietor of Mount Vernon on the Potomac* (Albany, NY: Joel Munsell's Sons, 1892), 39–42.

6. Ibid., 58.

7. Ibid., 58–62.

8. GW to Robert Dinwiddie, 10 June 1752 (*Papers, Colonial Series,* 1:50).

9. GW to Robert Dinwiddie, 20 March 1754 (*Papers, Colonial Series,* 1:78); GW to Robert Dinwiddie, 9 March 1754 (*Papers, Colonial Series,* 1:73).

10. GW to Robert Dinwiddie, 18 May 1754 (*Papers, Colonial Series,* 1:99).

11. GW to William Fitzhugh, 15 November 1754 (*Papers, Colonial Series,* 1:226).

12. GW to John Augustine Washington, 14 May 1755 (*Papers, Colonial Series,* 1:277).

13. GW to Robert Orme, 2 April 1755 (*Papers, Colonial Series,* 1:246).

14. GW to Robert Orme, 2 April 1755 (*Papers, Colonial Series,* 1:246); GW to William Byrd, 20 April 1755 (*Papers, Colonial Series,* 1:249–251); GW to Carter Burwell, 20 April 1755 (*Papers, Colonial Series,* 1:252).

15. GW to Sarah Cary Fairfax, 30 April 1755 (*Papers, Colonial Series,* 1:261–262); GW to Thomas, Lord Fairfax, 6 May 1755 (*Papers, Colonial Series,* 1:265–266); GW to John Augustine Washington, 6 May 1755 (*Papers, Colonial Series,* 1:266–268); GW to Augustine Washington, 14 May 1755 (*Papers, Colonial Series,* 1:271–272).

16. Humphreys, *Life of General Washington*, 18; GW to Augustine Washington, 2 August 1755 (*Papers, Colonial Series*, 1:351); GW to Mary Ball Washington, 14 August 1755 (*Papers, Colonial Series*, 1:359).

17. GW to Warner Lewis, 14 August 1755 (*Papers, Colonial Series*, 1:362).

18. GW to Francis Fauquier, 5 August 1758 (*Papers, Colonial Series*, 5:370); John Forbes to Henry Bouquet, 23 September 1758 (*Papers, Colonial Series*, 6:24).

## Chapter Two: Love and Investment

1. GW to Richard Washington, 15 April 1757 (*Papers, Colonial Series*, 4:132–134).

2. Quoted in Patricia Brady, *Martha Washington: An American Life* (New York: Viking, 2005), 57.

3. GW to Richard Washington, 18 March 1758 (*Papers, Colonial Series*, 5:105–106).

4. GW to John Alton, 5 April 1759 (*Papers, Colonial Series*, 6:200).

5. Combined County Inventory of Slaves and Personal Property in the Estate (*Papers, Colonial Series*, 6:220–232).

6. Quoted in Freeman, *George Washington*, 3:16–17.

7. GW to Robert Cary & Company, 1 May 1759 (*Papers, Colonial Series*, 6:316).

8. Invoice to Robert Cary & Company, 1 May 1759 (*Papers, Colonial Series*, 6:317–318).

9. Ibid.

10. Ibid.

11. GW to Robert Cary & Company, 20 September 1759 (*Papers, Colonial Series*, 6:350–352).

12. Invoice to Robert Cary & Company, 20 September 1759 (*Papers, Colonial Series*, 6:352–358).

13. Ibid.; GW to Richard Washington, 20 September 1759 (*Papers, Colonial Series*, 6:358–359).

14. Capel & Osgood Hanbury to GW, 1 October 1759 (*Papers, Colonial Series*, 6:366–367).

15. Joseph Valentine to GW, 9 August 1760 (*Papers, Colonial Series*, 6:446); GW to Robert Cary & Company, 20 June 1762 (*Papers, Colonial Series*, 7:140); GW to Burwell Bassett, 28 August 1762 (*Papers, Colonial Series*, 7:147).

16. GW to Robert Cary & Company, 10 August 1760 (*Papers, Colonial Series*, 6:448); GW to Robert Cary & Company, 28 September 1760 (*Papers, Colonial Series*, 6:460).

17. GW to Robert Cary & Company, 26 April 1763 (*Papers, Colonial Series*, 7:202–205).

18. GW to Robert Cary & Company, 10 August 1764 (*Papers, Colonial Series*, 7:323–326).

19. Diary, 9 April 1760 (*Diaries*, 1:265).

20. Plan of Philip Mazzei's Agricultural Company, 1774 (*Jefferson Papers*, 1:156–159); GW to Philip Mazzei, 1 July 1779 (*Papers, Revolutionary War Series*, 21:320).

21. Memoranda, 17 September–15 November 1757 (*Papers, Colonial Series*, 4:405).

22. Invoice from Robert Cary & Company, 15 March 1760 (*Papers, Colonial Series*, 6:394); invoice from Robert Cary & Company, 10 April 1762 (*Papers, Colonial Series*, 7:127).

23. GW to Robert Stewart, 2 May 1763 (*Papers, Colonial Series*, 7:217).

24. GW to Jonathan Boucher, 9 July 1771 (*Papers, Colonial Series*, 8:495).

25. GW to Robert Cary & Company, 20 September 1765 (*Papers, Colonial Series*, 7:398–402).

26. Ibid.

27. GW to Capel & Osgood Hanbury, 20 September 1765 (*Papers, Colonial Series*, 7:394).

28. GW to Robert Cary & Company, 1 June 1774 (*Papers, Colonial Series*, 10:83).

29. Diary, 14 April, 1 May 1760 (*Diaries*, 1:266–267, 275).

30. GW to Robert Cary & Company, 13 February 1764 (*Papers, Colonial Series*, 7:286).

31. Thomas Newton, Jr., to GW, 22 March 1773 (*Papers, Colonial Series*, 9:203).

32. GW to Robert McMickan, 10 May 1774 (*Papers, Colonial Series*, 10:55).

33. Diary, 3 January 1760 (*Diaries*, 1:214).

34. GW to Charles Washington, 15 August 1764 (*Papers, Colonial Series,* 7:331); Diary, 16 May 1768, 22 April 1769 (*Diaries,* 2:61, 146).

35. GW to Arthur Young, 12 December 1793 (*Papers, Presidential Series,* 14:506).

36. GW to Capel & Osgood Hanbury, 5 May 1768 (*Papers, Colonial Series,* 8:85).

37. GW to Robert Cary & Company, 20 June 1768 (*Papers, Colonial Series,* 8:100).

38. Dismal Swamp Diary, 1763 (*Diaries,* 1:319–326).

39. Ibid.

40. GW to William Crawford, 17 September 1767 (*Papers, Colonial Series,* 8:27–28).

41. Diary, 13 October, 15 October 1770 (*Diaries,* 2:289–290).

42. Diary, 14 October, 25 October 1770 (*Diaries,* 2:290, 299).

43. GW to James Wood, 20 February 1774 (*Papers, Colonial Series,* 9:490).

## Chapter Three: The Road to Economic Freedom

1. GW to Robert Cary & Company, 21 July 1766 (*Papers, Colonial Series,* 7:456–457).

2. GW to Capel & Osgood Hanbury, 25 July 1767 (*Papers, Colonial Series,* 8:15).

3. Capel & Osgood Hanbury to GW, 20 October 1767 (*Papers, Colonial Series,* 8:44).

4. Arthur Lee to GW, 15 June 1777 (*Papers, Revolutionary War Series,* 10:43).

5. GW to George Mason, 5 April 1769 (*Papers, Colonial Series,* 8:177–181).

6. Ibid.

7. Quoted in *Diaries,* 2:152.

8. Quoted in Paul Longmore, *The Invention of George Washington* (Charlottesville: University of Virginia Press, 1999), 94–95.

9. GW to Robert Cary & Company, 20 August 1770 (*Papers, Colonial Series,* 8:371).

10. GW to Robert Cary & Company, 1 June 1774 (*Papers, Colonial Series,* 10:83).

11. GW to George William Fairfax, 10 June 1774 (*Papers, Colonial Series,* 10:96–97).

12. GW to Bryan Fairfax, 4 July 1774 (*Papers, Colonial Series,* 10:109).

13. Ibid.

14. Ibid.

15. Fairfax County Resolves, 18 July 1774 (*Papers, Colonial Series,* 10:119–128).

16. Ibid.

17. Ibid.

18. Ibid.

19. GW to Robert McKenzie, 9 October 1774 (*Papers, Colonial Series,* 10:171–172).

20. Quoted in Longmore, *Invention of George Washington,* 148.

21. Quoted in Longmore, *Invention of George Washington,* 151.

22. GW to John Augustine Washington, 25 March 1775 (*Papers, Colonial Series,* 10:308); GW to George William Fairfax, 31 May 1775 (*Papers, Colonial Series,* 10:367–368).

23. Invoice from Robert Cary & Company, 20 December 1765 (*Papers, Colonial Series,* 7:420).

## Chapter Four: Money: The Sinews of War

1. Quoted in *Papers, Revolutionary War Series,* 1:2.

2. GW to the New York Provincial Congress, 26 June 1775 (*Papers, Revolutionary War Series,* 1:41).

3. GW to Martha Washington, 18 June 1775 (*Papers, Revolutionary War Series,* 1:3–4).

4. GW to Burwell Bassett, 19 June 1775 (*Papers, Revolutionary War Series,* 1:13).

5. GW to John Hancock, 10–11 July 1775 (*Papers, Revolutionary War Series,* 1:88–89).

6. Address to the Continental Congress, 16 June 1775 (*Papers, Revolutionary War Series,* 1:1–3).

7. GW to Robert Morris, 14 August 1777 (*Papers, Revolutionary War Series,* 10:610).

8. GW's Revolutionary War Expense Account Book, 1776–1780 (Library of Congress: Washington Papers, Series 5).

9. GW to John Cochran, 16 August 1779 (Edward G. Lengel, ed., *This Glorious Struggle: George Washington's Revolutionary War Letters* [New York: Smithsonian Books, 2007], 187); Caleb Gibbs to John Chaloner, February 1780 (*Papers, Revolutionary War Series,* 24:315).

10. Quoted in Edward G. Lengel, *General George Washington: A Military Life* (New York: Random House, 2005), 282–283, 286–287.

11. GW to John Hancock, 24 January 1776 (*Papers, Revolutionary War Series,* 3:179).

12. GW to John Hancock, 11 July 1776 (*Papers, Revolutionary War Series,* 5:266–267).

13. GW to John Hancock, 20 June 1776 (*Papers, Revolutionary War Series,* 5:56).

14. General Orders, 7 August 1775 (*Papers, Revolutionary War Series,* 1:260).

15. GW to John Hancock, 4–5 August 1775 (*Papers, Revolutionary War Series,* 1:260).

16. GW to the Massachusetts Council, 29 August 1775 (*Papers, Revolutionary War Series,* 1:376–377).

17. General Orders, 5 July 1775 (*Papers, Revolutionary War Series,* 1:63).

18. General Orders, 25 April 1776 (*Papers, Revolutionary War Series,* 4:123).

19. GW to Jonathan Trumbull, Sr., 4 August 1775 (*Papers, Revolutionary War Series,* 1:244); GW to John Augustine Washington, 13 October 1775 (*Papers, Revolutionary War Series,* 2:161).

20. John Hancock to GW, 20 October 1775 (*Papers, Revolutionary War Series,* 2:212–213).

21. GW to Nicholas Cooke, 4 August 1775 (*Papers, Revolutionary War Series,* 1:221).

22. GW to Joseph Trumbull, 9 June 1776 (*Papers, Revolutionary War Series,* 4:479).

23. GW to John Jay, 23 April 1779 (*Papers, Revolutionary War Series,* 20:175).

24. GW to John Augustine Washington, 27 July 1775 (*Papers, Revolutionary War Series,* 1:183).

25. GW to John Augustine Washington, 10 September 1775 (*Papers, Revolutionary War Series,* 1:447–448).

26. GW to Joseph Reed, 28 November 1775 (*Papers, Revolutionary War Series,* 2:449).

27. GW to John Hancock, 21 September 1775 (*Papers, Revolutionary War Series,* 2:28).

28. GW to the Falmouth Committee of Public Safety, 24 October 1775 (*Papers, Revolutionary War Series,* 2:225–226); GW to Philip Schuyler, 26 October 1775 (*Papers, Revolutionary War Series,* 2:239).

29. GW to William Ramsay, 10–16 November 1775 (*Papers, Revolutionary War Series,* 2:345).

30. GW to Joseph Reed, 31 January 1776 (*Papers, Revolutionary War Series,* 3:228).

31. GW to Joseph Reed, 14 January 1776 (*Papers, Revolutionary War Series,* 3:90).

32. GW to John Hancock, 24 March 1776 (*Papers, Revolutionary War Series,* 3:523); GW to Philip Schuyler, 3 April 1776 (*Papers, Revolutionary War Series,* 4:29).

33. GW to John Augustine Washington, 31 March 1776 (*Papers, Revolutionary War Series,* 3:569–570).

34. GW to the New York Committee of Public Safety, 17 April 1776 (*Papers, Revolutionary War Series,* 4:77).

35. GW to John Hancock, 22 April 1776 (*Papers, Revolutionary War Series,* 4:106).

36. GW to John Augustine Washington, 31 May–4 June 1776 (*Papers, Revolutionary War Series,* 4:413).

37. GW to Lund Washington, 19 August 1776 (*Papers, Revolutionary War Series,* 6:83).

38. General Orders, 23 August 1776 (*Papers, Revolutionary War Series,* 6:109–110).

39. GW to John Hancock, 25 September 1776 (*Papers, Revolutionary War Series,* 6:393–400).

40. Ibid.

41. GW to John Hancock, 5 December 1776 (*Papers, Revolutionary War Series,* 7:263); GW to John Hancock, 25 September 1776 (*Papers, Revolutionary War Series,* 6:393–400).

42. GW to John Hancock, 25 September 1776 (*Papers, Revolutionary War Series,* 6:393–400).

43. GW to John Hancock, 11 November 1776 (*Papers, Revolutionary War Series,* 7:142).

44. GW to Lund Washington, 10–17 December 1776 (*Papers, Revolutionary War Series,* 7:291); GW to Jonathan Trumbull, Sr., 12 December 1776 (*Papers, Revolutionary War Series,* 7:321); GW to the Pennsylvania Council of Safety, 15 December 1776 (*Papers, Revolutionary War Series,* 7:347).

45. GW to Robert Morris, 25 December 1776 (*Papers, Revolutionary War Series,* 7:440).

46. GW to William Heath, 18 December 1776 (*Papers, Revolutionary War Series,* 7:367).

47. GW to Jonathan Trumbull, Sr., 14 December 1776 (*Papers, Revolutionary War Series,* 7:340), quoted in Lengel, *General George Washington,* 180.

48. GW to John Hancock, 1 January 1777 (*Papers, Revolutionary War Series,* 7:504).

49. John Hancock to GW, 15 January 1777 (*Papers, Revolutionary War Series,* 8:73).

50. GW to William Heath, 23 May 1777 (*Papers, Revolutionary War Series,* 9:504–505); GW to Richard Henry Lee, 24–26 April 1777 (*Papers, Revolutionary War Series,* 9:256).

51. Anthony Wayne to GW, 25 November 1777 (*Papers, Revolutionary War Series,* 12:403); Henry Knox to GW, 26 November 1777 (*Papers, Revolutionary War Series,* 12:415); GW to John Parke Custis, 14 November 1777 (*Papers, Revolutionary War Series,* 12:249).

52. Nathanael Greene to GW, 1 December 1777 (*Papers, Revolutionary War Series,* 12:462).

53. GW to a Continental Congress Camp Committee, 29 January 1778 (*Papers, Revolutionary War Series,* 13:399).

54. GW to James Mease, 21 January 1778 (*Papers, Revolutionary War Series,* 13:305); GW to Henry Knox, 8 January 1778 (*Papers, Revolutionary War Series,* 13:180–181); GW to William Grayson, 3 May 1777 (*Papers, Revolutionary War Series,* 9:332).

55. GW to James Potter, 12 January 1778 (*Papers, Revolutionary War Series,* 13:209).

56. General Orders, 20 January 1778 (*Papers, Revolutionary War Series,* 13:286).

57. GW to Henry Laurens, 5 January 1778 (*Papers, Revolutionary War Series,* 13:147).

58. Daniel Roberdeau to GW, 4 June 1778 (*Papers, Revolutionary War Series,* 15:314–315).

59. GW to Gouverneur Morris, 5 September 1778 (*Papers, Revolutionary War Series,* 16:529); GW to Anthony Wayne, 19 August 1777 (*Papers, Revolutionary War Series,* 11:9).

60. Quoted in *Papers, Revolutionary War Series,* 13:694.

## Chapter Five: Victory Without Peace

1. GW to James Lovell, 29 March 1778 (*Papers, Revolutionary War Series,* 14:356); GW to George Baylor, 15 May 1778 (*Papers, Revolutionary War Series,* 15:124).

2. GW to John Banister, 21 April 1778 (*Papers, Revolutionary War Series,* 14:574–576).

3. Ibid.

4. Ibid.

5. GW to Gouverneur Morris, 4 October 1778 (*Papers, Revolutionary War Series,* 17:253–254).

6. Henry Laurens to GW, 20 November 1778 (*Papers, Revolutionary War Series,* 18:231–232).

7. Ibid.; GW to the Continental Congress Committee of Conference, 13 January 1779 (*Papers, Revolutionary War Series,* 18:628).

8. GW to James Warren, 31 March 1779 (*Papers, Revolutionary War Series,* 19:673–674).

9. GW to Benjamin Harrison, 5–7 May 1779 (*Papers, Revolutionary War Series,* 20:332–333).

10. GW to John Sullivan, 4 February 1781 (Fitzpatrick, *Writings,* 21:181–183).

11. Ibid.

12. Quoted in Michael Cecere, "How Lund Washington Saved Mount Vernon" (*Journal of the American Revolution,* 14 April 2014, http://allthingsliberty.com/2014/04/how-lund-washington-saved-mount-vernon/).

13. Diary, 14 August 1781 (*Diaries*, 3:409).

14. Quoted in Lengel, *General George Washington*, 344.

15. GW to John Augustine Washington, May 1778 (*Papers, Revolutionary War Series*, 15:286), quoted in Lengel, *General George Washington*, 345.

16. GW to the Officers of the Army, 15 March 1783 (Fitzpatrick, *Writings*, 26:227).

17. Circular to the States, 8 June 1783 (Fitzpatrick, *Writings*, 26:483–496).

18. Ibid.

## Chapter Six: An Estate Grows, a Nation Stumbles

1. GW to Martha Washington, 18 June 1775 (*Papers, Revolutionary War Series*, 1:5).

2. GW to Lund Washington, 20 August 1775 (*Papers, Revolutionary War Series*, 1:335–337).

3. GW to John Parke Custis, 28 September 1777 (*Papers, Revolutionary War Series*, 11:341).

4. GW to John Parke Custis, 26 May 1778 (*Papers, Revolutionary War Series*, 15:224–225); GW to Lund Washington, 15 August 1778 (*Papers, Revolutionary War Series*, 16:315).

5. GW to John Parke Custis, 3 August 1778 (*Papers, Revolutionary War Series*, 16:230–231).

6. GW to John Parke Custis, 12 October 1778 (*Papers, Revolutionary War Series*, 17:353); GW to Lund Washington, 15 August 1778 (*Papers, Revolutionary War Series*, 16:315); GW to Lund Washington, 24–26 February 1779 (*Papers, Revolutionary War Series*, 19:258–259).

7. GW to Lund Washington, 26 November 1775 (*Papers, Revolutionary War Series*, 2:432).

8. GW to Fielding Lewis, Jr., 27 February 1784 (*Papers, Confederation Series*, 1:161).

9. GW to Charles Lee, 4 April 1788 (*Papers, Confederation Series*, 6:198).

10. GW to Richard Conway, 4 March 1789 (*Papers, Presidential Series*, 1:361).

11. GW to George William Fairfax, 10 November 1785 (*Papers, Confederation Series*, 3:349).

12. GW to Charles Carter, 20 January 1788 (*Papers, Confederation Series*, 6:48–49).

13. Ibid.

14. GW to George William Fairfax, 30 June 1785 (*Papers, Confederation Series*, 3:87–92).

15. George William Fairfax to GW, 23 January 1786 (*Papers, Confederation Series*, 3:517–521).

16. Quoted in Elizabeth Pinney Hunt, ed., *Arthur Young on Industry and Economics* (Bryn Mawr, PA, 1926), 9; Arthur Young, *The Autobiography of Arthur Young*, ed. Mathilda Betham-Edwards (London: Smith, Elder, 1898), 27.

17. Young, *Autobiography of Arthur Young*, 29.

18. Hunt, *Arthur Young on Industry and Economics*, 13.

19. Ibid.

20. Ibid., 14–20.

21. Quoted in ibid., 24.

22. GW to Samuel Chamberline, 3 April 1788 (*Papers, Confederation Series*, 6:190).

23. Quoted in Hunt, *Arthur Young on Industry and Economics*, 24–25, 32–22.

24. Arthur Young to GW, 7 January 1786 (*Papers, Confederation Series*, 3:498–500).

25. GW to Arthur Young, 6 August 1786 (*Papers, Confederation Series*, 4:196–200).

26. Charles Vancouver to GW, 5 November 1791 (*Papers, Presidential Series*, 9:142).

27. GW to John Beale Bordley, 17 August 1788 (*Papers, Confederation Series*, 6:450).

28. GW to Levi Hollingsworth, 20 September 1785 (*Papers, Confederation Series*, 3:268).

29. *Papers, Presidential Series*, 10:235, 11:230.

30. Farm Reports, 26 November 1785–15 April 1786 (*Papers, Confederation Series*, 3:389–409).

31. GW to William Fitzhugh, Jr., 15 May 1786 (*Papers, Confederation Series*, 4:52).

32. Lafayette to GW, 16 April 1785 (*Papers, Confederation Series*, 2:504); Samuel Morris to GW, 21 September 1787 (*Papers, Confederation Series*, 5:335–336).

33. Clement Biddle to GW, 16 October 1788 (*Papers, Presidential Series*, 1:48).

34. Arthur Young to GW, 1 July 1788 (*Papers, Confederation Series,* 5:405); Diary, 22 January 1790 (*Diaries,* 6:12–13).

35. GW to Tobias Lear, 26 June 1791 (*Papers, Presidential Series,* 8:300); Washington's Plan for a Barn, 28 October 1792 (*Papers, Presidential Series,* 11:280). See illustration in latter.

36. GW to William Drayton, 25 March 1786 (*Papers, Confederation Series,* 3:605–606).

37. Benjamin Lincoln to GW, 24 September 1788 (*Papers, Presidential Series,* 1:6).

38. GW to Trustees of the Alexandria Academy, 17 December 1785 (*Papers, Confederation Series,* 3:463–464).

39. GW to John Leigh, 9 January 1787 (*Papers, Confederation Series,* 4:314).

40. GW to Lund Washington, 15 August 1778 (*Papers, Revolutionary War Series,* 16:315).

41. GW to John Francis Mercer, 24 November 1786 (*Papers, Confederation Series,* 4:394).

42. GW to John Francis Mercer, 9 September 1786 (*Papers, Confederation Series,* 4:243).

43. GW to Edmund Randolph, 25 December 1786 (*Papers, Confederation Series,* 4:473).

44. James Jay to GW, 20 December 1784 (*Papers, Confederation Series,* 2:202–203).

45. GW to James Jay, 25 January 1785 (*Papers, Confederation Series,* 2:293).

46. GW to the Countess of Huntingdon, 27 February 1785 (*Papers, Confederation Series,* 2:394–395); Richard Henry Lee to GW, 27 February 1785 (*Papers, Confederation Series,* 2:395).

47. GW to Lafayette, 29 January 1789 (*Papers, Presidential Series,* 1:264).

48. GW to Clement Biddle, 20 July 1788 (*Papers, Confederation Series,* 6:387); GW to Tobias Lear, 7 November 1790 (*Papers, Presidential Series,* 6:635).

49. GW to David Humphreys, 25 July 1785 (*Papers, Confederation Series,* 3:148–149).

50. GW to Lafayette, 15 August 1786 (*Papers, Confederation Series,* 4:214–216).

51. Ibid.

52. Ibid.

53. GW to Moustier, 17 August 1788 (*Papers, Confederation Series,* 6:455–459).

54. Ibid.

55. To Chastellux, 5 September 1785 (*Papers, Confederation Series,* 3:228–229).

56. Sentiments on a Peace Establishment, May 1783 (Fitzpatrick, *Writings,* 26:374–398).

57. Ibid.

58. GW to John Marsden Pintard, 2 August 1786 (*Papers, Confederation Series,* 4:188–189); GW to Lafayette, 15 August 1786 (*Papers, Confederation Series,* 4:216).

59. GW to Thomas Jefferson, 29 March 1784 (*Papers, Confederation Series,* 1:239); GW to James Warren, 7 October 1785 (*Papers, Confederation Series,* 3:299–300).

60. Quoted in *Papers, Confederation Series,* 2:538.

61. GW to James McHenry, 22 August 1785 (*Papers, Confederation Series,* 3:198–199).

62. Diary, 6 September 1784 (*Diaries,* 4:9).

63. GW to Richard Henry Lee, 14 December 1784 (*Papers, Confederation Series,* 2:181–183).

64. Diary, 4 October 1784 (*Diaries,* 4:58).

65. Joel Achenbach, *The Grand Idea: George Washington's Potomac and the Race to the West* (New York: Simon & Schuster, 2004), 125.

66. GW to William Grayson, 22 August 1785 (*Papers, Confederation Series,* 3:193–194).

67. GW to Benjamin Harrison, 18 January 1784 (*Papers, Confederation Series,* 1:56); GW to Edward Newenham, 10 June 1784 (*Papers, Confederation Series,* 1:439).

68. GW to Henry Knox, 5 December 1784 (*Papers, Confederation Series,* 2:171–172), quoted in *Papers, Confederation Series,* 3:561–562.

69. GW to Henry Knox, 26 December 1786 (*Papers, Confederation Series,* 4:481); GW to Henry Lee, Jr., 31 October 1786 (*Papers, Confederation Series,* 4:318); GW to James Madison, 5 November 1786 (*Papers, Confederation Series,* 4:331).

70. Edmund Randolph to GW, 6 December 1786 (*Papers, Confederation Series,* 4:445).

71. Diary, 22 July 1787 (*Diaries,* 5:183); Peter Legaux to GW, 26 January 1791 (*Papers, Presidential Series,* 7:288–291).

72. Jonathan Elliott, ed., *The Debates in the Several State Conventions on the Adoption of the Federal Constitution,* 5 vols. (Philadelphia: J. B. Lippincott, 1836–1901), 3:44–45.

73. GW to William Barton, 7 September 1788 (*Papers, Confederation Series,* 6:503); GW to Benjamin Lincoln, 26 October 1788 (*Papers, Presidential Series,* 1:73).

## Chapter Seven: Building a National Economy: Washington's First Term

1. Diary, 16 April 1789 (*Diaries,* 5:445–447).

2. GW to the Citizens of Baltimore, 17 April 1789 (*Papers, Presidential Series,* 2:64); GW to the Delaware Society for Promoting Domestic Manufactures, 19–20 April 1789 (*Papers, Presidential Series,* 2:78–79).

3. GW to Edward Newenham, 29 August 1788 (*Papers, Confederation Series,* 6:487); GW to Lafayette, 18 June 1788 (*Papers, Confederation Series,* 6:337–338); GW to Thomas Jefferson, 31 August 1788 (*Papers, Confederation Series,* 6:494).

4. Quoted in *Papers, Presidential Series,* 1:261.

5. Quoted in *Papers, Presidential Series,* 1:260–261, 2:155–157; Diary, 20 October 1789 (*Diaries,* 5:468).

6. Undelivered First Inaugural Address: Fragments, 30 April 1789 (*Papers, Presidential Series,* 2:158–173).

7. Ibid.

8. Ibid.

9. First Inaugural Address: Final Version, 30 April 1789 (*Papers, Presidential Series,* 2:175).

10. Tobias Lear to John Field, 7 January 1791 (*Papers, Presidential Series,* 7:195).

11. Board of Treasury to GW, 9 June 1789 (*Papers, Presidential Series,* 2:456).

12. Board of Treasury to GW, 15 June 1789 (*Papers, Presidential Series,* 3:10, 25).

13. Memoranda on Thomas Jefferson's Letters, 27 August 1789 (*Papers, Presidential Series,* 4:494).

14. GW to Alexander Hamilton, 28 August 1788 (*Papers, Confederation Series,* 6:480–481).

15. H. Z. to GW, 24 March 1789 (*Papers, Presidential Series,* 1:441).

16. William Jackson to Clement Biddle, 2 May 1790 (*Papers, Presidential Series,* 5:393–396).

17. James Madison to GW, 21 February 1791 (*Papers, Presidential Series,* 7:395–397).

18. Opinion on the Constitutionality of an Act to Establish a Bank, 23 February 1791 (*Papers, Presidential Series,* 7:425–452); GW to Alexander Hamilton, 23 February 1791 (*Papers, Presidential Series,* 7:452).

19. GW to George Skene Keith, 22 June 1792 (*Papers, Presidential Series,* 10:492).

20. GW to the United States Senate and House of Representatives, 25 October 1791 (*Papers, Presidential Series,* 9:116).

21. Quoted in Ron Chernow, *Washington: A Life* (New York: Penguin, 2010), 631; quoted in *Papers, Presidential Series,* 7:395–397.

22. Diary, 5 October 1789 (*Diaries,* 5:453).

23. Thomas Fielder to GW, 29 October 1789 (*Papers, Presidential Series,* 4:219); GW to David Humphreys, 20 July 1791 (*Papers, Presidential Series,* 8:358–359); Thomas Fielder to GW, 29 August 1793 (*Papers, Presidential Series,* 13:574).

24. GW to Friedrich von Poellnitz, 23 March 1790 (*Papers, Presidential Series,* 5:274).

25. Charles Vancouver to GW, 5 November 1791 (*Papers, Presidential Series,* 9:144).

26. Thomas Jefferson to GW, 1 May 1791 (*Papers, Presidential Series,* 8:144).

27. GW to Arthur Young, 15 August 1791 (*Papers, Presidential Series,* 8:431).

28. Circular on the State of American Agriculture, 25 August 1791 (*Papers, Presidential Series*, 8:453–454).

29. GW to Tobias Lear, 6 May 1794 (*Papers, Presidential Series*, 16:26).

30. George F. Wehrs to GW, 25 January 1793 (*Papers, Presidential Series*, 12:47–51).

31. Tobias Lear to GW, 25 December 1793 (*Papers, Presidential Series*, 14:620–623).

32. Tobias Lear to GW, 26–30 January 1794 (*Papers, Presidential Series*, 15:117).

33. GW to Lafayette, 29 January 1789 (*Papers, Presidential Series*, 1:263).

34. GW to Robert Sinclair, 6 May 1792 (*Papers, Presidential Series*, 10:359).

35. GW to Thomas Jefferson, 13 February 1789 (*Papers, Presidential Series*, 1:299–300).

36. Ibid.

37. GW to Henry Dorsey Gough, 23 August 1797 (*Papers, Retirement Series*, 1:316).

38. Edmund Randolph to GW, 10 January 1791 (*Papers, Presidential Series*, 7:217).

39. GW to Alexander Hamilton, 14 October 1791 (*Papers, Presidential Series*, 9:79); GW to Henry Dorsey Gough, 4 February 1792 (*Papers, Presidential Series*, 9:527).

40. Thomas Jefferson's Memorandum of Conversations with Washington, 1 March 1792 (*Papers, Presidential Series*, 10:9).

41. B. Francis to GW, 25 May 1792 (*Papers, Presidential Series*, 10:415–418).

42. Undelivered First Inaugural Address: Fragments, 30 April 1789 (*Papers, Presidential Series*, 2:158–173).

43. GW to the United States Senate and House of Representatives, 25 October 1791 (*Papers, Presidential Series*, 9:215–216).

44. GW to the Earl of Buchan, 22 April 1793 (*Papers, Presidential Series*, 12:469–470).

45. GW to Arthur Young, 5 December 1791 (*Papers, Presidential Series*, 9:254–255).

46. GW to the United States Senate, 4 August 1790 (*Papers, Presidential Series*, 6:188–191).

47. GW to the United States Senate and House of Representatives, 25 October 1791 (*Papers, Presidential Series*, 9:112).

48. GW to Lafayette, 29 January 1789 (*Papers, Presidential Series*, 1:264).

49. GW to Thomas Jefferson, 31 August 1788 (*Papers, Confederation Series*, 6:494).

50. GW to Lafayette, 10 June 1792 (*Papers, Presidential Series*, 10:447–448).

51. James McHenry to GW, 17 July 1792 (*Papers, Presidential Series*, 10:548).

52. GW to John Christian Ehler, 10 October 1795 (*Papers, Presidential Series*, 19:365).

53. GW to Tench Tilghman, 17 August 1785 (*Papers, Confederation Series*, 3:187–189); Tench Tilghman to GW, 25 August 1785 (*Papers, Confederation Series*, 3:204–206); GW to Tench Tilghman, 29 August 1785 (*Papers, Confederation Series*, 3:208–209).

54. John O'Donnell to GW, 9 September 1790 (*Papers, Presidential Series*, 6:412).

55. GW to the United States Congress and House of Representatives, 8 December 1790 (*Papers, Presidential Series*, 7:45–47); Brown & Francis to GW, 13 December 1791 (*Papers, Presidential Series*, 9:387–388); GW to Brown & Francis, 7 January 1792 (*Papers, Presidential Series*, 12:155–157).

56. GW to Alexander Spotswood, 7 February 1792 (*Papers, Presidential Series*, 9:550).

57. Undelivered First Inaugural Address: Fragments, 30 April 1789 (*Papers, Presidential Series*, 2:158–173).

## Chapter Eight: Keeping the Peace: Washington's Second Term

1. GW to David Humphreys, 20 July 1791 (*Papers, Presidential Series*, 8:359).

2. Thomas Jefferson's Memorandum of Conversations with Washington, 1 March 1792 (*Papers, Presidential Series*, 10:6–8).

3. Thomas Jefferson to GW, 23 May 1792 (*Papers, Presidential Series*, 10:408–414).

4. Ibid.

5. Ibid.

6. Ibid.

7. Thomas Jefferson's Memorandum of Conversations with Washington, 10 July 1792 (*Papers, Presidential Series,* 10:535–537).

8. Ibid.

9. Ibid.

10. GW to Alexander Hamilton, 29 July 1792 (*Papers, Presidential Series,* 10:588–592).

11. Alexander Hamilton to GW, 18 August 1792 (*Papers, Presidential Series,* 11:12–13).

12. GW to Alexander Hamilton, 23 August 1792 (*Papers, Presidential Series,* 11:30); GW to Edmund Randolph, 26 August 1792 (*Papers, Presidential Series,* 11:45).

13. Alexander Hamilton to GW, 30 July–3 August 1792 (*Papers, Presidential Series,* 10:594–596); Thomas Jefferson to GW, 9 September 1792 (*Papers, Presidential Series,* 10:96–106).

14. Alexander Hamilton to GW, 30 July–3 August 1792 (*Papers, Presidential Series,* 10:594–596); Madison's Conversations with Washington, 5–25 May 1792 (*Papers, Presidential Series,* 10:349–354).

15. Elizabeth Willing Powel to GW, 17 November 1792 (*Papers, Presidential Series,* 11:395–397).

16. GW to the United States Congress and House of Representatives, 3 December 1793 (*Papers, Presidential Series,* 14:466).

17. Proclamation, 15 September 1792 (*Papers, Presidential Series,* 11:122–123).

18. Proclamation, 25 September 1794 (*Papers, Presidential Series,* 16:725–727).

19. Address to the United States Senate and House of Representatives, 6 November 1792 (*Papers, Presidential Series,* 11:345).

20. GW to Thomas Jefferson, 1 January 1788 (*Papers, Confederation Series,* 6:3).

21. GW to David Humphreys, 23 March 1793 (*Papers, Presidential Series,* 12:363).

22. GW to the Earl of Buchan, 22 April 1793 (*Papers, Presidential Series,* 12:469).

23. Philadelphia Merchants and Traders to GW, 16 May 1793 (*Papers, Presidential Series,* 12:599).

24. Quoted in *Papers, Presidential Series,* 14:636–637.

25. Tobias Lear to GW, 26–30 January 1794 (*Papers, Presidential Series,* 15:121).

26. Betty Washington Lewis to GW, 23 March 1794 (*Papers, Presidential Series,* 15:434).

27. GW to the United States Senate and House of Representatives, 3 December 1793 (*Papers, Presidential Series,* 14:464).

28. Alexander Hamilton to GW, 14 April 1794 (*Papers, Presidential Series,* 15:581–594).

29. GW to the United States Senate, 16 April 1794 (*Papers, Presidential Series,* 15:608–609).

30. Citizens West of the Allegheny Mountains to GW, December 1793 (*Papers, Presidential Series,* 14:655–656).

31. Alexander Hamilton to GW, 26 October 1795 (*Papers of Alexander Hamilton,* 19:350–352).

32. GW to Patrick Henry, 9 October 1795 (Fitzpatrick, *Writings,* 34:334–335); GW to James Anderson, 24 December 1795 (Fitzpatrick, *Writings,* 34:405–410).

33. Farewell Address, 19 September 1796 (Fitzpatrick, *Writings,* 35:214–238).

34. Ibid.

35. Ibid.

36. Ibid.

## Chapter Nine: The Road Home

1. Diary, 4 March 1797 (*Diaries,* 6:236); GW to James Anderson, 7 April 1797 (*Papers, Retirement Series,* 1:79).

2. GW to Elizabeth Willing Powel, 26 March 1797 (*Papers, Retirement Series*, 1:53).

3. GW to William Pearce, 18 December 1793 (*Papers, Presidential Series*, 14:561).

4. GW to Anthony Whitting, 21 April 1793 (*Papers, Presidential Series*, 12:464); GW to George Augustine Washington, 31 March 1789 (*Papers, Presidential Series*, 1:475); GW to Anthony Whitting, 5 May 1793 (*Papers, Presidential Series*, 12:524).

5. GW to James Anderson, 18 June 1797 (*Papers, Retirement Series*, 1:193).

6. James Anderson to GW, 21 June 1797 (*Papers, Retirement Series*, 1:200).

7. GW to James Anderson, 21 December 1797 (*Papers, Retirement Series*, 1:524–526); GW to James Anderson, 22 May 1798 (*Papers, Retirement Series*, 2:288).

8. GW to John Mason, 2 January 1798 (*Papers, Retirement Series*, 2:2).

9. GW to Tobias Lear, 6 May 1794 (*Papers, Presidential Series*, 16:28).

10. GW to Arthur Young, 18–21 June 1792 (*Papers, Presidential Series*, 10:461); GW to Anthony Whitting, 13–14 January 1793 (*Papers, Presidential Series*, 11:626); GW to William Pearce, 25 January 1795 (Fitzpatrick, *Writings*, 34:103–104).

11. Terms on Which the Farms at Mount Vernon May Be Obtained, 1 February 1796 (Fitzpatrick, *Writings*, 34:441–447).

12. GW to Patrick O'Flynn, 15 April 1798 (*Papers, Retirement Series*, 2:241–242); GW to Robert Lewis & Sons, 1 February 1785 (*Papers, Confederation Series*, 2:317–318); William Booker to GW, 6 June 1799 (*Papers, Retirement Series*, 4:102); William Roberts to GW, 21 June 1799 (*Papers, Retirement Series*, 4:139).

13. GW to James Anderson, 1 November 1798 (*Papers, Retirement Series*, 3:164).

14. GW to Clement Biddle, 28 April 1799 (*Papers, Retirement Series*, 4:28–29).

15. George Washington's Last Will and Testament, 9 July 1799 (*Papers, Retirement Series*, 4:517).

16. GW to George Washington Parke Custis, 7 January 1798 (*Papers, Retirement Series*, 2:4–5).

17. GW to George Washington Parke Custis, 19 March 1798 (*Papers, Retirement Series*, 2:149).

18. Joseph E. Fields, ed., *"Worthy Partner": The Papers of Martha Washington* (Westport, CT: Greenwood Press, 1994), 321–322.

19. George Washington's Last Will and Testament, 9 July 1799 (*Papers, Retirement Series*, 4:477–527).

20. GW to James Anderson, 13 December 1799 (*Papers, Retirement Series*, 4:455–477).

21. Tobias Lear's Narrative Accounts of the Death of George Washington, 15 December 1799 (*Papers, Retirement Series*, 4:542–555).

22. Ibid.

## Conclusion

1. Arthur Young to GW, 18 January 1792 (*Papers, Presidential Series*, 9:478–479).

2. Ibid.

# INDEX